EVE
WAS
SHAMED

HOW BRITISH JUSTICE
IS FAILING WOMEN

HELENA KENNEDY

Chatto & Windus
LONDON

1 3 5 7 9 10 8 6 4 2

Chatto & Windus, an imprint of Vintage,
20 Vauxhall Bridge Road,
London SW1V 2SA

Chatto & Windus is part of the Penguin Random House group of companies
whose addresses can be found at global.penguinrandomhouse.com.

Penguin
Random House
UK

First published in the United Kingdom by Chatto & Windus in 2018

penguin.co.uk/vintage

A CIP catalogue record for this book is available from the British Library

ISBN 9781784742225

Typeset in 11/17 pt Minion Pro
by Integra Software Services Pvt. Ltd, Pondicherry

Printed and bound in Great Britain by Clays Ltd, Elcograf S.p.A.

Penguin Random House is committed to a sustainable future for
our business, our readers and our planet. This book is made
from Forest Stewardship Council® certified paper.

EVE WAS SHAMED

To the new generations of feminists in the law

CONTENTS

INTRODUCTION

We all find our own way to feminism. I did not come to the Bar in the early seventies as a feminist looking for slights against women. When I started studying law I was not particularly conscious of women's issues, except inasmuch as they were part of my general concern about what happened to working-class people when they sought justice. I was a child of the Glasgow tenements with strong class politics, which informed my way of seeing law. When the women's movement gathered steam I was in my early twenties, I went to the meetings, read the books and carried the banners, but it was at the coal face that I really learned a deep and visceral under-standing of feminism, in the cells with my clients, in community advice centres and refuges, and most of all in courtrooms. Those experiences in turn fired memories from my childhood of blighted women's lives.

Two decades later I published *Eve Was Framed*, my book about women and the British justice system, and I was overwhelmed by the response. Laying out the law's failure to provide justice for women was highly contentious, especially within the profession and among the judiciary, but many women wrote to me, confiding in me their experiences of abuse and violence, which they had never taken to the courts. Some had told people in authority but had not been believed, though most remained silent because they knew that they would be accused of lying, exaggerating or fantasising. This response to the book seemed like a victory, but you don't need me to tell you that these concerns are exactly the same as the ones still raised by women today.

My passion to reshape the world has never subsided and, despite halting progress, I am still subject to surges of real hope. Over the last few decades the wall of silence about the abuse of women and children has been breached. Domestic violence and rape are now firmly located on the political and public agendas. And every now and again something happens which persuades me that at last we are reaching the uplands in the struggle for women's equality. The #MeToo campaign which went viral after the Harvey Weinstein scandal rocked Hollywood in 2017 has captured a mood that has been gathering force for several years, at least since the original Me Too movement was started by Tarana Burke in 1997. It is not just about celebrities and the abuse of the casting couch. It is about much more than predatory men with power in the film industry. It is about the way women have to live their lives and the debasing wretchedness of continuing gender inequality. The new element has been the Internet and social media. It has stirred a rage that has reverberated around the world and led to a huge wave of online disclosure. It has turned the spotlight on the harassment of models in the fashion industry and then moved on to Parliament, with political heads rolling and systems put in place to deal with sexual harassment there. No workplace seems safe from the naming and shaming of men abusing their power. It has turned to Oxfam, Save the Children and the charity world with the disclosure of male workers in crisis-stricken Haiti using young desperate women for prostitution and men in the upper reaches of these organisations behaving in disrespectful ways towards women. The whole Weinstein tsunami has been described as a 'watershed', a seismic response to law's failure.

The surge of confidence was growing well before the #MeToo campaign. There was the Oxford student Ione Wells who was attacked and almost raped in London. She threw off the mantle of anonymity and expressed a public refusal to be silenced and ashamed for being on the receiving end of a sexual assault. There are the incredible women from minority communities, like the Southall Black Sisters and members of the Iranian and Kurdish Women's Rights Organisation, who challenge discriminatory asylum and immigration policies as well as cultural practices like female genital mutilation, forced marriage and 'honour' killing, which are violations of human rights. Or the fabulous women in the Glasgow Disability Alliance who have unveiled the extent to which women with disabilities are exposed to dispropor-tionate sexual abuse and domestic violence. There is Laura Bates's brilliantly inventive Everyday Sexism Project, which provides a space for sharing the ways in which offensive remarks and conduct are a persistent feature of women's lives and are normalised. There has been the launch of the Women's Equality Party, and the creation of the Centre for Women's Justice by the tireless solicitor for women Harriet Wistrich. There are the students in universities who are demanding a change in the culture of entitlement they feel is enjoyed by young men. There is the growing clamour of voices in television and sport demanding that the salaries of men are published so that women doing the same jobs can see if they are getting equal pay.

It was in 2012 when the deceased celebrity entertainer Jimmy Savile was exposed as a paedophile and gross abuser of women and children that we seemed to reach a tipping point. As more cases emerged, suddenly the institutions – from the BBC to Parliament, from hospitals and schools to young offender institutions, from local authorities to universities and churches, all of which had colluded in keeping the lid on such crimes – were in retreat. Every one of these pillars of rectitude had put institutional reputation ahead of safeguarding women and children. The outrage was so deeply felt and the torrent of memories, anger and sorrow so great that a public debate raged, of a kind that had never taken place before. A public inquiry was set up by the then Home Secretary, Theresa May, in recognition of the extent of the problem. I kept hearing the same questions. How could so many predators have got away with it? Why did people do nothing? Was it because things were different then?

Now it was as though people had been waiting for permission to talk about their experiences and a flood of historic abuse and discrimination was laid bare. I thought then that maybe we were turning a corner.

The scandals of Rotherham, Rochdale, Oxford, Manchester, Newcastle and other cities were revealed, where girls, some as young as 13 and 14, were groomed and used for sex by gangs of men largely from ethnic minorities. The girls were white and usually from disadvantaged backgrounds, often in care homes. They would be staying out late, easily preyed upon in the night-time world of takeaway joints and minicabs. Plied with drink and drugs, given gifts of money or trinkets, they would be raped or coerced into sexual activity by men sometimes old enough to be their fathers. Yet they were treated by the authorities as girls making a lifestyle choice and the men avoided prosecution because the police did not think the girls or their families were credible witnesses. Again the question was asked. How could this have gone on without police action or intervention by social services? There were attempts to suggest this was culturally specific, as though it is only men from certain cultures who commit such crimes, when in fact these particular manifestations are just further examples of how 'pass-around' girls are a common feature of male gang networks. Many young Asian girls, like young white girls, suffer sexual abuse and, as we know, it is most commonly at the hands of people from their own family or community. A culture of impunity means serial abuse of women and girls has gone uninvestigated and unpunished for all my professional life. There is nothing racially or religiously inherent in male abuse. Yes, the police and social services were anxious in these cases not to be accused of racist conduct by pursuing Pakistanis or other ethnic minority men. The tabloids bleated about political correctness being the root cause of this systemic failure to pursue the offenders, and no doubt the police's past record of discrimination towards minority communities means they are now being trained not to repeat history, but these cases are not just about sensitivity to potential allegations of racism or worries about feeding racial bigotry. Lord Ken MacDonald QC, the former Director of Public Prosecutions, described the male offenders as the ones who were racist because their victims were white girls. Yet it was the vulnerability and apparent availability of the girls that made them easy prey rather than the colour of their skin or the fact that they were non-Muslims. At the core of these shameful episodes were the deep-seated attitudes about which I have written endlessly. Some women and girls are deemed unworthy of protection; some females are seen as fair game. Slut-shaming, shoulder-shrugging and victim-blaming are nothing new when women are sexually molested. And it happens to Muslim women, brown-skinned women and black women too. The police forces and social service departments that were involved had to examine their consciences and their practices in a way that had not happened before. Was this in fact the tipping point?

I think, too, about reading and watching the coverage not so long ago about the great athlete Oscar Pistorius, who shot his girlfriend in a fit of rage, or the footballer Ched Evans, who was acquitted on a retrial of rape, having been given the heads-up by a friend that there was a young woman available for sex who just happened to be very drunk, or the politician Dominique Strauss-Kahn, who walked away from a sexual assault allegation on an immigrant hotel worker claiming it was consensual, only to be later exposed as a man with an unquenchable appetite for aggressive sex with strangers. All these men were able to rally huge public support. I think of John Warboys, the taxi driver who was responsible for the assault of legions of women but was considered suitable for release by the Parole Board after nine years. Then there is Donald Trump, who boasted on tape that he liked to 'grab women by the pussy' and admitted he could do so without any consequences because of his power and fame; who also said that he thought women who had abortions deserved 'some form of punishment'. He then went on to become president of the United States, supported by swathes of men but also a large number of women who think he speaks for them. I read and watch female journalists, paid assassins, turn on women who speak out about the ways in which lecherous men grope them, or I hear senior women at the Bar say that young women who complain of roaming hands should not consider a career in law if they cannot deal with it, and then I wonder how long it will take before there is equality. For millennia women have been made to feel shame. They have been told that what happens to them is their fault and it is they who are blamed for their failures, their shortcomings, their conduct. That is the power of patriarchy. Male dominance is maintained by this stuff. Women are made to feel soiled. They absorb feelings of guilt. The voice in their heads is mouthing cultural norms created by men and sold to women. 'It must have been something about me that made him do that to me.'

While women are increasingly vocal and are refusing to be muzzled about the violence and abuse they experience, the extent of such crimes is not in decline. Two women a week are killed by a spouse or partner. The police receive one phone call per minute concerning domestic violence. Every seven minutes a woman is raped. New technology has brought the proliferation of pornography on a scale that is alarming and contagious. Boys and men are watching and sharing imagery on their phones in which intimacy is wholly debased and women treated as objects. They then act out what they see in their contact with women, thinking this is what good sex is like. The trafficking of women and children is being carried out on an industrial scale across the world and barely a town or city in the United Kingdom has escaped its reach. The truth is that a lot has happened but not enough has changed.

Patriarchy is a virus that lives deep in the body politic. We have to become more confident in naming it as one of the main blights on all our lives. For men and women both. Patriarchy is a system – a dynamic web – of ideas and relationships, a set of beliefs and a set of values. It explains the world to us from our earliest years and it informs us in the subtlest of ways as to what is good and attractive and what is bad and distasteful. We are all taught that men are rational and women emotional; the system then assigns more worth to reason than to emotion. Patriarchy tells us that the world is a dangerous place and men must be our protectors while at the same time being our greatest threat. This societal system is sustained by everyday sexism but is more than sexism. It embraces misogyny but it relies on more than misogyny. It produces inequality but its consequences run deeper than gender inequality.

As a belief system, patriarchy is very appealing to men but also to a lot of women because for some women it brings rewards. Even feminists have shied away from talk of patriarchy because it seems old hat, or like hostility towards men – all men. I avoided using the word when I wrote *Eve Was Framed* in 1992 because I thought this book will never be read if it is seen to come from a place of hostile ideology. That anxiety about how we will be perceived is what actually sustains patriarchy and enables it to survive.

Patriarchy while expressing admiration for femininity actually holds it in contempt.

All around us admiration is expressed for women who show outward signs of 'good mothering' and other indicators of 'real' feminine qualities, but masculinity is privileged over all forms of femininity (as well as over despised forms of masculinity). Margaret Thatcher was admired for being 'the only man in the room' according to a supporter because Conservative men look for masculinised forms of authority even in women. On this front, Theresa May was initially admired as a 'bloody difficult woman', but whenever she turns into 'poor Theresa May' her power seeps away. Her challenge of Putin over the poisoning of Russians on British soil lent her new potency in this male-skewed assessment. Admirers of the authoritarian leader take comfort from being foot soldiers, so long as they play this role to someone who displays powerful male qualities.

Our culture continues to harbour misogyny. Men are still being conditioned from an early age to feel a sense of superiority over women and to objectify them. They are often not even aware of it; it is so deeply encoded. 'Power is coded male', as Mary Beard the classics scholar has so eloquently pronounced. Boys around the world grow up being taught, in subtle ways, that women are less important and exist to satisfy men. And when grown, these boys are the folk who largely people our police forces, our prosecutorial services and our legislative systems. The simple fact is that men still dominate every pillar of power, from Parliament and the courts to the economy and the media. They crowd out the voices of women systematically, even on issues directly affecting women. Of course, the majority of men in the public arena denounce violence against women when required, but even the good guys, and there are many, rarely challenge degrading jokes, debasing images or sleazy comments which are the quotidian expression of the very stuff that feeds violence too. It is all part of a continuum. The culture of masculinity is so deeply ingrained in our hegemony that women also buy into it. It is all around us. At some level, everyday violence against women and objectification of women are tolerated because they are seen as an expression of manhood. Women are often held responsible. We 'make' men do it. We incite it by how we look and dress and by our very sexual being, by our wicked tongues and our devious ways. What does it mean when the Christian evangelical Mike Pence, vice president of the United States, says in the 21st century that he will not meet a woman alone, even if she is a leading politician or adviser? What is it he thinks Angela Merkel is going to do to him? Is it because he fears his own sexual appetites, or is he concerned that a false allegation might be made by her, or that it might give rise to scandal? What is the message he gives to the world in saying this?

Over the years I have learned that every surge for real change meets with a backlash. It is happening now. Currently the call is that the #MeToo campaign has gone too far. Men are being falsely accused and are given no recourse to justice, we are told. Well, it is true that we are not seeing much due process. Naming and shaming on the Internet is wild justice and can cause serious unfairness I have no doubt, but if we want to talk about failures of justice, I think women

9

can make a far greater claim. The #MeToo campaign is very much a response to law's failure. If women had confidence in the justice system and men really feared the shame and consequence of misconduct, we would not be seeing a resort to anonymous accusations, a few of which may be overstated or invalid. The other challenge is that the public shaming of men, particularly anonymously, is disproportionate when they have merely groped or talked dirty and this should not be compared to rape and other grievous assaults. Of course, there is no equivalence between gang rape and having your behind felt at a club or a cock pressed against you on the Tube, but it is all part of the soup in which inequality is suspended. Women of my generation learned survival mechanisms, avoidance techniques, self-safeguarding. We ran round tables, we walked off briskly. We pretended constant comments on our bodies meant nothing to us and hid our hurt. We survived pressure to have sex with men we were not interested in by saying we had to be up at dawn or had our periods. Why should women have to do this? Why should our daughters endure this behaviour and just put it down to a woman's lot in life?

The journalist Melanie Phillips took the actress Uma Thurman to task for joining the bands of women outing Weinstein rather late in the day, getting her fame in first. She described what she saw as complicity by women in sexual behaviour to advance their own careers and could not see how any self-respecting woman would ever work for a man who was disgusting in his conduct towards her. The answer according to Phillips is to walk away, refuse to be a victim, get another career, find another job. But women up and down the land are working for men who disrespect them because they feel they have little choice, not because they choose victimhood. Sometimes the job is too precious for financial reasons and sometimes the desire to succeed in the career you love leads women into dark places. They are left with self-disgust, shame and anger. That is what powerlessness does to people. Blaming the women is the recourse of those who have control and little humanity. Feeling disempowered has been too common an experience for many women. Melanie Phillips failed to understand that the #MeToo campaign is about women having had enough and actually refusing to be victims. They are involved in a form of civil disobedience and it should be seen as an alarm call.

The backlash against the new wave of feminism has seen the usual media suspects jump on the revelation that the police failed to disclose social media evidence from the electronic devices of complainants in a number of rape cases, which led to the cases being dropped. The headlines claimed that women were being exposed through their emails, their Snapchat photographs and their Tinder accounts as liars. The old claim that many women make up allegations of rape is on the front burner once again. No one is mentioning that there is also a failure by the prosecution to ask for the social media of the male accused, disclosing his use of hard porn and texts, exposing poisonous attitudes to women.

So here I am again, 25 years on, deeply frustrated that a new book on gender inequality and the law appears to be so urgently needed. Many things have improved. Undoubtedly. At the very least we have many more women in the law and on the Bench. But too many new challenges have arisen. In *Eve Was Shamed* I want to look again at the British justice system as it is experienced by women – whether as defendants, victims or practitioners – cataloguing the persistence of misogyny and stereotypes, and all the inequality that still exists, examining the continuing failures and the intersectionality of discrimination which multiplies the effects of gender discrimination when coupled with racism and class disadvantage and contempt for any person who is different. I think we have to look at the persistence of shame and the shaming of women. Women have an instinctive sense of shame when they are violated. It is a learned behaviour. Shame is a component of punishment for criminal behaviour, so why should women suffer shaming or experience shame when they have been at the receiving end of shameful behaviour by men? I want to suggest solutions for change whenever I see them, without undermining the principles which must underpin justice. But the bigger aim in this project is to move the current debate on.

We have had the huge, powerful and necessary outpouring, the sharing of stories and redrawing of boundaries, but what comes next? The lessons which have been learned have to be formalised and entrenched into society. There has to be systemic change in our places of work and all our institutions. But this is about more than tweaking the law, creating grievance procedures, strengthening human resource systems and changing governance structures. All of this must be done, but the bigger project is about creating deep cultural change which involves us all, men and women. Men and boys have to be helped to see how our cultures disfigure relationships and inflict deep wounds on them too. We must challenge the toxic masculinity that proliferates on the Internet, fostering violence and abuse. In its most extreme form this produces movements like Incel – involuntary celibates – which feed hatred against women amongst men who feel their old sexual and gender entitlements are being withdrawn. Their rage is leading to the aping of terrorist outrages, as we saw in Canada in May 2018 when a crowd was mown down with a vehicle.

The sham demands of a pernicious masculinity that from childhood shackles men to roles and behaviours which are damaging to them as well as us have to be exposed. Men are shamed into denying their own emotional needs and taught to cover vulnerability with bravado and toughness. Men who were abused as children by parents, carers, sports coaches, teachers and priests have also had to bury their pain for years. Those who have had the courage to name their abusers and testify against them have had to unearth buried layers of confusion and pain because those experiences upturned their own ideas of appropriate masculinity. Change has to embrace the way men too are encumbered and undermined by the burdens of expectation.

We have to ask: what is equality? What does it look like? What kind of equality do we want? And how might the law help in achieving it? These seem to me to be the most urgent questions we now face.

Equality certainly means getting more women into positions of power in all aspects of life – not just in a tokenist way, but creating genuine parity. It means more than improving numbers, however. Many of us have become successful in male worlds because we have learned to do jobs in the way men expect. Some of us can even outdo them at their own game. Having women learn to exercise power just as men do is not going to achieve real equality. Can we envisage a world where each of us is valued for who we are, for our individual human qualities, rather than our gender or race or caste or class? Valued not because we have learned to ape male rationality but because we have other kinds of intelligence and skills to bring to the table too? A world where we are all respected simply because of our common humanity? Equality means true and consensual sexual relations. It means working together without fear or expectation of exploitation of any kind. To re-engineer our systems we have to survey the landscape of law and recognise where it fails and why.

One of the great legal advances in the last 20 years has been the embrace of human rights into our domestic law. The European Convention of Human Rights was actually drafted by British lawyers in 1950, despite it being traduced as a foreign invention. The Human

Rights Act of 1998 introduced the Articles of the European Convention into the legal system of England and Wales. The Scotland Act of 1998 secured the same rights for the Scots and the Good Friday Agreement did likewise for the Northern Irish. The positive impact on the lives of UK citizens has been immeasurable. The main point of human rights principles is to create a template of values to work alongside the legal systems of different nations to protect the human needs of individuals. Where there were gaps in the protections afforded by domestic law, the courts have at their disposal potential remedies based on principle.

Women have benefitted hugely from the Human Rights Act because so many of its articles provide a corrective to the areas where the law has failed women. The right to life in the Human Rights Act was used in 2010 to secure the reopening of the inquest into the death of Naomi Bryant who was killed by Anthony Rice. The new inquest showed that the authorities had known he was a serial sex offender but had released him on licence without appropriate supervision when he was a clear risk to girls and women. The right to respect for family and private life was used to prevent the children of a domestic violence victim being taken into care by social services, who insisted she had made herself voluntarily homeless. Her violent husband pursued her relentlessly wherever she resettled, yet his behaviour was to mean the loss of her children and the children's loss of their mother. The Act was used to expose cruel and inhumane treatment, otherwise described as substandard care, of the elderly in Stafford Hospital. It was used to challenge failures in the Rotherham abuse scandal. It was used to reopen the investigation into the suicide of Private Cheryl James and the toxic and 'sexualised' atmosphere at Deepcut Army Barracks where she was training. The list goes on; but few women know the incredible uses they can make of these rights in pursuit of justice and equality – rights which some in power wish to take away.

Gender equality is within our grasp and law is one of the mechanisms that can be used to secure it. However, it requires persistence and constant review.

We live in a social system in which men hold primary power. They predominate in roles of political leadership and having Margaret Thatcher or Theresa May in charge has not augured a new world order, whatever we are told. Men hold all the main positions of moral authority, have social privilege and control of most property. Men still hold the reins over women and children in very many family homes. They control nearly every avenue of power, especially within mainstream institutions. If only they realised how much better it would be for them too if it were all changed, if the rules of the game altered. Imagine a world where it is taken for granted that men and women share power and no one is subject to another's dominion. Imagine we have equal legal rights to spend real time with our families, where there really is equal pay, where the pressures of the long-hours culture are removed, where pay in the caring professions was made so rewarding that it did not invariably fall to women to look after the elderly, the disabled or children in nurseries, nor that teaching in primary schools was a female role.

Sadly, there are still too many in the law who believe that the law is an objective set of rules, that law is neutral. The point of *Eve Was Framed* was to show that this claim of neutrality was bogus. Law was male because it was made by men, or with a male template, and only when law-making was reconsidered could law become just. But reforming the law with some legislative changes and the appointment of more women will not of itself resolve the deeply embedded problems with the law. There has to be a serious acknowledgement that legal cultures are premised on notions within society which are themselves excluding rather than including. There has to be a demolition job on the structural engineering of society.

When women of my generation first began to turn the spotlight on the treatment of women by law and in the law, we argued for law reform. We still need that, but what became increasingly clear is that law reform of itself is not the answer. Law is often part of the problem. We argued for equality but treating as equal those who are unequal does not produce equality. Equality is not about treating people the same. The European Court of Human Rights has said that equality is treating people who are in the same situation the same way, and treating people who are differently situated differently. Our Supreme Court used this distinction to decide that the bedroom tax (additional rent applied to council properties where there are more bedrooms than people registered at the address) would not apply to people with a disability or illness who needed overnight carers.

The problem is that too few administrators and employers and even courts understand this difference. We have to start talking about substantive equality, real equality, which acknowledges the historic or physical imbalances between men and women in our society, rather than formal equality. When the army first accepted women recruits to all regiments it thought equality would mean reacting to everyone as though they were the same. It then recognised that the stride and different physical capacities of a woman meant that the same timings for fitness runs could not be expected of men and women. Equality required making appropriate adjustments on objective assessments of capabilities. Real equality means treating 'as equals' – taking account of the context of our lives and the ways in which women can be deeply disadvantaged. The fact that only women can get pregnant is a special factor linked to gender, and dismissals for pregnancy must not be compared with a man being sick long term. Nor does equality mean reaching for the sentencing manual and doling out the same sentence for a man and a woman if the sentencing guidelines allow for no discretion or appreciation of women's reality. It does not mean expecting higher sexual morality from women than from men. It does not mean judging women on their clothing, their drunkenness, their skills as a parent, when none of those judgements are applied to males. It means recognising that for the most part women do low-paid work, that women give birth, that women do most of the caring within families, that women do not enjoy equal advancement within the workplace, that women's experiences from childhood may involve discrimination, that many women live in fear of violence and abuse from adolescence in a way that men do not. It does not assume that women who have consented to sex with many men will be content to have sex with any man. Doing justice requires lawyers and judges to understand the world in which we live. The evidence of continuing inequality is manifest in the cases that are recounted in this book. In order to construct a better vision of equality we have to become fully aware of the system's failings. It is important to emphasise that a new vision will not be achieved by purchasing justice for women at the cost of justice for men.

In the family courts, there have been enormous improvements for women, but sometimes the victories achieved have bizarre consequences because the wrongs they are seeking to redress are not fully understood by those who are asked to put the changes into practice. After a great deal of campaigning and pushing at the boundaries of legal precedent, a breakthrough took place in the eighties and nineties in relation to the distribution of assets after the breakdown of marriage. It was successfully argued that wives and partners who stay at home to care for children or who sacrifice their own careers to contribute to the success of their man should be appropriately compensated in any settlement, receiving not only a division of current assets but also a portion of future earnings and pension entitlements. The same principle should clearly apply where a male partner assumes the domestic role. However, in the spirit of gender equality the courts now interpret this to mean that when a couple divorces after their children are grown and both have had careers, if the woman earns more and has better prospects for the future she has to fork out to her husband even if she still took the greater role in childcare. There is also a failure to acknowledge that where both partners work, mothers still usually bear the responsibility of organising childcare and most of the domestic scene. Unfortunately, the struggles for equity in marriage and divorce are undermined by the highly publicised media reports of the few women who fortune-hunt for huge divorce settlements after short marriages to rich men.

Securing justice is not easy and nor should it be. It is obtained by giving a fair and unbiased appraisal of each person and situation, without relying on preconceived notions, whether the defendant is black or white, male or female, straight, trans or gay. Justice recognises the tension between the ideal of equality and the reality of people's lives. There are those who claim that the true classical symbol of Justice has her wearing a blindfold of impartiality but maybe that is why law fails. I have always preferred the image of Justice as an all-seeing goddess, as she appears above the Central Criminal Court at the Old Bailey, alert and aware of humanity in all its forms, taking everything into account, and thereby aiming for a higher ideal.

The law mirrors society with all its imperfections and it therefore reflects the subordination and lesser status of women, even today. But holding up a mirror can never be its sole function. The law affects as well as reflects, and all of those involved in the administration of justice have a special obligation to reject society's irrational prejudices. The law is symbolic, playing an important role in the internalising of ideas about what is right and natural. If the men of law say scantily dressed women or ones who are drunk or ones who hook up with guys on Tinder have been authors of their own misfortune, they reinforce that view in the man on the street. The law constructs beliefs about the roles of men and women in the home and at work which feed back into generally held attitudes about women.

True justice is about more than refereeing between two sides. It is about breathing life into the rules so that no side is at a disadvantage because of sex or race or any of the other impediments which deny justice.

1

EVE WAS FRAMED

Perhaps there's no better place to start our survey of inequality than with Eve. One of my maternal grandmother's old wives' maxims was that there would be no bad men if there were no bad women. After all, woman was responsible for the original sin. This world view, which would usually be expounded as she swept vigorously around me while I attempted homework on the kitchen table, filtered through our days.

I swallowed the idea that women should generally be expected to behave better than men, since there seemed ample evidence that they did so anyway, and I could see no harm in keeping up the standard. At every point in my Catholic girlhood the Virgin Mary was presented to us as our role model. Men were simply victims of their own appetites, hardly capable of free will when it came to sex or violence, and it was up to us to act as the restraining influence. However, my sense of natural justice baulked at the idea of holding women responsible for male transgressions. Why should women be considered the moral cornerstones of society? Does motherhood really carry with it such an overwhelming obligation? Ejection from Paradise is one thing, but a sentence of eternal damnation when the conviction had to be based on the uncorroborated testimony of a co-accused must surely constitute a breach of international standards on human rights. It was only later, when studying law, that I came to the conclusion that Eve had been framed.

Law comes out of deep cultural wells. The earliest sets of rules and laws laid down a subordinate role for women. Women were busy doing the procreating. The religions within our societies are the bedrock of law systems and all the major religions give women lower status, have myths of woman as the lure towards wickedness – the Eve. And then we have the compensatory myth promulgated by men of religion that women are in fact the better gender, too special in the schema to be burdened with certain kinds of power. More times than I can count, I have found myself in hot debate with priests, rabbis, Muslims, Hindus and many other people with deeply held faith, all of whom insist that their holy books prescribe a special role for women that allegedly places them on a pedestal of privilege. Better than equal, they claim. It may all sound outdated, but unspoken belief systems are rooted in the soil of 'proper womanhood', even though we have moved on. This does not mean we cannot be CEOs, doctors and lawyers too, but it still means our behaviour is expected to conform to entrenched notions of what is truly feminine or female.

Myths are tent pegs which secure the status quo. In the law, mythology operates almost as powerfully as legal precedent in inhibiting change. Mythology is a triumph of belief over reality, depending for its survival not on evidence but on constant reiteration. Myths are not the same as lies, in that they do not involve deliberate falsification. They endure because they serve social needs. The notion that judges, and the institutions of law in which they are forged, are invariably impartial is pervasive and unreal, but it is supposed to sustain our faith in the legal system.

Mythologies do change. They also vary between different groupings, but what matters are the dominant myths which receive institutional reinforcement daily in the administration of justice. But for those mythologies to change a concerted effort to reform from within is required. Most legislation and case law nowadays has the semblance of neutrality, and some legislative changes are designed to improve the position of women, but the letter of the law can easily become a cloak for the reality.

For me, coming to the Bar was almost an accident. A law degree was an escape route from the original plan to study English in Glasgow, and was devised after weeks of panic in London where I was doing a summer job. There, I had breathed the air of other possibilities, a world beyond. It was 1968 and student uprisings were happening everywhere, from Paris to Grosvenor Square. There was opposition to the Vietnam War and the talk was of revolutionary change. It was intoxicating and I did not want to miss out. But the pleasure my family had taken in the first of us going to higher education meant that any proposed alternative to my original plan of studying at home had to satisfy their anxieties about the unknown, and fulfil their hopes that I might end up with a good job.

The only professional women they or I had ever known were school-teachers, who in those days seemed to have a better material life than any other women we knew. Yet there was a certain predictability in heading towards teaching which made me want to resist it. I wanted to do what was not expected of me. The only other person I knew with a degree had read law, and its mysteries had caught my imagination. I was seduced by the drama of the Bar.

My father, a soft-hearted, intelligent man, had left school, like my mother, at 14. He worked as a dispatch hand in the print industry and was active in his union. I remember his passionate belief in the Labour movement and his pride in the changes which had been won in his lifetime. He thrilled to the idea of my doing law, especially when I said I wanted to be a trade union lawyer. I'm not sure where I picked up that idea from, but it seemed like a way of being professional without sounding too highfalutin.

My mother was surprisingly quiet at my decision. To her, London was purgatory, if not hell, and she muttered about things coming to a sorry pass. She had much more faith in holy water than the legal system, and merely getting involved in that world alarmed her. Her line was that any normal person would be thrilled at the chance of being a lady teacher, and she ignored my refrain about not knowing any boys who had that ambition.

When some of my relatives were told I had joined 'Gray's Inn' and was studying for the 'Bar', they imagined I had gone in for hotel management or catering and could not understand why anyone would pass up Glasgow University to do such a thing. The mysteries of the legal system in Scotland, let alone England, had rarely impinged on our lives, save for shamed references to cousin Bertie, who had ingeniously wired up his electricity to the street lighting and seen the inside of Barlinnie. Against this well-meaning resistance I just had to succeed; however miserable I was, there could be no complaining. And was I miserable! Like childbirth, nothing had really prepared me for it.

I had not been in criminal practice for long before I realised that special rules apply in, for example, rape cases; I saw some male jurors winking their support for my male client before the alleged victim had even finished her evidence. I also learned very quickly, like every other lawyer worth her salt and her fee, that the nearer I could get to painting a female client as a paragon of traditional womanhood, the more likely she was to experience the quality of mercy. If a woman with a weakness for bovver boots could be persuaded into wearing pearls and a broderie anglaise blouse she might just tip the judicial scales in her favour.

The first case I ever handled was for a woman who was pleading guilty in the magistrates' court to shoplifting. The items were children's clothes, and I was reassured by all the old hands that nothing much would happen to her; women always got off lightly and she would probably be fined, even if she did have a couple of previous convictions. I arrived at court and found my client in a state of great anxiety because she had not been able to make any arrangements for her children. It turned out that she had a suspended sentence of imprisonment outstanding which, in some bid to deny the inevitability of going to jail, she had failed to mention to my instructing solicitor. Like so many poor women, she had no resources to pay a fine and the courts had on previous occasions run through what they saw as the alternatives: a conditional discharge, then a probation order, then a suspended sentence and now the real McCoy. In this miserable first experience, I watched my despairing client being taken off to Holloway, weeping for her children.

It does not do wonders for your confidence when your first client is packed off to jail, however hopeless the case, but I hung on in there, doing a particularly active trade (which I thoroughly enjoyed) in my early years representing fellow Scots, marauding tartan-clad supporters who had been involved in displays of male camaraderie after Cup Finals. I suppose I was instructed on the assumption that I would be able to translate. While every other woman in the law tells stories of being taken for the solicitor's secretary, I was generally taken for the defendant's sister. Young black women in the law tell me the same assumption is made about them. I also had a significant clientele of Glaswegian prostitutes, whose families all thought they were down south working with the Civil Service. Some of them sent home money for babies their mothers were rearing for them; others had children living with them whom they looked after perfectly well, despite all belief to the contrary.

The early years of every barrister's practice are spent gaining experience in the lower courts. As a woman intent on criminal work I often found myself in the juvenile and magistrates' courts representing women and children, because in the dispersal of legal crumbs by solicitors or clerks the soft end of offending went to the girls. Even as I have progressed up the ladder into serious crime I have always represented a proportionately higher number of women and young people, since in the expectations of the courtroom it is an appropriate role to play.

The arrangements and language of the law would bemuse any bystander, and when you add to that the whole complicated system of courts, with its different divisions ranging from the local magistrates' court to the Court of Appeal, it was no wonder my relatives were bewildered. It sounded like a queer profession where you had to eat dinners as well as pass exams to qualify, something only the English could have thought up. I stepped from the equivalent of a comprehensive school in no mean city into the pages of an Evelyn Waugh novel.

Lectures were the least of my problems, providing a happy respite from social contact. The Inn robing room, where we put on a legal gown for dining, was the real class divider. Here, like the Queen, women carefully knotted silk headscarves in front of their chins rather than under them, and talked about weekend house parties and 'cockers-pees', which after enough eavesdropping I realised were nothing more vulgar than cocktail parties.

Sixties radicalism had certainly not had its way in the Inns of Court. Down the road at the London School of Economics, students were in revolt at how the school was governed; everywhere young people were demonstrating – against the war in Vietnam, then at its height, and against apartheid, demanding disinvestment in South Africa. Meanwhile at Gray's Inn, except among a very few, the main topics of conversation were the Field Club Ball and the Fencing Club. There was even a Smoking Concert after dinner during each Trinity term, from which women were excluded because of the ribald nature of the proceedings. Hall was supposed to represent the heart of life as a Bar student. Here, in the rarefied atmosphere of the beautiful wood-panelled room, dining was to present the opportunity for exchanging learned legal footnotes and scholarly opinions on case law.

I did not know anyone in practice at the English Bar when I started, which is the experience of most ordinary folk, and I did not know where to begin when it came to beginning life as a barrister. So I persuaded a friend who qualified the year before me to introduce me to his pupil-master, whom I then bludgeoned into taking me on, despite his warning that I would hate it in his chambers. He was absolutely right.

Chambers are the rooms in which barristers work, traditionally cloistered within the Inns. There is an architectural coherence about these male institutions: public schools, Oxbridge colleges, Inns of Court, Houses of Parliament. They combine opulence with austerity. The entrances to many sets of chambers resemble the closes of Scottish tenements, stark and bare-boarded. The conditions within are usually cramped like a book- and leather-bound womb. The lavatories might interest the public health inspectorate. Within sets of chambers, each barrister is self-employed, but there is a unity and interdependence, particularly in the early stages of practice, with work switching between barristers. Chambers, therefore, means more than shared offices and involves embracing the corporate identity of your brethren.

The clerks in my pupillage chambers did not like women and acted as though I were a piece of flotsam that had drifted in by mistake. Standing in the clerks' room trying to secure their attention was like trying to get served in the Harrods perfume department when you are wearing your old anorak. There were no other women, and the male barristers minded the invasion of their all-male sanctum. The discrimination was blatant, and some sets of chambers openly declared a no-women policy.

The story for black, Asian and minority ethnic (BAME) barristers was even worse. In 1979 there were only 200 ethnic minority barristers in independent practice. Most of those practised from chambers entirely comprised of those from ethnic minorities, and their work came largely from the minority communities. A committee was set up at the Bar to look at racial discrimination. In 1989 the Bar Council commissioned a survey which showed that in multi-racial Britain more than half the chambers did not have a single black or Asian tenant and that 53% of non-white barristers were ghettoised in a small number of chambers. This empirical research led to the fiercely debated Bar policy of setting a target of at least 5% ethnic minority lawyers in all chambers.

This positive action has resulted in huge change. According to the most recent statistics on diversity at the Bar, BAME barristers make up around 12% of the profession. BAME pupils account for around 16% of all pupils, a figure which is broadly in line with the ethnic make-up of England and Wales as a whole. Yet racial inequality continues to limit access to the upper echelons of the Bar, with ethnic minority barristers still representing only 6% of Queen's Counsels (QCs), the profession's most senior practitioners.

It is difficult to find concrete information on the class background of barristers. There is no universally accepted metric by which socio-economic status can be measured. Even asking education-related questions as a proxy for class ones produces limited results, with barristers playing their cards close to their chests. In the most recent round of monitoring questionnaires, nearly 70% of the barristers who responded did not disclose whether they went to a private school, or had university-educated parents. Nevertheless, the Bar Standards Board had enough information to conclude that, even in the unlikely event that all the non-responders had attended state schools, a disproportionate percentage of barristers are privately educated when compared with the country as a whole. Other studies have estimated the proportion of privately educated barristers and Counsel to be as high as 75%. The same percentage of High Court and Court of Appeal judges are products of public school, and the same proportion went to Oxford and Cambridge. Occasionally the less privileged do join the ranks, and that number is slowly growing. As of 2016, two out of 12 Supreme Court justices were grammar-school, as opposed to privately, educated. However, the men on the bench often find it hard to even imagine the lives of the really disadvantaged or the young. The average age of judges in this country is between 60 and 65, which coincides with the time when most other people are retiring. And according to the most recent official judicial diversity statistics, only 22 High Court judges out of 106 are women, with women making up only 9 out of 38 judges in the Court of Appeal. Across the High Court and Court of Appeal, there are only two judges who are not white. Everyone on the Supreme Court is white.

It is hard to avoid the conclusion that still too few men and women from different backgrounds find their way into practice. The introduction of tuition fees has made it much worse for students today, who come out of university with massive debts before they even embark on pupillage. The proliferation of universities since 1993, when the former polytechnics were able to acquire university status, has meant a huge expansion in the offer of law degrees to students. Policymakers, convinced that the future lay in knowledge economies, encouraged many more of our young to acquire higher education. Since higher education changed my life I have been a great supporter of widening participation. Unfortunately, opportunities to actually become professional lawyers have not been commensurate. The increased supply of law graduates has coincided with disgraceful cuts to legal aid and a constriction in recruitment by chambers and law firms of newly qualified lawyers. After obtaining a law degree or doing a law conversion course a student who wants to practise law faces a choice of acquiring a vocational diploma either for the Bar or to become a solicitor. The private providers with whom students must undertake this training charge enormous fees. So, for many, further debt is acquired. After this outlay and additional set of exams they must then secure a 'pupillage' in chambers for practical training at the Bar or a training contract with a firm of solicitors. Places are now few and far between and competition is fierce. My long-standing fear has been that the combined deterrents of financial burden and scarcity of places will turn the Bar back into the preserve of the well-to-do.

The wealth gap is being to some extent plugged by the estimated £5 million in funding and scholarships now provided by the Inns each year. These scholarships are vital in ensuring that the Bar doesn't end up as a career that is out of the reach to all but the very few, and they are an important statement of the Inns' commitment to ensuring equality of access to the profession. Some scholarships are reserved for students who come from disadvantaged backgrounds, have a disability, or plan to undertake publicly funded work. The vast majority take the applicant's financial means into account. Yet there are problems here, too. Even though chambers are now obliged to provide financing for a number of pupils, the effect of this has been to reduce the number of pupillages because of the cost to chambers. Another problem is that most students are obliged to spend their awards on their vocational training, leading to a revolving door between the Inns' coffers and the bank accounts of the private providers. As a result, the Inns are now seeking to reintroduce their own in-house training, at a significantly reduced cost.

There were no generous scholarships available when I was starting out. And it was clear to me that I was not likely to be taken on as a tenant, a fully recognised member who has his/her name on the door and thus officially becomes one of the barristers practising from those chambers. Obtaining a tenancy was extremely difficult, because the number of those emerging from pupillage and looking for tenancies considerably outstripped that of available spaces. So I joined forces with five other novice practitioners of radical inclination and decided to establish a new set of chambers in 1974. We were from the outset committed to gender equality and there were three men and three women – all of us feminists. We were also keen to break with the normal ways of organising chambers. Even in chambers where there were women, men often got preferential treatment because of the biases of the clerks. We found a very junior clerk to manage our work, and innocently launched into practice.

I have been involved in the creation of three new sets of chambers. In all of them we sought to challenge discrimination; we pioneered maternity leave and introduced before any other chambers the payment of pupils. After 10 years with the first set of chambers, Garden Court, in 1984 I joined Michael Mansfield in another new endeavour, Tooks

Court, where we made a strong commitment to ethnic diversity. Len Woodley QC, who would become one of the first two black QCs in the country, was one of our leading members, and half of our juniors were from an ethnic minority background. Then in 1989 I moved to Dr Johnson's Buildings – the chambers of John Mortimer QC – where a group were planning yet another new enterprise, which became Doughty Street Chambers. This group were already engaging with international human rights. I was keen to develop my practice in this area and worked with some of them through Charter 88 on the creation of a British bill of rights, which became the Human Rights Act. Our new set was created in 1990 and I became a QC one year later.

One of the key principles in each of these chambers was that we would not entertain having clerks paid on a percentage of the fees paid to individual barristers as it gave them too much power to determine who got work and what kind of work it should be. Traditionally, clerks earned 10% of their barristers' earnings. Over the years this was slowly eroded to 7% or even 5%, but still very high sums were involved. Others earned a percentage of their chambers' turnover, which meant they could make as much as QCs, sometimes in excess of £500,000. Not surprisingly, they held on to their sinecures with an iron grip.

Since clerks so often viewed women as a bad investment – women might take time out to have babies and time off during school holidays – and would channel women's practices into softer areas of law as they saw it, I felt clerks had to be salaried. That way we could do public interest work without the financial clock ticking and large amounts of pro bono work too. In Doughty Street we organised chambers like a very modern business with a practice manager and administrator. We reshaped chambers so that we had conference rooms rather than individual rooms for many of the barristers and a shared library and librarian for research. Senior members employed PAs to help run their professional life, and we paid an overall percentage of our incomes into chambers instead of rent. We were also outside of the Temples. We wanted a whole new efficient way of operating.

Before long, others followed suit. In the 1990s, to survive the removal of monopoly rights, with accountants and solicitors and in-house corporate lawyers increasingly taking on areas of work traditionally handled by the Bar, chambers realised they had to be more competitive and businesslike. They were being forced away from the quill pen and into intimacy with new technology. They needed a different infrastructure. Clerks were increasingly replaced by salaried practice managers and chief administrators, often women, who came from experience in the City and marketing and who were only too willing to realise the potential of women in the law so long as it was a money-spinner. A new generation of clerks emerged which saw women as a resource not to be wasted. Yet none of this meant that the old problems were entirely eradicated. Even today, there are reports of women barristers finding it difficult to obtain the kind and quality of work they want. The suspicion lingers that in some chambers the best cases go to the remaining clerks' favoured, invariably male, barristers.

Many of the problems women and others have faced in the legal profession are similar to those encountered in any job. The law is not the only profession in which people have got jobs through having the right social connections, or knowing the right people or having gone to Oxbridge. Nor is it the only occupation in which style, appearance, demeanour and self-confidence play a large part in success. As Mary Beard, the classical scholar, pointed out in her book *Women and Power*, the roots of misogyny go back to ancient times where it was made clear that the voices of women were unwelcome in public discourse. However, as well as the traditional legal and cultural obstacles, there are also structural problems. Women have to overcome the handicaps created by the already established tracks which divide the profession into elite and non-elite areas, and where they find themselves more readily functioning in areas that are undeservedly less prestigious, such as family law, child protection and low-level crime.

In 1990 I stood for election to the Bar Council specifically on the platform that I wanted to raise issues affecting women. I had realised that the only way to create real change was to engage with the institutions where power lies. Once I was a member of the council I argued for the creation of a women's committee, like the one which existed on race discrimination. I was accused of political correctness – an argument invariably made by those who want to maintain the old order. The male leader of the North Eastern Circuit – the grouping of barristers practising in the Newcastle and York area – berated me for having the audacity to speak for all women and insisted that the women of his circuit were perfectly happy, thank you, and did not need me to complain on their behalf. I would have preferred to have heard it from them, and in private. The point of a committee was that it would draw in many different women and that is when you see change.

With the support of the new Association of Women Barristers, and Anthony Scrivener QC, who was then chairman of the Bar, we secured the creation of a committee in 1992 under Sir Stephen Sedley, an enlightened judge. Women experienced discrimination when they applied for pupillage, when they applied for tenancies, when they applied for silk and when it came to the appointment of judges. The research was conclusive and confirmed what many of us knew. The remit of our original committee has since been expanded to encompass a wide range of equality, diversity and social mobility issues, and is all the better for it.

Since then there has been real change. Gender discrimination moved into the mainstream. From 2012, all chambers have been required to maintain a comprehensive equality policy, with an appointed equality officer, and to monitor their performance against a wide range of equality criteria. Compliance has been patchy, with a 2016 survey finding that 50% of chambers were failing to adhere to all or some of the equality rules. It does seem that the Bar itself is slowly beginning to recognise that principles of fairness, as well as the need to secure the best candidates, require the equitable treatment of men and women, yet intersectionality is an issue at the Bar as everywhere. Young women from working-class backgrounds find it harder because of the financial burdens in getting started, and young black women face additional hurdles. The combination of different types of discrimination can be especially insidious and persistent, and the answer is particularly hard to crack.

Despite protestations that discrimination is a thing of the past, change has not gone to the core. Today women represent nearly 50% of practising solicitors and 37% of barristers. Yet throughout their careers women in the law earn significantly less than men. Female solicitors are still failing to gain promotion in sufficient numbers.

Women participate less in the interstices of the law – the circuit dinners, the cricket matches, the golf, the wine committees, the Bar Council and specialist Bar associations. They are likely to know fewer judges socially and will not be championed in their career rise in the same way that men are. Legal cultures are premised on notions which are themselves exclusive. A woman MP, acknowledging similar problems in the House of Commons, described men 'talking up' an aspirant male colleague in a way that would rarely be done for a woman. The lubrication of patronage is not as readily available to facilitate the rise of women. Although there are considerably more women than men at the junior end of the profession, women are much less likely to reach the holy grail of partnership, which is the most senior and best remunerated status a solicitor can hold. Despite significant progress in some regions and sectors, women accounted for only 33% of partners in law firms in 2015. The picture is much worse in the biggest City firms, where it is not uncommon for female representation in the partnership to dip below 20%. Women's pay is also driven by the areas of law in which they function, with women more likely to develop specialisms that are less glamorous and less well paid.

It is a similar story at the Bar. Only around 14% of QCs are women. As of 2013, women made up 61% of family law practitioners, who often undertake poorly paid, publicly funded work. Meanwhile, 75% of the barristers bagging the lucrative commercial and chancery work are men. Until comparatively recently women played no part at all in the construction and content of the law, but even now their role in law-making is seriously limited. Before 2003 there was no woman at all in the Appellate Committee of the House of Lords, our highest court. The appointment of the brilliant Brenda Hale to Their Lordships' ranks was long overdue. In 2009 the committee was abolished and the Supreme Court was established with 12 justices and again Brenda Hale remained the sole woman. It took eight more years before she was joined by Jill Black in 2017, making just two women at the apex of our legal system. Fortunately, the parliamentary role in law-making has been improved by the increasing presence of women in the legislature as MPs and peers. Female representation in Parliament reached a record high following the 2017 general election, and the fact that as I write the prime minister and the Scottish and Northern Irish First Ministers are all women shows that genuine progress is being made. Yet men still dominate, with women still only making up 32% of elected MPs.

Research conducted and published in 1998 showed that between the ages of 29 and 36, the number of women leaving the Bar was twice that of men. Depressingly, the picture is much the same 20 years on. Women continue to have a disproportionately higher attrition rate than men, with nearly 70% of female barristers who participated in a 2016 study claiming to have at some point considered leaving the Bar, and if current industry conditions prevail, we are unlikely ever to achieve a 50:50 gender balance among all practising barristers.

For many years, the lack of research on the topic required us to make (fairly obvious) guesses as to the reasons why women were leaving the Bar in such droves. Today, studies have confirmed long-held suspicions; women's most commonly cited reasons for leaving include family commitments and the difficulties of combining the long-hours culture of life at the Bar with caring responsibilities. As self-employed professionals, barristers are not entitled to the same maternity protections available to most people. Under new Bar equality rules, all chambers are required to have a maternity leave policy, which must provide for rent breaks and a minimum period of leave. Within these fairly broad parameters, however, chambers can set their own policies. And then there is the age-old problem of 'out of sight, out of mind', with women on maternity leave often feeling out of the loop or overlooked. All in all, it is not surprising that nearly three-quarters of women from the 2016 survey stated that taking maternity or parental leave impacted on their practice or career progression. In 2017, the decision was taken to change the Bar equality rules to enable all self-employed barristers to take one year's parental leave, regardless of whether their spouse or partner also takes parental leave. It is to be tentatively hoped that this rule change will go some way towards reducing the disadvantages experienced by new mothers at the Bar.

Women also leave the 'magic circle' City law firms in their thirties citing dissatisfaction with the nature of the work, saying they find it unfulfilling. While this may be true, research suggests that the 'adaptive principle' may be operating as well, whereby women recognise the limits on their opportunities for promotion in a given environment and leave because they are adapting their views of the work to those limitations. Crucially, losing women in significant numbers for any of these reasons also dilutes the pool from which judges will be drawn five or ten years down the road.

It is true that the last five years have seen a concerted effort to both understand and improve women's prospects at the Bar. The increased emphasis on gathering diversity data has been critical to this effort, as has mandatory equal opportunities policies. Yet the problem remains one of how to implement good intentions; a quick glance below the surface reveals that there are often inadequate structures to turn the aspiration of equality into a reality. In the law schools there have been more female law students than men for a number of years now, and they are coming through with excellent qualifications, often far better than the men. Some of those now coming to the Bar are mature women making a courageous career change. They deserve to be in a profession which is flexible enough to embrace their family responsibilities as well as their talent. A new generation of men at the Bar also think differently about fatherhood. They too want to spend time with their children and many are living with women who expect them to take their share of the domestic load. A self-employed profession like the Bar should be eminently suited to new ways of working and it is time the Bar mothered some creative structural change.

Another problem about the self-employed Bar is that each step up the ladder relies upon relationships of goodwill. Securing briefs means being smart and good at the job but it also means being liked by solicitors or by a senior counsel who chooses you as his or her junior on a big case. Getting a pupillage or a tenancy again involves having people rooting for you, being your champion. These goodwill relationships lend themselves to exploitation. The misuse of a young lawyer's determination to impress can lead to unfair work demands but also inappropriate requests of a sexual nature, especially if you are a young woman. Sexual harassment is common in the legal profession. Working with someone privately on very challenging cases can easily lead to the relinquishing of appropriate boundaries. Young women tell stories of QCs presumptuously booking double rooms when they go out of town with them to do cases or of solicitors promising briefs in high-profile cases if favours are received.

The raised public profile of sexual harassment cases in 2017 has brought into existence Behind the Robe, an organisation to which victims of abuse at the Bar can turn for guidance. The fear that reporting misconduct will blight their careers or lead to reprisals has stopped complainants taking steps against this abuse of power. Until now it has also been unclear where to turn as everyone is self-employed. Unfortunately, senior women in the victims' chambers are sometimes unsupportive, recounting their own ability to beat away sex pests when they were young and insisting that if a woman cannot deal with a sexual nuisance she should not be at the Bar. This is the kind of comment that adds to the feelings of misery and self-doubt that haunt women who experience harassment or bullying. Clear policies are now being created across the legal profession, and chambers should be asking abusers and harassers to leave if misconduct is established. The Equality Act 2010 makes it clear that a sexually-laden environment constitutes discrimination at work.

As I started to practise law, it became increasingly clear to me that, wherever they stand in the courtroom, women have to fight harder to gain the same authority or credibility as their male counterparts. As soon as it was announced that the alibi witness was a wife, girlfriend or female family member, eyes would often roll to the heavens in tacit agreement that her testimony would be worthless. I used to think that women police officers would be seen as especially worthy of trust, given that they have not been tainted by police corruption scandals and are portrayed in television dramas like *Prime Suspect* and *Happy Valley* as tough but tender and ethically unimpeachable. However, women in the police force tell me this is not true. It is assumed that, like women in the family, they are seen as *less* trustworthy, they will lie to save the skin of male colleagues, or be even more ruthless when on a crusade to convict an accused. Female lawyers often describe being patronised and marginalised, their legal arguments given greater weight when repeated in the mouths of male colleagues. It happens in all the main institutions. In the House of Commons, male politicians still feel entitled to make 'woof-woof' noises at their female colleagues, or advise them to 'calm down, dear'.

The Bar is not an easy choice for women, for reasons other than the same old prejudices. It can be very hard to compete publicly and enter into open debate with men. We are still not educated adequately for it. We are still training women not to offend. Women on public platforms or around board tables are still not heard because they rarely make full use of their authority and too often use language which men do not hear.

Advocacy is about communicating and persuading, something women can do as well as men – they are often more down to earth and less pompous. It requires the marshalling of material, research, the ability to charge your argument with imagery. It involves an inter-play of the cerebral and the emotional, with a shifting of emphasis between the two, depending on your recipients. You have to be quick on your feet and have a good memory. Confidence and skill in advo-cacy come from doing it repeatedly, but irascible judges don't make the going easy. I try to encourage female pupils to watch other women in court, to show them that they do not have to behave like men or function in any way that feels unnatural.

But criminal advocacy can raise a particular problem for women precisely because it is the most adversarial arena in the court system. You have to enjoy the taste of blood and some on the bench feel uncomfortable with assertive women, an ambivalence that becomes very clear when arguments are heated. Not long ago, in cases involving a female barrister on both sides, interventions of the 'come now, ladies' variety were common, said in a tone which suggested that some kind of catfight was breaking out. Even today, genteel charm is still the expected role; aggression is considered phallic, certainly unattractive in a woman. The way we continue to socialise girls means they are taught to avoid confrontation and encouraged to please. Both can be useful skills in advocacy, but in courtroom battles you also have to be bold, and having a cross daddy figure up there on the bench can create a real identity problem.

Quite unjustly, women continue to be not as highly rated as advocates as are men. Samuel Johnson's old adage still holds: like performing dogs, the surprise is not that they might do it well but that they do it at all. In my student days *Glanville Williams: Learning the Law* was set reading and in it he unabashedly asserted that women were not usually suited to the Bar because their voices did not have the right timbre and were hard on the ear. Subsequent versions were trimmed of the offending remarks but not before their poison had been swallowed by generations of women. Yet, as recently as 2001, a civil judge in the Royal Courts of Justice, Master Robert Turner, wrote a guide to advocacy which criticised women lawyers for being too quietly spoken. The possibility that he might be a touch deaf had not occurred to him.

Fortunately, women are becoming much less vulnerable to the criticism that only tough old boots survive in the criminal courts. I was constantly told by colleagues that the word among certain judges was that I was a terrible virago who ate small boys for breakfast. Whoever this woman was that filled them with terror, she became particularly confusing when she was pregnant. The contradictory myths about women are profoundly in conflict when an advocate fighting her corner is also a symbol of fecundity. There is a tangible difference in atmosphere. Juries are bemused and interested; judges are benign, and worry about being seen to argue with you. I was tempted to make it a permanent state in the interests of my clients.

One very tangible challenge for women lawyers is language. There is far too much pomp and circumstance in British courts, but after discussing courtroom experience with female attorneys in the USA I can appreciate that there are benefits to be gained from some degree of formality. It is a question of getting the balance right. One of the major complaints by American female lawyers is that they are often undermined in court by being referred to as 'honey' by their male colleagues, and even by judges – not a problem I have ever encountered in the Old Bailey, where the hardship was much more likely to be about being acknowledged at all, lawyers too often being collectively referred to as 'gentlemen'. That said, I also know many women who dislike the English practice of addressing all female advocates as 'Miss'. This infantilising and irritatingly persistent label applies across the board, irrespective of a woman's age, seniority or family status. I recently had a judge reprimand me in a petulant, headmasterish way in open court. I had seen him do this before to another woman QC in a previous trial. One of the shocking statistics in a recent survey was that 22% of women at the Bar reported bullying. This judge had in fact been quite bullying to all the counsel but he seemed to have a particular problem in knowing how to deal with senior women of his own age. Seniority makes it possible sometimes for a QC to say what younger lawyers can't. When the jury went out, I told him I found it unacceptable to be spoken to in a condescending way in front of a jury when I was old enough to be the mother of some of them. He was utterly dumb-founded and slouched off the bench very confused, but it affected his demeanour towards all counsel thereafter. If judges want respect they must not abuse their authority; they need to treat others with respect even if they disagree with an argument or find a case distasteful; they have to learn to treat grown women appropriately.

Perhaps with too much accommodation, I learned to live with the assertion that the male pronoun includes the female before realising that, if the law and courtroom analogies are always couched in male pronouns, it is more difficult for juries to see women embraced by their application. Even the relatively recent Sexual Offences Act 2003 uses the pronoun 'he' throughout when referring to the complainant in rape when it is usually women who are the victims. It makes no sense to the listener.

Language often perpetuates hidden values, and a conscious effort has to be made to make professional language include women. Studies have shown that when women read job advertisements which use the male pronoun they do not see themselves as applicants. A young student barrister recently told me of how, in a mock trial competition, she had unthinkingly referred to the female judge throughout as 'M'Lud'. She completed her submissions and sat down, whereupon she was morti-fied to be informed of her mistake. She later explained that she had simply become accustomed to using the male pronoun in her advocacy exercises, all of which had taken place before male judges, and where the tutors spoke all the time of M'Lud.

The United States, Canada and Australia led the way in ensuring that new legislation was drafted in inclusive language, while also committing to updating and revising existing legislation. By a written ministerial statement issued by the then Justice Secretary, Jack Straw, in 2007, the UK government finally accepted that use of the male pronoun to refer to both men and women risked reinforcing historic gender stereotypes, and announced its commitment to using gender-neutral legislative language as far as possible. One problem about using he/she in domestic violence or rape is that it gives the impression that the offences are just as often committed by women as men when the opposite is true and the reality is therefore disguised. The good news is that our judges are coming to accept the symbolic effect of language. There are encouraging reports of enlightened male judges asking counsel to refer to a predominantly female appellate bench as 'Your Ladyships'.

In the scramble up the professional ladder, becoming a Queen's Counsel is an important milestone. A successful barrister will consider applying after about 20 years, but the transition is not automatic and only a small proportion of practising barristers 'take silk', as donning the new robe is called. The procedure, like everything in the law, was histori-cally wrapped in secrecy and involved applying to the Lord Chancellor to be considered by him for appointment. Soundings were taken from the judges to assess your standing – and the sound might be a raspberry if you were a rocker of boats or a person not fitting the mould. No reasons were given for refusal; some barristers waited years before being appointed.

Thanks to reforms introduced in 2004, the process by which today's leading lights are identified is much more transparent, and applicants are provided with stage-by-stage guidance on the selection process. Just as sunlight is said to be the best of disinfectants, this new transparency has trained a spotlight upon the dark crevices in which secretive and therefore questionable value judgements previously operated. Yet as I have already shown, the number of women who make it through this selection process is still depressingly low. More must be done to encourage women to actually apply to take silk; female barristers commonly cite lack of confidence as a key reason for not applying. Applicants both male and female can still be very secretive about whether they have applied, considering a refusal a vote of no confidence. I was open about being refused on my first application, and spoke about it when asked on *Woman's Hour* in 1990 because I believed, and still do, that furtiveness feeds unacceptable practices and secrecy is far too rife in the law. Perhaps the powers that be feared I would go on to make an annual announcement over the airwaves about being turned down, so they relented in 1991.

Having more women on the top rung of the practitioners' ladder is as significant for women as increasing the number of female judges. Lawyers in silk take on the most demanding and important cases, many of which have real social reverberations.

In the studies of Dr R. M. Kanter, reported in the *Harvard Women's Law Journal*, whenever people of any social type are proportionally scarce (i.e. less than 20% of the total), the dynamics of tokenism are set in motion. Token appointees are more visible and worry about being seen to fail. They are also faced with the choice of accepting comparative isolation or becoming a member of the dominant group at the price of denying their own identity and accepting a definition of themselves as 'exceptional'. The flattery of being labelled in that way can be quite intoxicating for women – the 'queen bee' syndrome – but it also creates a pressure which means that, while in that role, she is not able to fight for her rights as a woman or to stand up for her sex. Instead, there is an incentive for her to turn her back on other women, either literally or figuratively, in order to protect her place.

Women who have made it insist their achievements were gained on merit, a questionable value. More and more women understandably ask whether their skills are undervalued in a system where 'merit' is defined by men. One of the truisms hauled out of the fire in discussions about suitability for the rank of QC or for the bench is whether someone has 'authority', a stamp which usually involves a stern demeanour and a very loud voice. Does someone with a strong Geordie accent lack authority? Or someone with a tiny stature? Another murky criterion is 'decisiveness'. Does that mean bold, quick decision-making or quiet reflection? Is too much reliance placed on skills of oratory? Is advocacy really necessary for the bench? To diversify the bench, experienced solicitors are now being encouraged to apply but then they find that the criteria laid down by judges who were former barristers is used to exclude them.

In 2000 a Commission for Judicial Appointments was created whose job was to audit selection procedures and act as an ombudsman for the judicial and silk appointments process but not to make appointments. The commission, chaired by Sir Colin Campbell, found that the criteria for making silk appointments was so unsystematic as to be subjective and that some consultees' comments appeared to be influenced by a perception of a 'silk mould', which meant that 'successful applicants had to conform to expectations as to appearance, dress, educational or social background and other irrelevant factors'. These consultees were all judges and grandees at the Bar who like some self-perpetuating oligarchy were clearly only endorsing people like themselves. It was a form of cloning. Ninety-seven per cent of those consulted about suitability were male, white and from a narrow social group. A small number of barristers' chambers had a stranglehold on influence:

effectively seen as silk and judge incubators. The result of belonging to those chambers is that the judges and practitioners regularly mingled and the grooming for appointments started early. Close study shows that a hard core of chambers monopolised the appointment process and their idea of what constitutes excellence was immutable. The number of women was low, and black faces rare.

In his first annual report in 2002, Sir Colin showed the system to be a real scandal, with unsupported and sometimes unattributable tittle-tattle and comment recorded against people to their detriment: 'Too primly spinsterish, though her other qualities are self-evident.' 'She's off-puttingly headmistressy.' 'She does not always dress appropriately.' 'Down and out scruffy.' The eight commissioners, who had wide experience in industry, academia and the Civil Service, 'had not in twenty years of experience come across comments like them'. As can be imagined, the disclosures did nothing to dispel concern about the whole process of taking 'soundings' as a method for advancing careers. In other professions people applied for jobs and produced references.

Significant legislative change was brought about by the Constitutional Reform Act 2005, which required the establishment of an independent Judicial Appointments Commission (JAC). Set up in 2006, the JAC is composed of lay and judicial members and has responsibility for appointing judges at all levels save to the Supreme Court, for which ad hoc selection committees are convened. It uses a mix of paper and interview assessments to select candidates to be recommended for appointment. If the Lord Chancellor or the relevant senior judge declines to follow the JAC's recommendation, they must give reasons. While the JAC has a statutory duty to have regard to the need to encourage diversity in the judiciary, it is obliged to select judges 'solely on merit'. Where two applicants are ranked as being of equal merit, a 'tie-break' provision can be applied, which entitles the JAC to choose the candidate who will increase judicial diversity.

Prior to its creation, Sir Colin Campbell expressed serious concerns that the JAC was structurally flawed, and that it risked perpetuating the old problems. As Sir Colin pointed out: 'Some people are worried that the new commission might just be a shell in which traditional practices might continue.'

Sadly, he has been proved right. As we have seen, the rate of diversification of the judiciary, particularly at senior levels, has remained woefully slow. When the suggestion was made that well-qualified women might be fast-tracked, Lord Sumption baulked at the idea but commented that it may well take 50 years for gender parity to be fully achieved within the judiciary. At the current pace of change, this is a significant underestimate.

I strongly believe that this slow progress is in large part due to the old chestnut that people must only be appointed on merit. Like other institutions, the law uses the meritocracy argument to deflect challenges about how it makes its appointments. Merit is a notion which on its face is unobjectionable. It is presented as another of those neutral concepts, an apolitical criterion of personal worth. Yet the concept of merit is not self-defining, and nor is it inherently objective. Rather, it is a question of who defines excellence. No one can help relying on their own experiences, values and preconceptions when assessing the merit of others. The risk is that the supposedly neutral criterion of merit becomes a vehicle by which the norms of the dominant group are entrenched. I refuse to accept that there are fewer women with sufficient merit to fill the top jobs.

So what can be done? Many talented and dedicated lawyers and policymakers, both male and female, myself included, have refused to throw our hands up in despair. A 2014 Labour Party report by two QCs, Geoffrey Bindman and Karon Monaghan, points out that the JAC's conceptions of merit do not embrace the importance of diversity for the judiciary as a whole. They suggest that the value of a candidate to the creation of a diverse judiciary should itself be regarded as an element of merit. Another of their suggestions is the introduction of a quota system to ensure proportionate representation of women and minorities within the judicial system. The idea of judicial quotas is predictably unpopular. Lord Sumption was reported in the *Evening Standard* as urging patience and cautioning against the transformation of the judicial system overnight. Apparently, His Lordship was worried that the men would feel as though the cards were stacked against them.

I am in favour of quotas because I think that otherwise we will wait forever for real change. I am particularly amused by the story that female or BAME judges selected to fulfil a quota will be regarded as less able than their colleagues and they will feel they got there by some unfair mechanism. Unfair! What is unfair is what has been going on for millennia. How able are the current incumbents? I get depressed when I hear women say they do not want to be appointed on anything but merit, as though some miraculously just system appointed the men currently in office. I know that quotas will not immediately receive a welcome, but we do need immediate change. A recent report by JUSTICE, a law reform and human rights organisation of which I am president, offers an alternative, less intrusive way of achieving gender parity in the judiciary. The authors argue for 'targets with teeth'; manageable diversity goals aimed at ensuring that a publicly stated proportion of judicial appointments are women, or drawn from other under-represented groups, with any failure to comply requiring an explanation by the relevant appointments body. JUSTICE argues that each court should have an 'appointable pool' of candidates who are willing and qualified to serve as, for example, High Court judges. Judges would then be drawn from the pool as and when vacancies arise, with women, ethnic minority or specialist candidates being given priority at least in the short term. These are innovative ideas propounded by people who are taking the lack of representation in the judiciary very seriously indeed.

When Baroness Hale gave the Independent and Bar Law Reform Lecture in London in November 2004, she quoted Chief Justice Beverley McLachlan of the Supreme Court of Canada who gave a rationale for women 'as judges'.

> The most important reason why I believe we need women on our benches is because we need the perspectives that women can bring to judging. This is because jurists are human beings, and, as such, are informed and influenced by their backgrounds, community and experiences. For cultural, biological, social and historic reasons women do have different experiences than men.

With increased numbers of women at every level in the law it would function differently; men would ease up on many of their attitudes, and myths would be shattered. If judges during their luncheon recess were sitting round a table talking about their cases with many more women and being ribbed for their arcane views, they might start taking stock of a different kind of experience. Isolated women cannot challenge that culture.

It is essential for people to see women in positions of power. We have to stop sending out the message that only a special breed of person can get to be a lawyer or a judge, and that they all wear dark suits and talk with marbles in their mouths. We can only hope to gain the public's confidence if that kind of remoteness from the real world is addressed.

The smell of the gentleman's club permeates every crevice of the Inns of Court. It is hard to untangle the web of very fine biases which are insinuated, like that smell, into the system. As Mary Robinson, the former president of Ireland and an eminent human rights lawyer, has said:

> Every society maintains an invisible life where attitudes and assumptions are formed. Every society is hostage to this unseen place, where fear conquers reason and old attitudes remain entrenched. It is here that the chance phrases and small asides are made which say so little and reveal so much.
>
> If we are to go forward we need to look at attitudes and the language which expresses attitude ... If we are to strike a balance, if we are to readjust participation and enrich our society with dialogue, we have to revise this way of thinking.

2

THE GOOD WIFE AND MOTHER

There was a little girl, who had a little curl
Right in the middle of her forehead.
When she was good, she was very, very good
But when she was bad she was horrid.

When Jeffrey Archer, the former Conservative Party chairman, sued the *Star* for libel in 1987 over his alleged association with a prostitute, his wife gave evidence on his behalf. She indicated discreetly that she and her husband enjoyed a full married life, speaking with delicacy about the indelicate. She was the exemplar of the 'good wife', standing by her husband as the wives of John Profumo and Cecil Parkinson had done before her. She was dressed unassumingly but with great care, attractive without being striking.

Mr Justice Caulfield was moved to lyricism when he dealt with Mary Archer's evidence. Giving his directions to the jury ('giving directions' is when the judge instructs the jury on how to approach the evidence in the case), he suggested to them that their vision of her in the witness box would never disappear. Indeed, His Lordship became quite rapturous. 'Has she fragrance? Would she have, without the strain of this, radiance?' His personal view that Mrs Archer's scent could expunge any whiff of scandal was undisguised. Here was the flower of womanhood, whose moral worth shone like a flame in the murky world of tabloid newspapers, sex and call girls.

Monica Coghlan, the prostitute, was Mary Magdalene to Mrs Archer's Virgin Mary in this morality play. Her evidence did not evoke much sympathy and in the view of judge and jury was probably untruthful. Here was a woman who sold her body to the next buyer and who might lie for the right price.

Polar examples of the female sex, these two women created a contrast which was orchestrated by the press and which enabled Jeffrey Archer to recede from the centre of the courtroom drama. But in 2001, he was back before the courts charged with perjury. It transpired that he had lied in the libel action, having presented a false account of his movements on the night he had allegedly been with Monica. This time Mary had a tougher ride when she strode confidently into the witness box. No less fragrant, she was now portrayed as steely, calculating and manipulative. The stereotyping of women is an extraordinary phenomenon to behold and the lightning changes in how women are perceived can be the result of almost subliminal codes.

The good wife features regularly in our courts, usually as the other half of a male offender. For, as the songs and stories tell us, the love of a good woman can be the making of a man, and any hope of redemption is often deemed to lie with a criminal's wife. Wives are also brought forth as a measure of whether the man has reason to mend his ways. Hidden victims of the criminal justice system, they and their children, as well as their spouses, have sentences passed upon them. Every term of imprisonment means for them the loneliness of separation, bringing up a family without support, suffering financial hardship, and the misery of long journeys and unfulfilling visits to remote prisons.

Wives are rarely indicted for being passive beneficiaries of criminality. If a husband indulges in unconventional means of bringing home the bacon, more often than not it is accepted as unlikely that his wife will be able to prevent it. She usually has to play an active role before the police will charge her, though her safe passage can be the bargaining counter used effectively by the police to get the husband to 'cough'. Wives and womenfolk are the subject of frequent deals, where she goes home to the kids if the main contender sees sense and takes the rap. In 2010, the former Scottish Socialist Party leader Tommy Sheridan and his wife Gail found themselves charged with perjury. It was alleged that the pair had lied during a defamation case, brought against the *News of the World* in 2006 after the tabloid accused the politician of being an adulterer who visited swingers' clubs. The charges against Gail Sheridan were ultimately dropped, but not before prosecutors reportedly put considerable pressure on her husband to plead guilty in return for his wife walking free.

When the good wife does appear in the dock, it is usually because she has allowed her love for her husband to 'seduce' her into crime, helping him to escape custody, harbouring him from the forces of law or concealing stolen items. Because the image of the faithful and supportive – if misguided – wife is so powerful, defence lawyers always try to turn a female client into just such a one. The use of the term 'common-law wife' is insinuated into proceedings precisely for this purpose, intended to communicate those positive aspects of womanliness that combine to create the archetypal wife. Judges and juries alike have a soft spot for this romanticised ideal; when charged with playing some ancillary role the good wife is often acquitted.

This is what gives rise to the misguided claim that women benefit from chivalry. But in reality the good wife stereotype only assists women who fit the mould. In 2004 family members of a man who had committed a suicide bombing in Tel Aviv were put on trial, including his wife. I acted for the brother of the bomber. The allegation was that as his wife, intimately involved with him, she must have known that he was going off to kill himself and others in an act of terrorism. A new law introduced after 11 September 2001 placed a duty on people to inform on others if they suspected anything connected with terrorism. Failure to inform was made, and remains, a criminal offence even for a wife. Wives of IRA men, who probably knew when their other half disappeared for weeks that they were part of an active service unit, were never prosecuted because it was accepted that to do so would be futile and counterproductive in the community. Expecting a woman who has the care of a family and profound emotional loyalties to pop down to the police station to 'grass' on her man was implausible. The Muslim community not surprisingly felt that the legal change with its new approach to wives was specially designed as an assault upon it and was affronted by the appearance of this devout young mother bereft by her husband's death. The clincher in her acquittal was the irrefutable evidence that after the birth of her newest baby she had gone to her doctor to have a contraceptive coil fitted – not the act of a faithful wife who knew her young husband was on his way to his death.

Some wives can be too accommodating. When the Liberal Democrat MP and Cabinet minister in the coalition government Chris Huhne left his wife Vicky Pryce in June 2010, she slipped to the media the information that she had taken speeding points for her husband to prevent him losing his driving licence, which would have caused him difficulties in his busy political life. She tried to put the information of his criminal malfeasance into the public domain in a way that damaged him but did not boomerang back and bring down the forces of law on her own head.

The whole business brought both Huhne and Pryce before the courts for perverting the course of justice; the MP pleaded guilty, thereby putting an end to his political career but Pryce contested the case before a jury, maintaining she had been subjected to marital coercion. The jury did not believe her and convicted. She was sentenced to eight months' imprisonment, served nine weeks, and wrote a strong book about the senselessness of imprisoning so many women who had committed low-level crime. Drawing on her own expertise as an economist, she called the book *Prisonomics* and concentrated on the fact that, as well as wasting lives, it made poor financial sense. The case gave rise to an interesting public debate about whether marital coercion was an old-fashioned defence to crime which had had its day given the modern emancipation of women. However, it was pointed out by many of us that while it may have been hard for a jury to believe that the redoubtable Vicky Pryce would be coerced by anyone, many women are forced under threat by spouses to commit all sorts of offences and the defence still had its place in the law. What was also notable about the case was the vituperative comments by the trial judge who clearly formed a poor view of Pryce and characterised her as a 'vengeful', 'controlling', 'manipulative' and 'devious' woman. All words that have haunted the case law over the centuries when dealing with women.

In the gamut of crime, women usually commit less serious offences. They also tend to play supportive roles: harbouring and handling stolen goods, carrying drugs, providing safe houses, cashing stolen cheques. As in the world of legitimate enterprises, they are on the payroll but are rarely the paymaster, a syndrome that is usually reflected in shorter sentences but has nothing to do with the kindness of judges. While Joyti De Laurey, the personal assistant to a director of Goldman Sachs, may have spirited away over £4 million without her banker boss noticing, few women embark on such bold embezzlement. White-collar criminals usually have a wife at home laundering their shirts. The attitude of the court to a female accused still depends on the kind of woman she is perceived to be. In itself this is no different from the conscious and unconscious approach to any defendant, who is judged according to all sorts of hidden criteria, such as whether they are employable or whether they show enough respect to the court. But for a woman, the assessment of her worth is enmeshed in very limiting ideas. If she challenges conventions in any significant way, she is seen as threatening or, at the least, disappointing. A mere hint in court that a woman might be a bad mother, a bit of a whore or emotionally unstable, and she is lost.

Preconceived ideas about 'good' women have always affected judges' decisions. When wavering between a prison sentence and a community order, many judges play the sugar-and-spice game of deciding what this little girl is made of. The tests they apply commonly revolve around our clients' functions as wives, mothers and daughters. Women who break the rules by being dissolute or unfaithful, or by otherwise not fulfilling their wifely functions, are bad wives. The courts do not like bad wives. 'Mistresses' and casual girlfriends fare little better, with their negative connotations of adulterous relationships and promiscuity. Single women pose special problems. Here the issue is whether they lead orderly or disorderly lives, hold down jobs and have community or family ties.

Good mothers get credit from the court. Yet the principles applied in deciding whether or not someone is a good mother are essentially middle class. The emphasis is less on how many hours women spend prattling with their children or rolling together on the floor than on cleanliness and homemaking skills. Pre-sentencing reports, written by people who know the market with which they are dealing, make references to the spick-and-span council flat, the well-kept home, the neatly arranged ornaments and the scrubbed children. If a woman's children are in care her failure is already established, and whatever circumstances led to the separation are largely ignored.

The compulsion to make women fulfil accepted criteria of decent womanhood is a great temptation to lawyers and experts alike, who in colluding with it succumb to a paternalism which effectively marginalises women. The prosecutions in the last 20 years of Sally Clark, Angela Cannings and Trupti Patel – all mothers accused of killing their babies – are a case in point. The common feature in these three shocking cases, besides the fact that each woman had lost more than one baby in circumstances that are commonly described as cot deaths, was that men in the police, medicine and the law jumped to conclusions about the capacity of these women as mothers. The burden of proof was reversed and there was an assumption of guilt rather than the presumption of innocence.

These women failed to fit the straitjacket of 'natural' mothers according to some fantasy of how natural mothers conduct themselves.

They were questioned as to the frequency of the cuddles they administered and comments were made on the amount of tears shed. Perceived lack of emotion was read as callousness. Over and over again Sally Clark was described as a career woman who had a luxury dream home as though there was clearly no place for babies in her world. Sally Clark and Angela Cannings were both convicted of murdering their babies and sentenced to life imprisonment until their convictions were overturned in 2003. Sally Clark had served three years and Angela Cannings served one year before the convictions were quashed. Trupti Patel, a pharmacist, was acquitted by a jury in May 2003 despite prosecution claims that 'against nature or instinct' she too had smothered her children. At her trial she called her aged grandmother from India, who testified that she had lost five of her 12 children in early infancy, which suggested strongly that there could be some sort of genetic reason for the unexpected deaths. The cause of sudden infant death syndrome is still unknown.

Sally Clark's first appeal was unsuccessful. Yet her friends and lawyers laboured away until they turned up a medical report which had not been made available at her trial; it showed that her second baby, Harry, had an infection at the time of his death. On seeing the test results – which had mysteriously never been disclosed – two eminent pathologists stated that in their view Harry died of natural causes. No one had ever doubted that the earlier death of Christopher was anything other than natural until doctors began to 'think dirty' because a second baby died. Sir Roy Meadow, the star witness for the prosecution, had testified that two deaths were unnatural, telling the jury that there was a 'one in 73 million chance' that both deaths had occurred naturally, something that could only happen once in every hundred years. This statistic was the smoking gun that convicted Sally Clark. In one soundbite the jury had a compelling case against her.

The jury, some of whom were openly weeping, convicted her by 10–2 after two days' deliberation. The statistic was grossly inaccurate. It is more rather than less likely that a mother who has suffered one cot death will suffer another. The true odds were not one in 73 million but one in 60. No one had challenged Sir Roy Meadow on where he had got his statistics, despite his wandering far outside of his field of expertise. He was subsequently struck off by the General Medical Council for serious professional misconduct, albeit to be later reinstated upon appeal.

When Sally Clark's husband visited her in prison and told her that exculpatory evidence had been found, her first reaction was not 'Thank goodness, I'm coming home' but to burst into tears and ask whether Harry had suffered. In 2007, Sally Clark was found dead at her home. The coroner's report recorded a verdict of accidental death by reason of acute alcohol intoxication. According to her family, she had never managed to come to terms with being falsely accused of murdering her children.

The sudden infant death lawsuits were cases where evidential gaps were filled with strange notions about how natural mothers should behave. Ideas about instinctive mothering floated through the courts. The fault did not just lie with doctors or lawyers; the police often fell from grace too. I chaired a working group for the Royal College of Pathology and the Royal College of Paediatrics and Child Health in the aftermath to examine medical, legal and police practice in such cases. I heard accounts from mothers who wakened to find their baby dead and were immediately the subject of suspicion – with crime-scene yellow tape being placed across the door almost as soon as the ambulance had taken the lifeless baby to hospital. Unlike other situations where a person is found dead and the body is left until professional help arrives, distraught parents try to breathe life into it, clean away vomit and mucus, pass the baby between them, splash it with water, put a finger in its mouth to see if something is blocking its airway. To police officers the removal of nightclothes and cleaning away of evidence may seem highly suspicious but parents do not want their baby in cold, wet clothes even if it is dead. They do not want its face crusted with detritus. Evidentially it may be unhelpful but to expect rationality is to lose connection with real lives.

Unfortunately not much has changed since the great scandals of the late nineties. In 2005 Suzanne Holdsworth was convicted of murdering a two-year-old boy, Kyle Fisher, whom she was babysitting for a neighbour. The allegation was that she had beaten his head repeatedly against a wooden banister at her home in Hartlepool. She was given life imprisonment and served three years before her conviction was quashed in 2008 when new medical evidence was presented showing that it was much more likely that Kyle had died of an epileptic fit. The police had jumped to the conclusion that, if the boy was with her when he died, she had clearly done something to him. Her panicked 999 call registered her as saying he was having a fit, which the police assumed was the result of violence. At the post-mortem a pathologist recorded the brain as normal at the time of death. What came to light was that Kyle had suffered an accident not long before his death, which had nothing whatsoever to do with Suzanne Holdsworth. It had happened in his own home and was the result of a fall out of his pushchair onto a fire prong which had pierced his eye socket and penetrated the brain. As a result there was bleeding in the child's skull and water on his brain. Indeed, in photographs taken shortly before his death the little boy's head is enlarged and his eye is clearly drooping, which was explained by doctors at the appeal as being caused by the swelling brain pressing down through the eye socket.

It transpired that the boy was due to have surgery because of the swollen brain and the likely risk of seizures. Although the police claimed they had spoken to the hospital surgeon, he had no record or memory of such a call and was quite clear he would have told the police about the brain injuries and likelihood of seizure. The original autopsy identified no bruising or abrasions to Kyle's skin despite the claim that Suzanne must have beaten him against the banister. No DNA sampling was done of the banister to look for tiny particles of skin. The miscarriage of justice was explained as shoddy police work but it was more than that. The police, for whatever reason, preferred to believe that this woman was guilty of cruel and vicious behaviour towards a child.

In some cases, class divisions as well as gender expectations are at the root of the court's inability to understand how the offences were committed. I remember a case in which a mother of four children was convicted of cutting her son with a breadknife. The woman's children had different fathers, none of whom was around, and two of the children were of mixed race. The family was living on the breadline, in a flat without electricity, and the oldest boy, who was eight, was already showing signs of problem behaviour. Social services confirmed that a change of personnel had resulted in a period with no social work support. A doctor testified that the injury to the boy's head was not serious and would have involved little force. A schoolteacher wrote to the court to describe the effort the woman was putting into helping her children to read. She had minimal previous history of offending. Nevertheless, she was sentenced to 18 months' imprisonment. There is a chasm of misunderstanding between the privileged professionals who work the system and the offender bringing up children alone without financial and emotional resources. The misery of that existence and the toll it can take is rarely appreciated.

The idea that women can be subject to their hormones was the traditional way of explaining otherwise inexplicable behaviour. The special crime of infanticide, available only to a woman who is responsible for the death of her newly born baby, recognises that 'at the time of the act or omission she had not fully recovered from the effect of giving birth or the effect of lactation and for this reason the balance of her mind was disturbed'. The offence was introduced as part of the Homicide Act in 1957 because it was appreciated that a charge of murder was wholly inappropriate, but the charge is confined to the first 12 months of a baby's life.

The availability of contraception and abortion, as well as a change in attitude to the entire issue of illegitimacy, has meant a reduction in cases of infanticide. Girls and young women are not always so ridden with shame and fear of parental response. It makes all the more poignant the Irish case of 15-year-old Anne Lovett, who died in a churchyard in Granard, County Longford, where she had furtively gone to give birth, or the 16-year-old girl who was desperate to hide her pregnancy from her parents and, after giving birth in the bathroom of their home, choked the baby boy to death. Over the years I have represented a number of young girls who have kept their state of pregnancy secret, almost deluding themselves into believing that they were not carrying a child. They have then killed their baby after giving birth in lonely, desperate circumstances, silently enduring the trauma and pain of labour. In one case the girl was in such a state of shock after the birth that she stuffed the baby in her hockey bag, and when the bag moved, in her crazed state she hit it with the hockey stick. The judge spoke to me after the sentencing for infanticide by giving her a conditional discharge and murmured that in the old days the family doctor would just have buried the baby at the bottom of his garden and the family could have got on with their lives. Shame at pregnancy outside marriage, for adult women at least, has largely disappeared in many communities and we should relish the fact. But in some the stigma of dishonour is still so strong that the suffering is unbearable. In another case the accused was a Bangladeshi girl, 14 years old and terrified of telling anyone she had been raped by an uncle. She threw the baby from the bathroom window of a high-rise flat in the seconds after giving birth.

The death of a baby is highly emotive. As a society we have a duty to protect the most vulnerable among us especially if they have no voice and cannot complain of their suffering. In the vast majority of cases where a baby dies it is as a result of natural causes. In most cases where a baby has been killed the mother is suffering from postnatal depression and has spiralled into a nadir of hopelessness. Usually the mother is overwhelmed with guilt and just wants to die herself.

The young woman who stole baby Abbie Humphreys from a maternity ward in 1994 became a hate figure to the public because of the terrible pain and anguish she inflicted on the baby's parents, but she was a sad, mentally unwell girl whose own miscarriage and failure to produce a healthy baby had propelled her into a serious delusional disorder. Instead of telling her family and boyfriend that she had lost her baby, she acted out an extraordinary fantasy pregnancy, filling her trousers with old clothing to simulate a swelling stomach and decorating a nursery for her expected child. The stoning of the prison van which brought her to the court may have assuaged primitive feelings among fellow citizens but courts have to reach beyond atavistic impulses to punish in order to deliver justice. This was a terrible crime but it was the product of mental illness; the judge's response – making a probation order and sending her as a condition to a place where she could have psychiatric treatment – was wholly appropriate.

The pressure to fulfil society's expectation weighs heavily on women. I have represented two very different women who had undergone years of in vitro fertilisation without success and finally adopted children whom they subsequently harmed. One child died; the other is permanently brain-damaged. In each case the years of pursuing motherhood led to heightened expectations and an idealised notion of what it would be like to mother a child. Their personal sense of failure when confronted with the reality of parenting stimulated a mental breakdown in both women. In another case I acted for a young woman who pleaded guilty to the attempted murder of her baby daughter. My client had been so violently abused by her boyfriend that she was demented with terror and could not take any more. She wanted a way out for both of them, took an overdose and tried to smother the sleeping baby. When the baby vomited she was stricken by what she was doing and phoned the police. She ended up in the dock while he was appearing on *Top of the Pops* in a music video, but his behaviour was never exposed; he was covered with anonymity because to name him would have identified the child.

Since the creation of the special female crime of infanticide, the law has come to a greater understanding of mental impairment. However, the infanticide law reflects a paternalistic and generalised approach to women's psychology and physiology, and it is probably time that it is removed from the statute books and absorbed into a reformed Homicide Act. Childbirth and lactation do not dissolve women's brains, but postnatal depression is a recognised disorder and would fulfil the criteria for diminished responsibility in appropriate cases.

Thirty years ago, a young woman of 19 called Ann Reynolds killed her mother shortly after giving birth to a baby whom she had surrendered for adoption. The girl had concealed her pregnancy and taken herself off to a hospital in a nearby town to give birth secretly. In the period that followed, she clearly suffered puerperal depression, and one night, after a confrontation with her mother, she killed her as she slept. She was convicted of murder, the jury having rejected her defence of diminished responsibility, but released on appeal after a campaign by local women led to the involvement of experts, who testified as to her hormonal imbalance, with the emphasis on a chronic premenstrual condition.

Since then, premenstrual syndrome (PMS) has figured a number of times as a defence or mitigation to crime, and in two well-publicised cases has successfully reduced a charge of murder to manslaughter. Christine English crushed her former lover against a telegraph pole with her car, and Sandra Craddock killed another barmaid at the place where she worked. Both pleas to manslaughter were accepted on the grounds of diminished responsibility due to PMS. Christine English received a conditional discharge and driving ban. At first Sandra Craddock's sentence was deferred for a period, during which she received progesterone therapy. The success of the treatment eventually resulted in her receiving a probation order. At a later stage, after a further conviction, her counsel sought in the Court of Appeal to establish PMS as a special defence in its own right, but the judges were having none of it – quite rightly, in my view.

The issue has created unrest among many men and women, the former seeing it as a 'get-out' and the latter as a reinforcement of the 'slaves to hormones' view of women. Because we feel differently about women committing crime, we have over the years gone to some lengths to avoid defining them as criminal, preferring the idea that they have emotional problems; they were mad rather than bad. The truth is that our desire to seek psychiatric explanations for women's crime was a way of trying to make it invisible, a profound expression of our worst fears about the social fabric falling apart. However, medicalising and pathologising women is a way of perpetuating the myth that they are victims of their own physiology and that the function of all women might be intrinsically impaired. The point which has to be emphasised is that these cases of a profoundly disturbed hormonal balance, in which women's physiology affects their mental state, are extremely rare. In my own practice I have used the condition in relation to my client's mental state only twice. In murder cases it can be raised only where evidence is strong that the hormonal imbalance is so extreme that the tests for diminished responsibility are fulfilled. There are probably just as many cases where exceedingly high testosterone levels in the male might account for outbursts of violence. It is just that, as usual, we are more predisposed to explore psychiatric explanations in women.

The workings of the female body and its potential for childbearing are sometimes justifiably used in special pleading for women, but it does have the double bind of being used to shackle women to very confining roles. Biology is commonly assumed to determine women's lives, and there are times when it feels as though it does. Women are rendered much more vulnerable by virtue of their physiology, and the real evidence for this is in the extent to which they are the victims rather than the perpetrators of violence. Most of the violence women experience is in the domestic setting and not on the street. The home is by far the most dangerous place for women.

Yet when it comes to sentencing, judges typically take insufficient account of the fact that women are still the primary carers of children and other family members, and fail to see that the sentencing system is formulated with men in mind. The organisation Women in Prison reports that women, ironically, sometimes receive harsher sentences than men because they are mothers. They may be deemed unsuitable for community service because they have young children, but then the courts, unable or unwilling to come up with an alternative punishment, send them to jail. On other occasions the courts might kill with kindness. The All-Party Parliamentary Group on Women in the Penal System found evidence of women being slapped with community orders festooned with multiple and onerous conditions. Imprisonment for failure to comply is all too often the inevitable result.

When I was first in practice it was claimed that women got off lightly in the courts. However, the lower sentences merely reflected the less serious nature of the offending. The early noughties saw a shocking escalation in the numbers of women being sent to prison. According to Home Office statistics the average female prison population in 1994 was 1,811. By 1999 it stood at 3,247, and in 2005 the number of female prisoners peaked at 4,467. This means the number of women being incarcerated has more than doubled in a period of 10 years without any significant change in the nature of women's offending. Between 2005 and 2015 there was a net increase of 6% in the number of prosecutions taken against women, and a net increase of 11% in the number of convictions for female offenders. Yet the proportion of women committing more serious offences fell by 5% in the same period. It is only very recently that this trend towards imprisoning women has shown any signs of slowing, with the female prison population in overall mild decline since 2005 and coming in at 4,007 on 30 June 2017. Let's hope this trend continues but it will only do so if there is a genuine reappraisal of sentencing and the crisis in the prison system.

The majority of sentenced female prisoners – 84% – are held for non-violent offences despite the constant refrain that prison should really only be used for violent offenders or those committing serious crime. In 2015, the average sentence length for female prisoners was 9.5 months, with 76% of women in prison on short sentences of less than 12 months. These are sentences which serve no earthly purpose other than retributive punishment. In the same year, the most common offence committed by women was shoplifting, which amounted to 80% of all female convictions for theft. Shockingly high numbers of women are also convicted for TV licence evasion. These prosecutions accounted for 36% of all women coming before courts in 2015, up from 20% in 2005. More likely to be at home when the TV licence inspector comes to call, women make up 70% of the defendants prosecuted for that offence.

Once in prison, women are more likely to self-harm. In the year ending March 2016, Ministry of Justice Safety in Custody statistics show a self-harm rate of 2,034 self-harm incidents per 1,000 female prisoners, compared to just 328 per 1,000 male prisoners. A National Audit Office report found that women in prison were 24 times more likely to take their own life than women in the community.

Why did the last 20 years see this disproportionate punishment of women? Some of it can be explained by an increase in the severity of sentences generally. This was caused by the political parties competing over who could be tougher on law and order and a general ratcheting up of sentencing with a shameful rhetoric about punishment by politicians. The tabloids' pursuit of judges who were deemed too lenient created a meaner culture in the courts and it was not helped by the perverse notion that women should just be treated like men, however different their circumstances. I have no doubt that in part we were seeing the crude equation that equality means no soft soaping of women, even if they have babies and young children or a history of being abused. Our call for gender equality has led to a ham-fisted, literal interpretation of equality without considering the context of the women's lives.

As I have already mentioned the idea that gender equality requires everybody to be treated in exactly the same way is a misconception.

Stung by allegations of subconscious sexism, many judges have allowed the pendulum to swing too far back the other way. Some are so keen to appear unbiased that they determinedly ignore the fact that the person standing in front of them in the dock is a woman, whether of the fragrant variety or otherwise. The result is that the particular needs and vulnerabilities of women offenders often go unconsidered in the sentencing process – such as the burden of childcare still being primarily shouldered by women. Some of the comments made by judges who participated in research by Shona Minson in 2014 suggest that this is partially driven by the perceived need to avoid giving women special treatment.

> 'We have to treat everyone equally so we can't make exceptions just because she has children.'
>
> 'I generally try to be gender neutral because there are always going to be individual considerations and they are not purely on a gender basis.'
>
> 'Let's not forget that fathers lose children too, so you know let's equal it up a bit and not make a sexist point.'

These comments miss the point completely. Yes a father loses his children when imprisoned but the question is whether he is the primary carer of those children. It is perfectly legitimate for a judge to acknowledge that a woman's childcare responsibilities make it less appropriate to give her a custodial sentence. Indeed, there are international human rights instruments and Supreme Court decisions that require the courts to do just that. Yet if judges are either unwilling or unable to recognise that treating men and women equally requires more than a simple one-size-fits-all approach, women will continue to receive sentences which are totally out of touch with the realities of their lives. Viewed from the perspective of the women involved, 'gender-blind' sentencing produces just as bad results as Mr Justice Caulfield's scratch-and-sniff approach.

The more sensitive judges know that custody will be devastating for a mother, but feel compelled by sentencing guidelines to send her to prison nonetheless. There are no separate sentencing guidelines for women offenders, and the existing guidelines make next to no mention of gender-specific issues. The result is a limited range of possibilities when it comes to sentencing women. Fines perpetuate the vicious circle of poverty, and are inappropriate for women who simply cannot pay. Prison should not be used for women who have committed non-violent crime, particularly those who have suffered abuse, have young children, or are addicted to drugs or alcohol. Community sentences, which can require women to do unpaid work in their local area, participate in drug or alcohol rehab programmes, or seek treatment for their mental health issues, are more effective than prison at preventing reoffending and targeting the root causes of women's crime. Despite this, community sentencing remains insufficiently adapted to women's needs. While there are many small-scale organisations, programmes and pilot schemes around the country doing sterling work, overall provision of women-specific community options is patchy at best – dependent on uncertain funding and unlikely to improve in the face of sustained budget cuts. Curfews save on the cost of probation officers, but can leave women vulnerable to domestic abuse for the 12 hours per day that they are confined to their homes.

Community service is especially difficult for a mother of small children; she may not have access to childcare facilities while she is doing her unpaid work or attending probation sessions. Little attention is paid to the need to schedule mandatory appointments during school hours. Research by the Prison Reform Trust has found evidence that women's childcare responsibilities are impacting on their ability to comply with their community sentences. The punishment may be imprisonment for breach, even where the original offence would never have merited a custodial sentence. All the research says that robust and comprehensive community sentencing options are the best response to the majority of women's crime, but plainly much more must be done to make them a viable sentencing option, particularly for women with children.

Where a woman's offending is minor, the police may decide not to prosecute in favour of issuing her with a caution, which can be made conditional on her attendance at a local women's centre. These centres provide supportive, usually women-only environments, in which women offenders can access the help they really need – to overcome substance addiction, improve their mental or sexual health, increase their self-confidence, re-enter education, or develop their parenting skills. An evaluation of a pilot scheme testing out this sort of conditional caution managed a compliance rate of around 75%, with evidence of improved self-esteem, reduced drinking and improved money management for the women involved, who said that they felt listened to, and believed in (Easton et al. for the Ministry of Justice, 2010). The development of the women-specific conditional caution is to be welcomed as an example of a criminal justice approach that is explicitly targeted at tackling the real reasons why women offend. But women's centres can only do as much as their dwindling resources allow, and police in areas with limited provision are unlikely to see mandatory referrals as a realistic option. The temptation to 'up-tariff' an offence is also problematic. The 2010 pilot evaluation found evidence that some women were given conditional cautions where a simple caution, coupled with the option to self-refer to a women's centre, would have been sufficient. Well-meaning but misguided attempts to help should not result in women offenders being subject to harsher penalties which all too often set them up to fail. The sad coda is that these centres are disappearing because of the austerity programmes.

As I document the many cases I have conducted, representing women who have harmed themselves or their children or partners, it is hard to find one who was not herself a victim or an extremely vulnerable person with serious psychological problems. In her seminal 2007 report into women in the criminal justice system, Baroness Jean Corston identified three types of vulnerable women: those who are vulnerable because of their domestic circumstances, including domestic violence; those made vulnerable by personal circumstances such as mental illness and substance abuse; and those made vulnerable by their socio-economic status as poor, isolated or unemployed. None of these women require traditional incarceration but they are squeezed into a system that was designed for male offenders.

Imprisonment is used as a means of social control, and that is particularly true in relation to women. For most people, prison is the end of a road paved with deprivation, disadvantage, abuse, discrimination and multiple social problems. Empty lives produce crime. In my life at the Criminal Bar I have spent rather a lot of time in prisons. For those of us who have no experience of prison it is hard to imagine what it means to lose your liberty, to surrender to a regime where the rules are not your rules, where your autonomy dissolves, where your battered self-worth spirals into further decline. Small matters taken for granted in the outside world become complicated and strangely insurmountable because of the requirements of the authorities. Your timetable is directed by others, privacy disappears, petty resentments build into serious conflict, and indignities are part of the daily round. It is my idea of hell.

Until it was shut down in 2016 I was a regular visitor to Holloway Prison, first as a barrister visiting my clients, and later as a member of the prison's Health Advisory Board. I saw the same issues arise repeatedly. Appalling family circumstances, histories of neglect, abuse and sexual exploitation, poor health, mental disorders, lack of support, inadequate housing or homelessness, poverty and debt, and little expectation of change. These are rarely women who make judges swoon over their metaphorical 'fragrance'. Poor, battered and abused, they are women who find themselves continually punished.

In the face of all this they often show remarkable resilience and courage and frequently do not fulfil the stereotype of victims, which can be why they end up in prison: because they are seen as 'bolshie' and in need of discipline. Of course there are some women who have had reasonably privileged lives who end up in jail, but they are few. However, virtually all women who go to prison come out damaged by the experience. The consequences of removal from their children, their families and their communities are immeasurable. They are overwhelmed with feelings of guilt and shame.

Women do not need to be locked up for hours on end in overcrowded prisons where self-harming, tearing into their own flesh with hairclips and bottle tops, is endemic. They do not need their medication to be pushed through the metal flap in the door as though they are lepers. It is argued that deaths in custody are a result of chronic underfunding and lack of staff in the prisons. Most of the women who kill themselves take overdoses or hang themselves but one woman who choked herself by swallowing toilet paper stands out particularly in the memory.

A women's prison in Cheshire, HMP Styal, became synonymous with the devastating impact which imprisonment can have on women's mental health. In a single 12-month period between 2002 and 2003, six of the prison's inmates took their own lives. The mother of one, Pauline Campbell, campaigned passionately on the subject after her daughter Sarah, who was only 18, committed suicide. Five years later Pauline killed herself by taking a fatal dose of antidepressants. Her body was found at her daughter's graveside. In 2008, Lisa Marley was remanded to HMP Styal pending her trial for common assault. Due to a history of mental illness and suicide attempts, she was placed in a supposedly reduced risk cell in the prison's Keller Unit. Less than 48 hours later, she hanged herself in her cell using bed sheets and the casing that surrounded her in-cell television. Officers detailed to keep Lisa under observation had failed to carry out the proper number of checks, or to report the red marks they noticed around her neck. A surprise inspection of HMP Styal in 2011 found that while overall the prison had improved, the Keller Unit was wholly unsuitable for safely holding its seriously mentally ill occupants, with officers often required to use force to remove ligatures from women intent on harming themselves. The Keller Unit was subsequently closed down. The Inquest Report documents the deaths of Emily Hartley and Sarah Reed, who both committed suicide in prison in 2016; Caroline Hunt and K.W. who also killed themselves did so in 2015; Diana Waplington in 2014 and Natasha Evans in 2013. Case record after case record in the report describe the mental anguish of the women who died and the failure of prisons and staff to deal adequately with their needs. The comments of coroners lamenting the system should be emblazoned on the wall of the Department of Justice.

It is as plain as day that court-based diversion schemes for women with mental health problems need urgent improvement and expansion. A standardised liaison and diversion service is currently in the process of being rolled out across England. It is supposed to spot offenders' substance addictions and mental health issues as early as possible, so that they can receive appropriate care and support as they progress through the system. The programme also aims to divert offenders away from prison by ensuring that judges and magistrates have the information they need to identify the best sentencing option. The infancy of the scheme makes it hard to tell how well it is working. Like other initiatives, however, its effectiveness will largely depend on whether it has the money and political backing needed to make it a success. It is no coincidence that the current spike in inmate suicides has come at a time of chronic underfunding for prisons and related services. The Prison Service is understaffed and undertrained. Officers have less opportunity to get to know prisoners individually and thus to spot the danger signs that a woman might take her own life.

Most of the women enter prison vulnerable to breakdown because of their personal histories but not all. The *Independent* newspaper's 2003 campaign on mental health documented the experience of Wendy Kramer, who was imprisoned for two and a half years for conspiring to supply drugs. She left prison with severe mental health problems despite having no previous history of mental illness.

> In prison I felt anxiety, panic, self-harm, suicide, depression – the unbelievable hurt inside your stomach which is what makes you bang your head against the wall. The main thing that gets to me is that there are a lot of women in there that shouldn't be. They aren't criminals; they are mentally ill.

Around 60% of women who are imprisoned have dependent children; it is estimated that over 17,200 children are separated from their mother by imprisonment every year. Whereas many men serve their sentences knowing their partners are taking care of their children, fewer than one in 10 children is cared for by their father while the mothers are inside. Just 5% of children stay in their own home once their mother is jailed.

In our family courts the philosophy is that the child comes first in any dispute. Children need their parents, and only in the most extreme circumstances should we break that bond. Yet in the criminal courts, and despite being legally required to consider the best interests of the child, officials often wash their hands of responsibility by saying that if her children suffer it is the criminal woman who is to blame. The family is presented as the foundation of society, to be supported and preserved. Women who transgress accepted roles and fail 'the family' unleash punitive responses.

The work of Dr Dora Black, the eminent child psychiatrist, who conducted studies on the mother and baby unit at Holloway Prison, explains that the trauma of separation of young children from their mothers frequently leads to mental illness or at the least to profound emotional problems when they reach adolescence. In England and Wales a maximum of 54 mothers can keep their babies with them in prison, though children cannot stay beyond the age of 18 months. Even where spaces are available, the process of getting one is far from straightforward, with the result that the units often operate below capacity. Some mothers are not aware that mother and baby units exist until they arrive in prison. Others report long delays between applying for a place in the unit and receiving the final decision, leading to high levels of worry and stress as they wait anxiously to find out whether they have been accepted. By and large, women have no idea what the decision-making process itself entails until they are presented to the board and asked to argue for their place.

The upshot of all this is that keeping your baby in prison is a privilege. Some states in the USA now recognise the right of every mother of an infant to have that child with her except where she has a history of child abuse or the child would suffer. It is extraordinary that this issue of children's rights has taken so long to be addressed. Babies should be with their mothers, and unless a woman has committed an offence of violence which would carry a significant sentence, a mother should not be imprisoned. When I say this I am met with the retort that women would deliberately get themselves pregnant to avoid jail. The people who say this are also up in arms at the idea of women using their pregnant status to get council houses. Yes, when we reach for principles to guide a civilised society there will always be those who cheat or play with the rules, but against them there are the many more who will be salvaged by more humane responses.

Mothers who do end up in prison find that the system offers them little humanity. Breastfeeding becomes humiliating when done under the gaze of a male prison officer. The late Denise Marshall worked for a charity called Birth Companions, which supports female prisoners during pregnancy and after the birth of their children. In a 2010 interview with the *Guardian*, she described some of the worries that prison mothers have alongside the ordinary stresses of childbirth. Will the doors be unlocked in time when they go into labour? Will they be disciplined for swearing at officers when carried away with the pain of childbirth? Countless times I have observed these stresses and others for myself. One of my visits to the mother and baby unit at the old Holloway Prison especially sticks in my mind. A young woman there told me of the nightmare of being remanded in custody for report when there was no place on the unit to accommodate her baby. She was released after 24 hours on an application for bail to the High Court. But for those 24 hours she was separated from the baby, which she was breastfeeding, and suffered the agony of engorged breasts and desperation at how the baby was coping without her. In the end she was sent down for nine months. Her offence was a fraud valued at £700, and although this time she was able to bring the baby into prison with her, her other child, a toddler, was left in the care of the father and was seriously disturbed by the separation.

Imprisoning mothers should be a last resort, but judges have different ideas as to what that means. Where a parent, male or female, has primary care of a child, the criminal courts should be required to obtain social inquiry reports on the impact upon the family of imprisonment. The hypocrisy of lauding the family and motherhood on the one hand while refusing adequately to acknowledge the social and economic supports necessary to sustain women in their motherhood role is a shameful reflection on the values of the justice system. For men and women alike, separation from the family is the worst aspect of imprisonment, but for women the guilt of failing their children exacts a special burden. Their offence is seen as being against more than the criminal law, and that is how they themselves feel it.

The sociologist Pat Carlen has recently examined what she brilliantly and sardonically describes as the 'carceral clawback' – the way in which the arguments for reducing the imprisonment of women have been subverted and used as a rationale for locking women up. She sees the boast – made by successive Home Secretaries – of 'making prison work' as the problem. The 'repairing gel', as she describes it, was to be the creation of programmes inside prisons to address the background problems of the women and indeed the men too. This has given sentencers a sense of justification and freedom to lock up women rather than find a community alternative; courts adopt what they think is a welfare approach by imprisoning the woman so that she can be helped. In truth, provision of these programmes is very scant because of overcrowding and can never be much use if the sentence is short. Judges and magistrates sleep more easily at night if they think Styal Prison is like a short stay at the Priory, but they are deluding themselves.

Any review of sentences on women shows that women are now getting heavier sentences for less serious offences. All the arguments women criminologists and lawyers made to persuade the courts and policymakers that the background of most women and their place in society explained their offending were used, not to avoid prison, but to justify imprisonment. The very language we used in developing a feminist critique of offending was appropriated and used to legitimise the use of prison. There is much talk of 'empowering' women prisoners and raising self-esteem. Yet as soon as a woman is assertive she is very quickly reminded she is a prisoner and that unquestioning compliance with the rules is the expectation.

Eight years of austerity have had a devastating impact on Britain's prisons, many of which are locked in a spiral of decline. The impact of savage budget cuts since 2010 has been felt right across the criminal justice system. Deteriorating prison hygiene, poor health care, inadequate resettlement support, cuts to community services, staffing crises and lack of mental health support leading to an increased risk of bullying, self-harm and suicide – the list is never-ending. Back in 2007 the Corston Report urged the creation of Women's Centres around the country to provide small locally based units for women offenders where they could receive one-to-one psychotherapy, address their addictions, receive skills training and prepare for a life in the community. Many were established, but when Chris Grayling was Justice Secretary he took a scythe to most of the supportive initiatives in the criminal justice system, including the provision of books to prisoners. Therapeutic work now operates on a shoestring and involves group therapy where women are less willing to reveal the true nature of the abuse they have experienced. The number of Women's Centres has not grown as planned and

Probation Services in the community have been de-professionalised and greatly reduced.

One of our responsibilities must be to ensure that those who have to be in prison have opportunities; to repair the black holes in their own experience which led to offending; many activities should be taking place in a more developed way. The government has been well intentioned in trying to make some provision – therapeutic programmes have been created addressing violence or past abuse, and there are domestic violence projects for both victim and offender, therapy addressing childhood trauma, issues of sexuality or substance abuse. Funding is a problem, increasingly restricted and allocated on a short-term basis, with even those programmes currently receiving grants unsure if they will get them renewed next year. Whether a prisoner can access such a programme is more in the hands of the gods than based on any real assessment of need. Yet ministers talk about these initiatives as if they were available on tap. The Scottish government is currently planning to demolish its one women's prison, Cornton Vale, in Stirling, and to rebuild it as a much smaller prison for a maximum of 80 female prisoners who have committed serious crime and must be detained in a secure prison setting. It is then the intention to build twenty therapeutic houses around the country where the regime will concentrate on the problems which brought the women before the courts. Only 15–20 women will be accommodated in each and the houses will be close to the families of the women staying there. Counselling, drug and alcohol rehabilitation programmes, job training and education will be available. There will be restorative justice initiatives so that women begin taking responsibility for their offending behaviour. The women will be able in time to work outside of the centres to gain experience in preparation for resettling in the community. It is the model which has been championed by prison reformers for years and as a pilot it could initiate real change throughout the UK.

However, political commitment to improving the lot of women in prison is irregular, coming in fits and starts rather than as part of a comprehensive and sustained strategy. In 2007, the Corston Report documented the appalling conditions experienced by some women in prison, and called for a radically different approach to women in the criminal justice system. One of its key recommendations was the replacement of women's prisons with custodial units dispersed around the country, along the lines of the Scottish plan. The small number of women's prisons meant that women were often incarcerated far away from home, making it difficult or impossible for family and children to visit. The government rejected the recommendation, and on average women prisoners today are jailed 64 miles away from where they live. Many of Jean Corston's other recommendations were accepted, although progress in implementing them has been disappointingly slow. Routine strip searches have ended, and there are pockets of very good work being done in some areas in terms of supporting and rehabilitating female offenders. But women are still incarcerated in large numbers for non-violent crimes, and campaign groups report that women are still being sent to prison 'for their own good'. Housing for women leaving prison also remains a major problem, with 60% of women left without a home to go to on release. The impetus for reform sparked by the Corston Report has been slowly draining away. In 2013 Nick Hardwick, who was then the Chief Inspector of Prisons, gave evidence to the House of Commons Justice Committee's inquiry on women offenders. It is hard to disagree with his observation that 'the whole business about prisons, and women's prisons in particular, has almost been forgotten in some of the [government's] thinking ... You feel that you are always having to remind people about this issue, rather than it being at the forefront of their minds.'

I am not blind to the inhumanity some women wreak on others, nor to their criminality. Women can be horrible, and some do batter their babies or kill their husbands unprovoked. But very few women commit violent or serious offences or are career criminals. The majority of those who are in prison should not be there. What is needed is the creation of real alternatives, such as appropriate community service, hostels and rehabilitation units. If the spirit of sentencing policy is truly that prisons are to be places for dealing with serious crime, particularly violence, then it should be translated into reality by the judges with support from politicians. Our female prisons could then virtually be emptied.

3

THE BATTERED WIFE

The experience of women offenders is only one side of the criminal justice coin. When it comes to crime women are more often offended against than offenders. Women who kill are rare. Women being killed is the common currency. Discounting gang violence, which is a wholly separate issue, it is women who are stalked and assaulted for no apparent reason in parks, women who are usually the prey of serial killers, female children who are the ones most often killed. Half of all female murder victims are killed by a current or former husband or lover. On average nearly two women die as a result of domestic violence each week.

Statistics show that in Britain 1.4 million women a year suffer domestic abuse and this is probably the tip of the iceberg. Half of disabled women report experiencing domestic abuse. Men suffer domestic violence too but female victims outnumber men two to one in Office of National Statistics' estimates but three to one in the numbers recorded by large police forces. A third of violent crime in London that results in injury is of a domestic nature. The police attend twice as many emergency calls for domestic violence there than they do for residential burglary.

Cases involving domestic abuse are an important gauge of entrenched attitudes about the proper roles of men and women. Whenever I speak at events in this country and around the world, women of all kinds and all ages raise the ways in which women's lives are blighted by fear of male violence.

One of the biggest barriers to combatting domestic violence has been the split between what is perceived as public, and therefore the law's business, and what is private, which shouldn't concern the law at all. The way in which people choose to conduct their private lives should be regulated as little as possible by the state and we have been happy to incorporate the ideas of liberal philosophy into our jurisprudence. Normally, it is only where private behaviour harms others that we condone the intervention of the law.

Yet this separation of the private and public worked against women, whose major sphere of activity was in the home. Marital behaviour behind closed doors was for a long time deemed a 'no-go' area for law enforcement. Instead, police turned a blind eye to domestic violence, failing to prosecute and taking little action against its perpetrators. Women were often failed in the areas where they were most vulnerable.

The critical importance of this private/public dichotomy was overlooked because lawyers and lawmakers could not see that not regulating was as significant as regulating. Finding remedies in law for the protection of women and their children poses a problem, because it usually involves greater intervention by the state and the possible erosion of defendants' rights. Policing the bedroom is not a course we should readily advocate, but there should never be any qualms when it is done at the behest of those who are being abused, or on their behalf by concerned parties. The whole point of human rights philosophy is that every human being should be valued and respected, and the state has a responsibility to ensure that some members of the community are not ill-using others. Modern rights discourse recognises that persecution and abuse is carried out not only by the state but by relatives and neighbours, and that the failure of the state to prevent inhumane behaviour becomes a tacit acceptance of it.

Until the arrival of the Human Rights Act, the police, who would have no problem entering premises believed to contain explosive substances, became very sensitive to the rights of man if the information related to domestic violence. It has not been easy shifting the culture to acknowledge that human rights is not only about obscenities which take place in Kosovo or Sudan, Somalia or Iraq, but also about the abuse of people closer to home.

Today, the barriers once erected around people's private lives are beginning to crumble as lawmakers become increasingly aware of the scope of domestic violence and its social cost. In 2004, research commissioned by then women's minister Jacqui Smith, and carried out by the sociologist Professor Sylvia Walby, lifted the lid on the shockingly high price of domestic violence. That research was updated in 2009, when the cost to the economy of time off work for domestic violence injuries was estimated at £1.9 billion a year. At the same time £3.8 billion was being spent on services for victims, such as physical and mental health care, social services and emergency housing.

It is telling that the female ministers who did so much to get domestic violence on the agenda had to focus on its economic costs to get through to male policymakers. But the spreading acceptance that something has to be done about domestic abuse is to be welcomed. The last decade has seen a flurry of legislative and police activity. Police now have the power to issue emergency notices requiring suspected abusers to stay away from their victims for 48 hours, extendable to 28 days upon application to the court; the idea is to give the victim breathing space to consider her options with the help of specialist support. The Serious Crime Act 2015 introduced a new offence which is designed to combat exactly this type of abuse. It criminalises 'coercive or controlling behaviour' towards a partner or family member, by which it means physical, sexual, psychological, financial or emotional abuse. Critically, this new legislation ends the law's myopic focus on violence as the defining characteristic of domestic abuse, to the exclusion of the fear, emotional manipulation, mind games and other controlling behaviours that form the background to the blows. In February 2018 Sally Challen had her conviction for the murder of her husband overturned and a retrial ordered on the grounds that there was evidence she was subjected to years of coercive and controlling behaviour.

Yes, violence is very often present in abusive relationships. But a woman who is beaten every Saturday night when her husband gets home from the pub is not only abused once a week. Campaigners and survivors have been saying this for years, but it has taken the law a long time to catch up. 'Did he hit you?' is an important question, but it is no longer the end of the enquiry. Women can now also check whether their partner has a history of physical abuse under the new domestic violence disclosure scheme, and stalking has found its way onto the statute books as a discrete criminal offence. New legislation is promised to establish a domestic violence and abuse commissioner.

But there is so much more to do. Every hour, the police receive an average of over 100 calls for assistance with domestic abuse. The real scale of the problem is likely to be much bigger; the 2015 Crime Survey for England and Wales estimated that 79% of people abused by their partners did not report the abuse to the police. Research carried out by Women's Aid suggested that almost two-thirds of the women referred to a refuge in London did not manage to get a place; outside London the situation is reported to be even worse. In addition, services for black and ethnic minority women in recent years have been disproportionately hit by cuts. More than 60% of women who have a secure tenancy lose it when they enter a refuge, while almost 90% find themselves in another kind of temporary accommodation when they leave. Housing officers in local authorities frequently treat victims of domestic abuse as voluntarily homeless, sending them to the back of the queue for social housing. 'Why did she go back to him?' is the recurrent question in the courts. The answer may be that she had nowhere else to go. New legislation and important-sounding government strategies are all well and good, but they are only half the battle. There remains a gulf between the best intentions of those in power, and their track record in translating policy into practice.

Prosecution rates for domestic abuse have always been poor. In 2015–16, the CPS prosecuted 70% of domestic abuse cases referred to it by police. But many instances of domestic abuse are not referred. Time and again following an assault men are given a 'talking-to' rather than being arrested. It used to be that when the police were called out to these situations they did not even record the incident, so that if a prosecution did proceed a history of previous violence was not available. Now there is a requirement to record everything, and police forces are asked to 'flag' crimes relating to domestic abuse. The requirement to record rates of domestic abuse, and the centralised collation of that data, is very new, and the analysis is further complicated by the fact that domestic abuse is not a specific criminal offence, but rather a range of behaviours which may constitute any number of offences depending on the perceptions of the police. It is therefore difficult to construct an exact statistical picture of the prevalence of domestic abuse. However, all the research suggests that there are still many more instances of domestic abuse than there are prosecutions.

Police, lawyers and judges used to regard prosecution as inappropriate because it was likely to accelerate the disintegration of the relationship or damage the family unit. However inappropriate, they often saw their role as helping to preserve the marriage. In a *World in Action* programme shown on television in 1990, about rape as part of the pattern of domestic violence within marriage, Sir Frederick Lawton, a retired Appeal Court judge, explained that if it were open to wives to bring prosecutions for rape, even against a background of domestic violence, it would prohibit any chance of rehabilitation of the marriage and would have a deleterious effect on children – as though rape itself, rather than the prosecution, might not already have had that effect. Such a view may seem antiquated today, but there are many who still feel that the criminal courts are not the right place for such issues because criminalising a partner has dire consequences for the whole family. Women themselves say that having a conviction will affect their husband's career and stigmatise their children, or result in them losing their children to care, so they postpone taking the steps which so often in the end become inevitable. Precisely these arguments about 'irreparable damage to the family' have been used to counter the introduction of every piece of reforming legislation for the benefit of women for the last 120 years, whether it was allowing a woman to divorce, hold property in her own name, gain the vote, or obtain the right to enter the professions and public life.

Another old line trotted out by those who dismissed domestic violence was that many women invite beatings because of nagging, because they pushed their man to the edge or because they were masochists. The nagging wife was put on the scales as a counterweight to the violent husband, although few die in direct consequence of a tongue-lashing. Indeed, most battered wives cannot afford the luxury of a grinding whinge because they know they will literally get it in the teeth. Sometimes they even instigate an assault to get it over with; they know a beating is coming but the waiting in terror is even more excruciating than the blows.

Domestic violence victims often blame themselves, and fear not being believed. They suffer in silence and cover up what is going on to doctors, family and neighbours. Their silence then becomes a stick with which they are beaten. Women are abused on average 35 times before seeking police support. When they do call the police, they are often unsatisfactory complainants, fearful of, or ambivalent about, pursuing a prosecution because of the potential implications. It is vital to properly understand this reluctance. When it is understood, it results in an increased focus on evidence-led prosecutions, which aim to secure enough independent evidence to prosecute the abuser even where the victim does not testify herself. Photographs of the victim's bruised face, smashed windows or overturned furniture are crucial. The Criminal Justice Act 2003 allows hearsay evidence into trials, making a much wider swathe of evidence usable; if the victim refuses to give evidence herself in court, police can now indirectly relay her account as recorded in a police officer's statement or via police body-cam footage.

Recordings of 999 calls are also becoming increasingly important. In 2014, Lee Barnaby attempted to strangle his girlfriend, Glenda Gibb, while she slept. Gibb dialled 999 three times within the space of about

15 minutes. The first two calls were made while Barnaby was still in her home; frightened and whispering down the line, she reported that he had attacked her, but refused to give her name. By the time the third call was made, the defendant had left the house and, finally, Glenda Gibb stated her name and address. When the police arrived, she wouldn't sign a statement, saying that Barnaby had beaten her up the last time she'd cooperated with the police. The prosecution went ahead without calling her as a witness, and the transcripts of the 999 calls were critical in securing Barnaby's conviction and sentence of 16 weeks in prison. On appeal, Barnaby argued that the 999 calls shouldn't have been admitted as evidence; the suggestion was that Glenda Gibb might have concocted the allegation and staged the calls to back it up. The divisional court gave this argument short shrift. The police had arrived at the scene just six minutes after Gibb's third phone call. They found her in an agitated state, with the red marks caused by the assault still visible around her neck. Moreover, the divisional court found that it was permissible not to call a victim of domestic abuse as a witness if there was a real risk that she might suffer further harm as a result of her cooperation with the prosecuting authorities. Barnaby's appeal was dismissed.

Disappointingly, not all police forces are pursuing evidence-led prosecutions with as much enthusiasm as they should be. A key problem is police failure to collect vital evidence when called to the scene of an incident. In 2014 HM Inspectorate of Constabulary (HMIC) conducted a review of police responses to domestic violence (*Everyone's Business*). It made for fairly shocking reading. Photographs of the victim's injuries taken at the time of the incident were only available in 46% of the 600 case files reviewed. In some forces, police officers did not even have access to a camera. In three out of 10 cases the attending officer filed a statement which did not include basic information like a description of the scene or the victim's injuries. The 999 call was only listened to in 16% of cases, and house-to-house inquiries only completed 23% of the time. Even when the victim is prepared to testify, a failure to collect corroborating evidence can prove fatal in court. The problem is even more acute when she is not.

Some headway has been made. A follow-up review published by HMIC in 2015 found indications of progress in a number of areas. However, there is so much more work for the police to do. Evidence-gathering remains inconsistent and often inadequate in many forces. Several forces use 999 call-handling systems which are unable to automatically identify potential repeat victims of domestic abuse, so that call handlers cannot identify the women at greatest risk. Repeat victims are regularly required to explain the full, distressing history of their abuse to first-response officers who have not been provided with any information from their case files.

In addition, too many officers simply equate domestic abuse with physical injury, and fail to spot signs that the victim is being psychologically controlled or manipulated by the perpetrator. They do not realise that victims of domestic abuse are often paralysed by fear, or totally dominated by their abusers. Asking these women to describe their abuse while the perpetrator is in the same house – or even in the same room – is often about as much use as not asking them at all. The question 'What do you want us to do?' is equally unhelpful, as it places the burden on the most vulnerable person there, the victim, to decide the course of action at a time when she may be physically hurt, in fear of the perpetrator, unaware of her options or simply unable to think straight. Police attitudes towards domestic abuse victims are also in need of urgent improvement. Victims report dealing with unsympathetic and rude officers, who cannot understand why they are making such a fuss if they don't want to press charges, or judge them for not having the 'sense' to leave.

I am not saying that every police officer has a terrible attitude, nor that police forces in general aren't interested in helping victims of domestic abuse. I know from experience that there are many well-intentioned officers, both on the front line and in specialist domestic abuse units, who try very hard to make sure that victims are supported. But there is a need for meaningful training to ensure that officers right across the board are able to understand domestic abuse and respond appropriately.

Above all, it is vital that the police take all complaints of domestic violence seriously. Women frequently complain of being fobbed off or waiting weeks for the police to respond to breaches of injunctions by their partners, for them only to be arrested weeks after the event. One victim is quoted in the 2014 HMIC report as saying: 'They didn't take it seriously until something happened in public. That's what happened to me – me and my kids living in fear, being locked in rooms and stuff – police not taking it seriously until he hit me in a club in the middle of everybody. Then they were there like that and arrested him like that. It was no different to what we experienced behind closed doors.'

Women's fears of being killed have to be taken seriously because they are often justified. On 18 November 2003 Alan Pemberton, a financial adviser, shot dead his wife Julia and his 17-year-old son William at their home. Julia Pemberton had suffered years of abuse and became so afraid of her husband that she handed over guns and kitchen knives belonging to him to the police. She took out an injunction against him and agreed to have a panic button installed. On the night of the attack Alan Pemberton arrived at the house with a shotgun and shot William five times in the chest when he tried to protect his mother. Julia Pemberton hid in a cupboard where she dialled 999. During the harrowing 16-minute call the operator told her the police were on their way. Julia could be heard saying she had 'about a minute before I die'. The operator heard her say 'he's coming now' and a man's voice say 'you fucking whore'. She was found with four shotgun wounds to the chest and lower back. After killing his son and wife Alan Pemberton turned the gun on himself. A letter was found in which he made it clear that he was taking revenge for her daring to end the marriage. The police did not turn up at the farmhouse for 40 minutes after the call and then waited a further five hours before entering the premises because they were waiting for an armed response unit. Following the inquest, Julia's brother Frank Mullane said that Thames Valley Police seemed to have 'a somewhat limited understanding of domestic violence'. He said that his sister had received 'next to nothing, if not nothing' in terms of support from the police and that the way the police kept records of abuse was so disorganised that no one looking at the case could take an overall view.

In December 2008, Maria Stubbings was murdered by her ex-boyfriend Marc Chivers. Chivers had already served one prison sentence in Germany for the murder of another woman, and was jailed again for seriously assaulting Maria shortly after they met. Once released, he soon began to bother Maria again, and when Maria injured her ribs, one friend did not believe her explanation that she had slipped on cooking oil. But when the friend reported her suspicions that Chivers had caused the injury, the police operator told her that nothing could be done as it was a 'domestic'. In the week immediately before her death, Maria contacted the police numerous times, reporting that Chivers had broken into her home in order to steal from her, and asking about how to get a restraining order against him. Despite noticing that Maria was acting strangely – including suddenly deciding to drop the burglary allegations – the police failed to investigate properly. On 19 December, officers found Maria dead in her home. Chivers had strangled her with a dog lead.

In November 2013, Anne-Marie Birch was strangled by her estranged husband Lee. In the two months leading up to her murder, Anne-Marie had contacted the police multiple times about her husband's behaviour. She told them that Lee had said that he would 'do her in' and that she should sleep with 'one eye open'. She told them that she was in fear for her life. She told them that he had been following her around, sending abusive texts, and spying on her from her back garden. She obtained a non-molestation order against him, and made the police aware that he was repeatedly in breach. More than once, she complained that nothing was being done despite her repeated reports. At 8.32 a.m. on 7 November 2013, Anne-Marie called the police to report that her husband was again in her garden. It was the last straw and she asked the police to arrest him. Anne-Marie was found dead in a field at 2.04 p.m. on the same day.

In August 2016, Shana Grice was murdered by an ex-boyfriend called Michael Lane. Lane had stalked Shana obsessively in the months before the murder: loitering outside her home, slashing her car tyres, sending threatening letters. He secretly installed a tracker device on her car. On one occasion, Lane hit Shana as he attempted to grab her mobile phone to check who she had been texting. Shana's numerous complaints to the police were treated dismissively and with scepticism. On one occasion, she was issued with a fixed penalty notice and a fine for wasting police time – her offence was to fail to disclose that she and Lane had been in a sexual relationship. At Lane's trial, Mr Justice Green was scathing in his criticism of the police response.

[Shana] was treated as the wrongdoer and having committed a criminal offence, and Michael Lane was treated as the victim. There was seemingly no appreciation on the part of those investigating that a young woman in a sexual relationship with a man could at one and the same time be vulnerable and at risk of serious harm. The Police jumped to conclusions and Shana was stereotyped.

During the trial Shana's family gave evidence that, after she was issued with the fine, Shana no longer felt the police would take her complaints seriously. She was right; when Lane later stole her house key so that he could sneak into her bedroom and watch her sleep, the police classified the incident as 'low risk'. Meanwhile, Lane continued to stalk Shana, safe in the knowledge that the police would not do anything. He eventually broke into Shana's house, slashed her throat and burned her body. It was only afterwards that it emerged that 12 other women had complained to the police about Lane in the three years before Shana was killed.

Independent reviews subsequently found serious police failings in the cases of Julia Pemberton, Maria Stubbings and Anne-Marie Birch. The review into Shana Grice's case is still ongoing, and I have no doubt that it will be similarly critical of the police response. The criticism is couched in predictably sanitised language – lack of training, failure to properly assess and manage risk, insufficient information sharing – but at root these cases are about the police's failure to pay attention to women who say they are afraid. The ceremonial wringing of hands after the event is not enough. Helen Pearson's stalker Joseph Willis did not manage to kill her when he attacked her with scissors in October 2013, but he was still able to stab her eight times in the back, face and neck before being pulled away by a passer-by. This was after a five-year campaign of harassment during which Helen had reported 125 separate incidents to police – including the day Willis left a dead cat on her doorstep, and the time he painted a wall near her home with the message 'die Helen die'. Helen Pearson later rejected an official police apology as 'meaningless'. It is not difficult to see why.

The police have to have their feet held to the fire on their responses to domestic violence. There should be a requirement for an officer to make an oral report of every call or mention of ill treatment or violence made by a woman, not merely to log a note that disappears into the computer systems; there should be a dedicated officer to receive such reports and whose role it is to ensure they are followed through. Demotion or dismissal of responsible officers should follow failure. There has to be a consequence for inaction when women make complaints or express fear. The Chief Constable of any police force that fails to deal with domestic violence adequately should expect to lose his job.

When she gets to court, the woman can meet a hostile environment. At one time if the husband was on bail, he would often sit in the hallway feet away from her, harassing his wife and coercing her into dropping the charges. Now the courts are much more aware of the problems and victims' support groups will provide companionship and a special room for the woman. But the same pressure may be exercised by the man's family or friends before she ever gets to court. Once in court, demonstrating physical evidence of the abuse can be difficult, with lawyers for the other side claiming recent fabrication or exaggeration. In every contested criminal case I have conducted over the years involving the battering of a woman, she is accused of inflating her account and exaggerating the extent of any violence. Corroboration of less than a handful of assaults is par for the course, and those often become the only instances of violence which are accepted.

The initial questioning of the woman sometimes feels clinical, justified by those who are supposed to be on her side as testing the strength of any case they could bring and letting her see what is going to come from those who will represent her partner. Many victims internalise the blame implied by authority figures and, naturally enough, often decide not to go through with a court case. Such failure to proceed can be met with irritation from the authorities. If a woman does steel herself to go through with it, it is precisely then that she needs support. This is when further violence might occur, because involving the police and the courts is a declaration of the right to control her own life, and if there is one thing that upsets a wife-beater it is a wife who asserts herself.

Police lawyers and judges still have difficulties in abandoning their stereotype of the abused woman as someone who is submissive and cowed. When the woman appears competent or has a bit of gumption or if she seems to be materially well off, there is a failure of the imagination as to how she could be victimised. Lawyers still say, 'She is a middle-class woman. It is not as though she could not afford alternative accommodation.' When, in 2013, the tabloid press published paparazzi pictures of Charles Saatchi holding Nigella Lawson by the neck in a Mayfair restaurant, it sparked a national debate about whether a woman as wealthy and glamorous as Nigella could possibly be a victim of domestic abuse. The incident may well have been innocent and wrongly interpreted, but what is well documented is that wealth and glamour are no protection from domestic abuse. In 2017 Mustafa Bashir appeared in the Crown court for sentencing, having admitted to assaulting his wife, Fakhara Karim. The court heard he had hit Fakhara with a cricket bat and made her drink bleach. He received an 18-month suspended sentence, as Judge Richard Mansell QC declared himself 'not convinced' that Fakhara Karim was vulnerable, relying on the fact that this 'plainly intelligent woman' had a 2.1 degree and a network of friends. It was clear that he could not reconcile Fakhara, who had reported being in fear for her life at the hands of Bashir, with his preconception of what a vulnerable woman looked like. Bashir was later imprisoned when it turned out that he had lied about having an offer to play professional cricket in order to avoid jail.

Domestic abuse cuts across all classes, ethnicities, sexualities, ages and social backgrounds. It can, and does, happen to anyone, and not all victims will show their trauma in the witness box. In almost every case in which I have been involved the woman presents herself in a very flat, unemotional way which can fail to arouse, in a judge or a jury, a full appreciation of her partner's behaviour towards her. Psychologists describe it as lack of 'affect'. Women are also often so filled with shame at the public exposure of what they see as their private failure that they may minimise the extent of their suffering.

Understanding domestic abuse plainly remains a challenge for the courts. To onlookers the response of the battered woman seems abnormal, but to her it is a rational response to her abnormal circumstances. Misconceptions litter the court and are reflected in the verdicts of juries: women have ample opportunities to leave; in some perverse way they like the pain; no real woman becomes so crushed by her abusive partner that her maternal instinct is extinguished. Continuing to live with the tormentor is seen as a testament to the acceptability of his behaviour. A constant refrain in the questioning is 'Why did you not leave?' This is something the woman herself can never answer coherently.

The answers are many and complex. Some women want to leave, but understand that it is too risky. The Femicide Census data shows that the time immediately following a break-up can be extremely dangerous for women; three-quarters of women who are killed by an ex-partner are killed within a year of their separation. Leaving home requires money and somewhere to go, and often women simply cannot get away. Refuges provide safe, women-only spaces, where victims can access emotional and practical support, out of reach of the clutches of their abusers, but demand for beds far outstrips supply. The charity Women's Aid estimates that on a typical day, 155 women and 103 children are turned away from refuges. Women must rely on the generosity of friends or family while they wait. If that is not an option some end up sleeping rough or returning to their abuser. Finding a suitable refuge space becomes even harder if a woman needs specialist support due to a disability, or has children.

Women with children often stay in a violent relationship because they fear that if they leave they will set up a situation which might result in the children being taken into care. According to Sandra Horley, the chief executive of Refuge, research shows that 90% of domestic violence incidents take place in the presence of children or with children in the next room. Being made to witness such events is another form of abuse. Yet women face a dilemma when it comes to leaving: if they abandon their children, they will fail as a mother; if they take them, they may face homelessness. It becomes a monumental step. In court even today few reasons are good enough to justify a woman leaving her children. The hostility towards a mother who contemplates doing this, even where she can no longer survive her husband's cruelty and has nowhere to bring children if she takes them with her, can annihilate her cause in a trial by jury.

The psychological effects of domestic abuse are still not sufficiently understood – effects which are often so severe as to render women incapable of taking the necessary steps to end the relationship. In the early stages women believe the violent incidents are isolated events. The male partners are remorseful and the women believe everything will improve. They usually rationalise the abuse as the result of excess alcohol or the stress their partner might be experiencing because of overwork, no work, a new baby (over 30% of domestic violence starts in or is exacerbated by pregnancy). They minimise the extent of the abuse to which they are subjected, as a coping device or because of self-blaming and their own sense of shame. They avoid going to the doctor, and cover their bruises. They provide innocent explanations to outsiders for injuries and concoct elaborate stories to distract attention from the abuse. Part of the pretence is to delude themselves, as they cannot face up to the horror of what is happening. A constant theme in the accounts of battered women who come before the courts is that they had lived in hope that everything would come right, that if they had a proper home, or a baby, or the baby was older, or the man had a job, or his job had fewer pressures, or they had more money, then the relationship would return to the romantic idyll of the courtship. Eventually the excuses – whether those made by the abuser or invented by the abused – are no longer convincing but by that time the cycle is so established it is impossible to break.

Recognising the psychological power that an abuser can wield over his victim is key to defeating the myth that domestic abuse only happens when wives and girlfriends are beaten and raped. At its root, domestic abuse is about control. It is true that many abusers exercise that control with their fists. But others establish their control by seeking emotional dominance over women, and this counts as domestic abuse just as much as a slap with the back of the hand. This kind of domestic abuse can happen in a huge variety of ways, and abusers may exert control over every aspect of a woman's life: who she can be friends with, where she can go, what she can wear, how much she can spend, who she can text, which websites she can use, when she can eat, what she can eat. Possessiveness and jealousy, which had been flattering at the start of the relationship, become oppressive and controlling. By slowly under-mining their victim's confidence, abusers slowly undo the woman's very sense of self, wearing her down until she is incapable of acting without permission. 'You're worthless' or 'You're nothing without me' are common refrains.

For women who are abused in this way, it can be very hard to put their trauma into words. Described in isolation, many instances of such abuse can seem trivial to those without personal experience of the daily grind of humiliation and indignity. A recent storyline in Radio 4's long-running drama *The Archers*, developed with advice from specialist chari-ties, put this type of abuse at its very heart. When Rob Titchener moved to the fictional village of Ambridge in 2013, and took up with local cheesemaker Helen, few in the audience could have guessed at the controlling husband he would turn out to be. But over the course of a three-year storyline, the programme tracked the evolution of the couple's relationship, with listeners following in real time as Rob slowly and systematically dismantled Helen's autonomy. The gradual, almost imper-ceptible, escalation of incidents – from refusing to eat a meal which Helen had prepared, to telling her what to wear, to exploiting her history of anorexia by needling her about her pregnancy weight, to preventing her from driving – allowed the audience to understand the cumulative effects of emotional abuse. By the time Helen finally snapped and stabbed Rob, during an argument in which he told her to kill herself and threat-ened to harm her son, listeners could see themselves in her shoes. When she was put on trial for attempted murder, millions tuned in to cheer her acquittal.

Helen's story had a discernible impact on the public's perceptions of domestic violence. At its height, the National Domestic Violence Helpline reported a 17% spike in calls. By making Rob emotionally manipulative rather than violent – hints of physical and sexual violence were only confirmed at the very end of the story, when Helen revealed from the dock that Rob was a serial rapist – *The Archers* exploded the stereotype of the battered wife. Other domestic abuse myths were challenged in the process; Helen didn't live in isolation on a council estate, but was a middle-class woman with friends and family nearby. As for Rob, he wasn't an obvious monster, but a man who presented a charming face to the rest of the world. The storyline brought the innovation of the Serious Crime Act 2015, and the crime of coercive and controlling behaviour, to a wide audience.

Groundbreaking though this legislation is, it is not without problems. Two years after its introduction official figures in March 2017 showed that only eight out of 43 police forces had introduced a national training programme, and this lack of training is reflected in the low number of prosecutions under the new offences. In response to a Freedom of Information request from the Bureau of Investigative Journalists only 29 forces responded and disclosed that altogether 532 charges had been brought. Six forces had brought five charges or fewer.

A number of female academics have expressed concern that it will prove difficult to implement in practice, with judges and juries failing to recognise the more nuanced elements of coercion. It is also seriously worrying that, in cases of non-violent abuse, the accused will have a defence if he believed that he was acting in the victim's best interests, and his behaviour was reasonable in all the circumstances. Ingenious defence counsel will soon find ways to portray their clients as a misunderstood gentleman who took the abused under his wing, the model of concern and romantic attentiveness. They may well be believed; Vanessa Bettinson, of De Montfort University, has pointed out that this defence leaves considerable scope for the prejudices of the jury, who will undoubtedly bring their own preconceptions concerning relationships to bear when deciding what counts as reasonable behaviour. The role of the judge is going to be particularly important in directing the jury about the true meaning of coercion and how the autonomy of another can be overborne.

Whenever the topic of domestic abuse comes up, there is always somebody – usually male – who is quick to point out that men are abused too. Studies on the domestic abuse of men generate lots of column inches, and the headlines are usually along the lines of 'Revealed: the male cost of domestic violence', the unwritten accusation being that we women are monopolising victimhood for our own ends. Even men who would not dream of using violence against their own wives become very defensive. It is much easier to treat domestic abuse as an isolated aberration that randomly affects individuals regardless of their gender, rather than to acknowledge it as a problem rooted in sexual imbalance.

Of course, violence against men does take place; the 2016 Crime Survey for England and Wales found that 14% of men had experienced some form of domestic abuse since the age of 16. The figure for women is 25%. It is difficult to know whether the violence is comparable and how many men are put in crippling fear of crossing their partner. Some men, just like women, remain in abusive relationships because they do not want to leave their children. All domestic abuse is wrong, and all men who experience it deserve support just as much as female victims. Yet to pretend it is an equivalent problem is a denial of the underlying issues. Indeed, in 2002, the claim that men are just as much victims of domestic abuse as women was exploded by the research of Dr David Gadd et al. for the Scottish Executive (*Domestic Abuse against Men in Scotland*). Their conclusion was that while some men did endure genuinely harrowing experiences, very few experienced prolonged forms of domestic abuse and very few lived in fear. They added that some members of the group of men who are hit by partners are in fact more terrifying than terrified. The 2016 crime survey figures treat all instances of domestic abuse as equal. They do not distinguish between a slap in the heat of an argument, a full-on assault or coercive behaviour which involves psychological abuse. It is hardly surprising that the battering, real battering, of men at the hands of women remains rare, given the history of heterosexual relationships, the power disparity which has existed between men and women, the socialisation of the sexes and the physical disadvantages of women. However, it will be interesting to see whether significant numbers of women find themselves prosecuted for psychological abuse or coercion once the police get the hang of what to look for in investigating the offence.

Over many years, the musician Bob Geldof, to his credit, highlighted the importance of positive fathering and the role men should play, even after separation, in the upbringing of their children, but although it was never his intention his campaign provided shelter for men who have entrenched ideas about the role of the paterfamilias, who want contact in order to perpetuate control over the family. Many of the Fathers4Justice argue that there should be a presumption in all cases of shared parenting. In most cases that should be so, but we must not forget the significant number of children who depend on women for protection and emotional well-being. It cannot be assumed that domestic abuse, and its impact, stops as soon as a couple have separated. A recent briefing by the All-Party Parliamentary Group on Domestic Violence found that many family courts were adopting a 'contact at all costs' approach, sometimes at the expense of protecting the child from domestic abuse. This was despite domestic abuse being an issue in at least 70% of family court cases.

For many years, the charity Women's Aid has been documenting cases of children killed as a result of unsafe contact with fathers who were domestic abusers. Between 1994 and 2015 there were an estimated

48 such deaths. They include the four children of Claude Mubiangata, the youngest of whom was three years old. In July 2002 Mubiangata locked himself and the children in his car and set it alight. In February of that same year, Stuart Wilson took his sons to a golf course near Handsworth and slit the throat of Brad who was seven, then plunged a screwdriver into the neck of eight-year-old Brett. It happened shortly after he had met with his wife, beaten her up and made off with his children saying he would teach her 'a lesson she would never forget'. Wilson was put on trial but killed himself before its conclusion. Like Othello, these men are victims of their own pathological jealousy and make victims of the people they love. Again, in July 2002, Mark Bradley, from Dorset, killed his wife, his children and himself on hearing that she had had an affair and wanted a separation. In London, in 2011, José Pimenta pushed his two young sons off a fourth-floor balcony and then jumped himself when his estranged wife told him she had begun a new relationship. Their thinking is: 'If I can't have the children, you can't either.' In 2014, Claire Throssell lost her sons Jack and Paul in a house fire deliberately started by their father shortly after the family split up. She had told a judge of her fear that her ex-husband would harm the boys. She has since campaigned to end unsafe child contact with domestic abusers.

Even the very process of determining visiting rights gives abusers another opportunity to exert control over their victims. Many survivors of domestic abuse report being physically or verbally assaulted by their ex-partners in or outside the family courts. Deep cuts to legal aid have led to an increase in the number of people representing themselves in family courts, as they are unable to afford a barrister. This means that victims of domestic abuse can end up being cross-examined by their abusers. It is hard to conceive of how traumatic it must be to have to do battle with your abuser across the witness box. Encouragingly, new legislation has been promised to bring an end to the direct cross-examination of victims by their abusers in family courts, but pressure must be kept up to ensure that the law makes it onto the statute books. Criminal courts would never dream of letting this happen, and it must be stopped in the family courts too.

In New Zealand there is a rebuttable presumption of no-contact in cases where there has been domestic violence and it is for the violent partner to show that there is no risk to the family. This makes sense to me, given the evidence of continuing harassment and abuse in so many cases where violence has been part of the family dynamic. Where there is a history of domestic violence towards a partner the default position should be that there is no access to children until a proper risk assessment is conducted by suitably qualified professionals. This is the position increasingly being adopted across common law jurisdictions.

With horrifying regularity, cases of child-killing come before the courts. The components have surprisingly few variables. The couple are usually young. In the majority of cases the child is a girl, and the male partner is a stepfather. The death is usually preceded by protracted neglect and abuse before a final brutal assault. The cases which stand out in our minds are, of course, those where social service departments, underfunded and under pressure, are severely criticised and formal inquiries follow. Among these are the cases of Jasmine Beckford, whose stepfather, Maurice, was jailed in March 1985 for 10 years for her manslaughter, and whose mother, Beverly Lorrington, received 18 months for wilful neglect; Heidi Koseda, whose stepfather, Nicholas Price, was sentenced to life imprisonment in September 1985 with a recommendation that he serve a minimum of 15 years and whose mother, Rosemarie Koseda, pleaded guilty to manslaughter and was detained under the Mental Health Act. The cases continue to occur with regularity. In 2007 Baby P (Peter) died at the hands of his mother, her lover and their lodger, and in the year that followed the NSPCC passed 11,243 suspected child protection cases to the police. Two-year-old Sanam Navsarka suffered more than 100 injuries in the four weeks leading up to her death in May 2008. Her mother received a nine-year sentence for manslaughter and her mother's partner a life sentence for murder. The wicked stepmother is the spectre that has haunted us all since childhood. Yet in the courts it is the male equivalent – the step-father or mother's boyfriend – who appears with greater regularity.

However, natural fathers appear in the dock with frequency too. In 2013, Ben Butler killed his six-year-old daughter Ellie with a blow to the head which caused catastrophic skull and brain injuries. It was the final, fatal, injury to a little girl who had suffered months of physical and verbal abuse from her father. Ellie had been returned to the custody of her parents only a year earlier, following protracted care proceedings in which the family court wrongly concluded that Butler was not an abusive father. Jennie Gray, Ellie's mother, did not report the abuse, and was herself subject to violent physical and verbal attacks at the hands of Butler. Having killed his daughter, Butler methodically arranged the scene to make it appear as though her death was acci-dental, even arranging for Ellie's younger sibling to 'discover' Ellie as she lay dead on the floor. Butler received life imprisonment for Ellie's murder with a minimum term of 23 years. Sentencing, Mr Justice Wilkie told Butler that he was 'a self-absorbed, ill-tempered, violent and domineering man' who regarded his children and partner as 'trophies having no role other than to fit in with your infantile and sentimentalised fantasy of family life with you as patriarch whose every whim was to be responded to appropriately'. The judge also found that

Jennie Gray was totally beholden to, and dominated by, Butler, and she had lied to the police on his behalf out of stupid, naive loyalty. She received 42 months in prison for child cruelty and perverting the course of justice.

Public anger towards the men who commit these crimes against defenceless children is matched by bewilderment and disgust at the role of the women. The questions which spring into the minds of us all are repeatedly asked in court. Why didn't you protect the child? Why didn't you seek the help of police, doctors, health visitors, social workers or even just a friend? Why did you cover up your partner's behaviour? Why did you protect him rather than your own baby? How could you allow him to harm repeatedly the child you had borne?

The women themselves do not know the answers to these questions. They have usually been beaten or emotionally battered by their men and are the passive partners in volatile relationships. Often they are grateful for the attention of the men in their lives, however abusive that attention might be. Their low sense of their own worth often emanates from childhood experiences. The children they bear become extensions of themselves, and I suspect this is particularly the case with female children. The apparent collusion in violence towards their offspring has often seemed to me to be a consolidation of what they have come to expect for themselves. This is reinforced by the cross-examination of women in such cases, which frequently operates on the premise that a certain level of violence towards her was acceptable while hitting a child is not.

These mothers have become incapable of taking action, incapacitated by the effects of long-term physical or mental abuse. A psychological freezing means they lose their ability to take the protective steps that another mother could initiate. Their partners are perceived by them to be omnipotent, so that any move out of line will provoke punishment, and avoidance becomes paramount, even if it means failing to protect a child. They learn to be helpless and hopeless, convinced that any attempt to escape will mean the infliction of more torture on them all. She believes nothing will prevail upon her husband to stop, and that any challenge to him will destroy her, and it should not be forgotten that in very many cases nothing does stop abusive men, and battered women do end up dead.

In January 1992 my client Sally Emery stood trial with her boyfriend Brian Hedman charged with ill-treatment of their child Chanel, who died as a result of a ruptured bowel. The baby bore the signs of terrible abuse: fractured ribs, old and fresh injuries. Sally Emery initially lied to the police, covering up for Hedman, but at her trial she gave a classic and horrifying history of being battered herself and described how this was extended to the baby within months of her birth. The fact that Emery had two O levels was used in comparison with Hedman's low IQ to suggest that she would be the more in control within the relationship. Her frozen demeanour and failure to cry in police interviews, so characteristic of those who are abused, was invoked to show her hardness. Her lying to cover for her abuser, of whom she was so terrified, indicated her proficiency at deceit. With the assistance of expert testimony, it was accepted that she was not the perpetrator of the assaults on her child. In fact Brian Hedman had punched Chanel in the gut because the baby had not shown enough appreciation of the Christmas present he had bought and seemed more interested in the paper. She was 10 months old. Emery was sentenced to four years' imprisonment for failing to protect her child.

The mothers in child abuse cases such as these spend the weeks and months after the child's death immersed in a legal process that is directed towards assessing the extent of criminal responsibility; little room is left to deal with their grief and personal guilt. Sally Emery cried out from the witness box, 'I feel guilty. I want to be punished.'

There used to be a serious loophole in the law of homicide where a child was killed and neither parent took responsibility. If neither testified against the other, both could end up being acquitted because of the absence of direct evidence. A change in the law in 2004 now makes it a crime carrying 14 years to allow a child to die while in your care and custody. However, the concern is that a battered woman who remains in terror of her partner will be convicted rather than tell the truth about his culpability.

The toll of domestic violence is immeasurable and it is universal. I frequently lecture abroad on violence against women and girls and the need for legal reform. There is no country where domestic violence is not a dirty secret. And there are few places where women do not express surprise that domestic violence is a problem here. 'In Britain,' they exclaim, shocked that we too have violence against women behind closed doors, here in this respected and sceptred isle.

4

ASKING FOR IT

I t is in rape that the law crashes up against the rawest display of the continuing power imbalance between men and women. It is the perfect example of the inadequacy of legal reform in challenging the more immutable forces operating in the system. The conviction rate for rape in Britain is still the lowest for all serious crime, despite increased reporting. Over the past decade the numbers of reported rapes have doubled but only 7% of complaints ever lead to conviction. Very few rape cases proceed to court because a huge number are withdrawn. This is often because women cannot face the legal process. Despite all the efforts to improve the system, the stumbling block is that the woman knows that cross-examination will publicly expose her to all the double standards that confront women in our society and it will be her word against his. As recently as 2013 when Neil Wilson, 41, was convicted of underage sex with a 13-year-old girl, she was described by the prosecutor, yes the prosecutor, as 'predatory in all her actions and sexually experienced'. The accused was consequently given an eight-month suspended sentence. The inclination to blame the victim, whatever her age, lives on – it is the classic response to crime in the private arena. Nowhere is this more clearly visible than in the handling of rape cases. Women know that it is difficult to secure a conviction; they make their own calculations as to whether they are prepared to go through with it. Of the cases which do proceed to trial, the conviction rate in rape is 37% when the general conviction rate for crime across the board is 73%.

The word 'no' is at the core of a rape trial. A 'no' may be taken for granted when a respectable woman is attacked by a total stranger in a dimly lit street, but since the vast majority of rapes are committed by men known to the victim, consent in rape trials has always been an issue which makes men very nervous. Where does seduction end and rape begin? It is like the old lawyer's joke about how to tread the fine line between tax evasion, which is criminal, and tax avoidance, which is every reasonable man's goal in life. As with rape and seduction, it is all supposed to be a matter of technique. Getting a woman to submit is an acceptable part of the sexual game plan, and straying across the line a ready peril for any man with a healthy sexual appetite. The notion that women, having been pressed into submission, will melt into the experience and find pleasure in it often erases responsibility for violence, fear and humiliation.

When I first started practising at the Bar attitudes were much more stark than they are now. At legal dinners, rape jokes used to be constant. Did you hear the one about the woman who claimed she was raped and ran from a house clutching a doormat to cover her nakedness? Counsel for the defence asked if there was a 'Welcome' on her mat.

Or the old chestnut about the woman who was describing the act of penetration by her attacker. 'He put his penis into me,' she said. 'Well, let's leave it there until after lunch,' suggested His Lordship.

The behaviour of real judges in court was often scarcely better. Despite advice from their brethren that they should watch out for mantraps containing snarling feminists, judges used to take on the furies like demented lemmings, oblivious to the likely rage which would follow their inane comments. They would say extraordinary things – that women who dressed sexily were 'contributory negligent' or that women who did not want sex 'just had to keep their legs shut'. After every outrageous statement made by a judge in a rape trial there would be calls for sackings and questions in the House. The judge in question would be publicly silent but privately bewildered, asking colleagues where he went wrong.

A lot has changed since then, and there is agreement that sexual activity should be based on mutuality, with no coercion acceptable. Today's judges are much more savvy and circumspect about their utterances. They understand that women's anger about the handling of rape cases is not confined to wild feminists but is an indignation shared by most women, including their own wives and daughters. However, myths and stereotypes still plague the process.

'Victim of his libido' is a recurring theme in the mitigation plea for a convicted rapist. If a woman has been in any way familiar, we are presented with the old idea of man, the overheated engine, incapable of switching off. We are to treat him as the functional equivalent of a handgun, something intrinsically dangerous. The same hackneyed thinking underpins the new market in protective products – from anti-rape knickers featuring reinforced fabric and combination locks, to nail polish that changes colour when dipped in a spiked drink, to hairy stockings designed to quell a rapist's ardour. Products like these only make sense if we accept that rape is a fact of life, from which we women bear responsibility for protecting ourselves. But rape is not inevitable. Men who rape are responsible for their own actions, and the focus must always be on holding them fully to account.

In the view of some men, a woman's 'no' is covered in ambiguity, not to be taken seriously if she is vivacious, friendly and seems to be 'up for it'; if she dresses provocatively; if she goes out late at night or has had sex with others before. There is an irrational theorem that if a woman has sex with Tom and Dick she is more likely to have sex with Harry. It is hard to get across the idea that a woman is entitled to have sex with the whole of the football team but draw the line at the goalie. Having a lot of sex also apparently does something to a woman's capacity for truth. Sometimes, according to the Boy's Own theories about women, an initial refusal is a female ploy to play hard to get in case men think they are easy or cheap. It is not enough to say 'no'. The underlying belief is that deep down women want sex but do not always know their own minds. Until as recently as 1991 a married woman's 'no' was meaningless, since a wife was not supposed to deny her husband his conjugal rights. There was deemed to be no such thing as rape within marriage. The real problem is that it is an exercise of male power to subject a woman to sex, and when women say 'no', they challenge that power.

Even in the last 10 years, attitudes to sex have shifted in ways that can be very alien to the older generation of judge or juror. Once the preserve of those with greater sexual experience, oral sex has become mainstream and expected among young people, sometimes the first sexual act girls engage in. The very language of sex has lost much of its potency, and sexually vivid and aggressive words are now common-place in much casual conversation. In online communications from emails and texts to tweets and WhatsApp, people describe sexual activity and desires in ways that are shocking to many older people. Modern television programmes are more explicit, with sex treated increasingly like every other commodity, something to which you are entitled. The biggest hit TV show of recent times, *Game of Thrones*, has been criticised by feminists as gratuitous and sensationalist in its use of rape. A new wave of self-proclaimed 'pickup artists' school their students online and at masterclasses in questionable methods for getting women into bed. Every year, one or two horrendously misjudged advertisements cause controversy by appearing to condone rape or sexual assault – like the US department store advert that encouraged men to spike their friend's Christmas drink, or the online retailer that invited customers to take advantage of its sale offers with the slogan 'Rape Us Now'. It is not just consensual sex that sells.

The way women are socialised not to offend also helps keep the lines blurred. We are still encouraged to be sensitive to the feelings of men, to avoid telling them they are simply not fancied. Excuses are supposed to be better than rejection and confused messages may be communicated. 'I can't, I've got my period' – 'I have to go home' – 'I already have a boyfriend.' The recitation is endless: all to avoid saying the hurtful 'no'.

As a rule, such blurred lines don't come into play in the trial of the stranger-rape, happening at knifepoint in the dark of night. Everyone, male and female alike, is united in their sense of outrage. Yet even in these cases, distinctions drawn between worthy and unworthy women affect the strength of that outrage, as we saw in the investigation and media coverage of the Yorkshire Ripper case in 1981. The whole tone of the police appeals to the public changed once it became clear that the victims were not 'only' prostitutes and that all women were at risk.

Still today the police frequently fail to act on women's complaints and put countless other women at risk. Former black-cab driver John

Worboys was a prolific sexual offender who drugged and sexually assaulted scores of women in the back of his London taxi. Claiming to have won the lottery, Worboys persuaded women travelling alone to toast his good fortune with champagne that he had laced with sedatives, before raping and assaulting his unconscious victims. Despite an allegation of sexual assault being made as early as May 2003, the police failed to arrest and charge Worboys until February 2008. In July 2007, Worboys was arrested on suspicion of sexual assault, but was subsequently released and went on to assault seven more women before finally being charged and convicted of rape and sexual assault. An investigation by the Independent Police Complaints Commission found numerous failings in the police's handling of the complaints. Inconsistencies in Worboys's account were never followed up, there was no search of his home or taxi, and he was not re-interviewed when new information relating to the case came to light. The police mindset appears to have been that a black-cab driver simply wouldn't get up to this sort of thing because his cab has to be licensed. Similar institutional failings left serial offender Kirk Reid free to assault an estimated 80–100 women in south London between 2001 and 2008, despite being known to the police since 2002. Reid was eventually convicted of two rapes and 24 sexual assaults in 2009.

The Worboys and Reid cases help to demonstrate why the official CPS rape conviction rate of 57.9% only tells part of the story. That figure refers to the conviction rate in cases where the police decide to refer a rape allegation to the CPS, and the CPS decides to prosecute. It provides a snapshot of conviction rates among the strongest cases, but reveals nothing about cases of unreported rape, or cases in which women struggle to get their complaints heard. According to figures compiled by the Home Office, the Ministry of Justice and the Office for National Statistics in January 2013 in 'An Overview of Sexual

Offending', approximately 85,000 women and 12,000 men are raped every year in England and Wales. That means 11 rapes per hour. One in five women between the ages of 16 and 59 has experienced some form of sexual violence since the age of 16. The Ministry of Justice estimates that only 15% of women who suffer serious sexual assault report it. Large numbers of rapes also go unreferred or unrecorded. The pressure on police to meet inflexible targets can be intense. In 2013, it emerged that officers based in Southwark's specialist sexual offences unit had been encouraging women to retract their allegations of rape, so that no crime was recorded and the proportion of recorded crimes proceeding to prosecution was artificially inflated. The same year, a serving police constable called James Patrick blew the whistle on widespread under-recording of crime by the Metropolitan Police, including in relation to rape. In evidence given to the Home Affairs Public Administration Select Committee, PC Patrick stated that sexual offence victims who were vulnerable because of mental health or substance abuse issues were particular targets of police pressure to retract.

Since these revelations and the public debate around Jimmy Savile, Rolf Harris and Harvey Weinstein, official statistics have shown a sharp increase in the number of recorded rapes. This is largely due to improvements in police recording practices, as well as the increased willingness of victims to come forward.

But this improvement in recording has not been matched by a corresponding spike in conviction rates. One of the serious problems for women is that their own phones, computers and tablets can often provide material that can be used evidentially to undermine their credibility. It is also the case that while women have become much more sexually independent and confident, they are still judged differently from men when it comes to their sexual behaviour.

In December 2017 the case against a young man called Liam Allan was stopped mid trial when it came to light that the police had failed to disclose vital evidence of text messages, in which the young woman who accused him of rape had described rape fantasies to other men, and told a friend about the acts with Liam Allan, saying, 'It wasn't against my will or anything.' The police officer conducting the case had failed to pass on the material from the woman's phone to the CPS and it was only disclosed when the prosecutor asked if there was any relevant content on her mobile phone. The police have a duty to pass to the prosecution any material which will assist the prosecution or the defence. The evidence had been available for two years so not surprisingly the man who was accused had a deep grievance about the fact that it hadn't happened. In the same week another case was dropped at a sexual abuse trial, again because of failure to disclose. The two cases raise important issues about police conduct in sex cases. There is nothing new in the police failing to disclose evidence which can exonerate an accused. In my own experience of many miscarriages of justice that is exactly what happened. Sometimes it is deliberate malfeasance but now it is often about under-resourcing of the police and prosecuting authorities. Swingeing cuts of 40% of the budget of the Ministry of Justice have left the system on its knees. There is currently serious concern that the police have little digital forensic capacity to examine computers and phones, and miscarriages of justice are taking place across the court system with wrongful convictions as well as wrongful acquittals. However, the tabloid press immediately jumped to the conclusion that this was all about political correctness with the police rushing to judgement on innocent men. I saw no such urgency to expose overzealous policing when it was Irish defendants in terrorist cases who were at the receiving end of non-disclosure or when it affected young black defendants in robbery cases. The pressing question is not why so many men are wrongly charged. It is why so few are charged at all. Why do so many alleged rapists continue to go unprosecuted?

In 2002 Professor Liz Kelly was commissioned by the Crown Prosecution Service Inspectorate to review research into rape in Britain and abroad so that we might have some understanding of the issue. Her review was included in the report of the Prosecution and Police Inspectorates and it suggested 'that at each stage of the legal process, stereotypes and prejudices play a part in decision making'. Since Professor Kelly's report, the CPS has appointed specially trained rape prosecutors, and police forces are increasingly training specialist officers who can provide sympathetic and expert support to rape victims. But the real problem, which persists today, is that the approach generally taken by the police and prosecutors is based on whether they believe a prosecution will succeed at trial. As PC Patrick commented in his evidence to the select committee:

[The police] are working to the charging standards, which is well beyond the remit of what we are there to do. We do not do deciding guilt. That is the court, that is the justice system. We gather evidence and put it before the justice system. Effectively, we are usurping that in some way by pre-empting it with our own decisions, based on those standards, which is inappropriate.

Inappropriate indeed. Yet when making decisions about how to record an alleged rape, or whether to seek a conviction, police and prosecutors routinely anticipate the kind of cross-examination to which the woman will be subjected and a judgement is made as to whether she will survive the test. This involves evaluating the complainant against the ideal victim, who is preferably sexually inexperienced or at least respectable. Respectability is becoming more and more difficult to characterise as women go clubbing, drink in 'unladylike' quantities and are also more prepared to have uncommitted sex than previous generations. They lay out their sexual activities in their texts and emails, distribute photographs of themselves undressed or with little on, or they may give expression to *Shades of Grey* fantasies of sadomasochism or even rape. Sadomasochism has its roots in subservience, inequality, feelings of guilt, shame and unworthiness. Men and women have absorbed these feelings, and misconstruing the voluntary surrendering of agency is utterly ill-conceived. None of those behaviours should prevent a woman saying 'no' when she does not want to have intercourse. Yet increasingly that seems to be the price paid for women choosing to be as sexually independent as men. Women are asked questions which are never put to men about why they were out alone in the street or in a pub or at a disco. They are asked about their clothing: the tightness of the fit, the absence of a bra. They are asked about their use of contraception. If a woman is middle-aged and perhaps divorced, frustration and loneliness are presented as motives for her consenting to sex with an unlikely partner.

Twenty years ago there was extensive debate about women being cross-examined on previous sexual relationships, and legislation was passed to limit this (section 41 of the Youth Justice and Criminal Evidence Act 1999), but much of the cross-examination which does not fall under that heading is almost as objectionable. Few women escape the inquisition and possible humiliation of cross-examination by the barrister of an inventive defendant. Well versed in the unspoken rules of the courtroom, defence counsel summon up pictures of the woman out on the town, scantily dressed and drunk on cider. They know that getting blitzed and binge drinking set the stage for an acquittal. In 2017 a retiring criminal judge called Lindsey

Kushner used her last trial to comment that while there was no excuse for rape, women were more vulnerable, and less likely to be believed, if they had been drinking. Her remarks caused a furore and were roundly condemned by campaigners for blaming victims not rapists. It is true that victim blaming is a real problem, but there is also no denying that, sadly, Judge Kushner was articulating one of the many unspoken prejudices that can and do affect a jury in a rape trial.

The victim is often totally unprepared for the defence's attack on her reputation, and the prosecution is not usually allowed to call evidence in support of her good character. Sometimes simply asking a question can be enormously damaging, even if the defence has no real evidence to back it up. 'Is it not the case that you were smoking cannabis earlier that evening?' 'You took Ecstasy at the club, didn't you?' 'You are a user of cocaine, are you not?' Juries assume the lawyer knows something; the denial still leaves a lurking doubt about the kind of woman she is.

In October 2004 two Surrey policemen stood trial for rape. They had been called out to help a woman who had been assaulted in a fracas in the street as she came out of a nightclub. By her own account she was very drunk, and one of her friends had wanted to accompany her when the police asked her to get in their car so that they could drive around to find her assailant. They refused to let the friend come. When the policemen, PC Mark Witcher and PC Andrew Lang, took her back to her flat, she thought they were going to take a statement but instead, according to the woman, they both raped and sexually assaulted her, pulling her around like a rag doll and shouting obscenities at her, telling her she was a slag. The men left laughing and afterwards boasted to colleagues in the police force that they had 'spit-roasted' her, both penetrating her at the same time, one orally, one vaginally.

It spoke volumes about the police culture that they felt uninhibited about recounting their behaviour.

Despite being on duty at the time, both officers contested the case on the basis that the woman consented; DNA from semen was found on her skirt which meant it would have been difficult for them to suggest that nothing had happened. In cross-examination, the woman was subjected to the usual litany about her clothing and her drunkenness. 'Why didn't you shout to waken the babysitter? Why didn't you go to the doctor? You were ashamed of what you had done, weren't you? You made this up because you were concerned that you would lose custody of your children, concerned about the new relationship you were enjoying at the time. You decided to turn this tale of consensual sex into one of rape, didn't you?' They were acquitted of rape. They were sentenced for having sex while on duty and it was then revealed that they were known in the force as sexual predators and the Assistant Chief Constable accepted that this allegation was not 'a one-off act.'

Defence counsel's words highlight the twist in the nailing of women. 'You are not a true victim. You are the victim of your own behaviour that evening,' he said. True victimhood has very demanding standards, and not all women are perceived to measure up. According to the 2013/14 Crime Survey for England and Wales, 27% of respondents believed that a victim of rape or sexual assault was at least partially responsible if they were drunk at the time. These harmful rape myths can continue to have an impact even if a conviction is secured. The Criminal Injuries Compensation Authority provides compensation for blameless victims of violent crimes. There are several documented instances of women having their compensation reduced because they had been drunk when they were raped.

Judges are now required to undergo specialist training before hearing rape trials, and they must ensure that no questioning of the complainant is carried out in an unduly harassing or degrading manner. The circumstances in which cross-examination of sexual history can take place might now be limited, but the ways that women can be denigrated in the eyes of a jury are extremely varied.

A woman might be asked whether her vagina was naturally lubricated to enable penetration, thereby encouraging the jury to infer that some gratification was being found in the sexual contact. Or her reliability as a witness is challenged on the basis that her true sexual nature and desires are so repressed that she has now reconstructed events and believes them herself. Her credibility is thus being challenged, not on the basis of her lying, but of her not even knowing that she is lying!

To explain away multiple acts of rape, a gang rape or physical injury, defence lawyers may even suggest to the jury that many women are turned on by group sex, enjoy kinky sex or a 'bit of rough'. There is no winning. Without the physical signs of resistance, such as bruising, it is (automatically) assumed that the victim consented or is subject to female rape fantasies; where she does bear the signs of attack she is challenged as a masochist.

And then of course we have the state of a victim's mental health. On the one hand psychiatry is mistrusted in the courtroom as hocus-pocus which distracts jurors from the main issues, but on the other it can prove very useful in undermining the value of testimony. The slightest hint of anything that might affect the mind can jeopardise a case.

I have heard it suggested to a woman in a rape case that she had a history of mental illness. This was in fact a breakdown under the pressure of taking her university finals, from which she rapidly recovered. The suggestion was used to undermine her, portraying her as someone whose mental stability was questionable and might lead to her making irrational allegations. Suggestions of instability cling to women much more readily than to men, and even a mention of going to psychotherapy in search of self-enlightenment is confused with mental illness. The leaps involved in such innuendo are never examined, and the damage can be irreparable unless the woman is given time to explain at length whole areas of her life which have no relevance to the proceedings.

One of the most shocking cases in recent times involved the trial in Belfast of four men who played for the Irish national rugby team. The complainant was a student who described in evidence going out with friends to celebrate the end of exams. They had gone to a club where that evening there were both soccer and rugby players at the bar. At the end of the evening there was an invitation to a party back at the home of one of the players, Patrick Jackson. In the course of the evening the young woman said she had gone to the bathroom upstairs and was pushed into a bedroom and then forward onto a bed by Jackson, who then pulled her trousers down and penetrated her vaginally from behind. He had also tried to force his fist into her vagina. A player called Stuart Olding then joined them and on her account forced her to perform oral sex on him while she was being penetrated by his teammate. Then a third man entered the room, Blane McIlroy, whom she described exposing himself, masturbating, and saying he wanted in on the action. When she ran from the room, pulling on her trousers, she was bleeding from her vagina onto her clothing. A fourth man called Rory Harrison saw the state she was in and got her into a taxi and dropped her off at home. The taxi driver testified that she was crying and sobbing in his cab. And that he heard Harrison on the phone say to someone 'She is with me now. She is not good. I'll call you in the morning.' The following day he texted her on the number he had asked her for the night before and she replied 'what happened last night was not consensual.' She was still bleeding from her vagina and said in evidence that, because she was face down, she could not see if a condom was used so she was anxious to have the morning after pill. She attended a clinic and when examined by a doctor she was found to have a tear to the wall of her vagina which was still bleeding 30 hours after the events. When the doctor testified he had to accept when questioned by the defence that he could not say if the tear was caused by penile penetration. This was because the men all claimed that no penetration whatsoever took place and she had simply voluntarily performed oral sex on two of them. The blood must have been from her period.

The men belonged to a WhatsApp group with a few other male friends. In an exchange the day after the events McIlroy posted: 'What the fuck was going on? Last night was hilarious.' A message has then been deleted but it seemed to have come from Harrison saying that the complainant was very distressed and alleging rape. McIlroy responded: 'Really. Fucks sake. Did you calm her? And where did she live?' Harrison replied: 'Make no joke. She is in hysteria.' He added that it wasn't going to end well. Other postings about the week asked: 'Any sluts get fucked?' The response from Olding was: 'Pumped a girl with Jacko on Monday. Roasted her. Then another on Thursday night.' 'Love Belfast sluts.' The claim of 'roasting', the Crown suggested, meant that while one accused was penetrating her vaginally another was penetrating her orally but this contradicted the account of the men who insisted there was no vaginal penetration. The defence claimed that this was just male banter, juvenile boasting, a sideshow which should have no relevance or evidential value.

The complainant was in the witness box being cross-examined for eight days. Her clothing was presented to the jury. Her briefs were shown to demonstrate that there was some blood on them, as in

127

evidence she had said she had not put them back on after they were pulled off with her trousers. The defence barristers claimed she must therefore have been having a period and the blood was not from damage caused by any forced penetration. The court, which is the biggest in the UK, had a public gallery with 100 spectators. The witness was behind a screen, as is now permitted in sexual cases, so at least she could not see the size of the crowd of onlookers, though she probably knew. Celebrity sportsmen turned up in the gallery to provide moral support to their friends in the dock. The complainant was accused of inventing the allegations because she was ashamed that she had participated in group sex. Minor contradictions were put to the woman who explained that 'In that situation you don't scream because you are so scared. You underestimate the shock you go into after being raped.' Her use of the impersonal 'you' allowed the defence to suggest she was recounting things she had read. Inconsistencies between the men also existed.

The men were acquitted to a rapturous response from their fans as they left the court. No one noticed what happened to the young woman. What we do know is that her protective anonymity was cancelled out as she was repeatedly named and shamed on social media. Whose shame are we talking about here?

It is not uncommon for rape to summon up long-learned fears whispered into the ears of boys about the fickleness and deceit of women – fears that women are vindictive and bitter, that they will stop at nothing to trap a man and stoop to anything to make him pay; fears that the line which separates rape from seduction is easily crossed, and any decent fellow is at the mercy of an unscrupulous female. A speaker from Fathers4Justice told the boys at my daughter's school that they should prepare their defences now for false allegations of rape because the law is now so skewed towards the female of the species that men are being wrongly imprisoned. In fact, the reverse is true. The number of women who claim to have been raped when they have not is extremely small, and is far outweighed by the number of men who rape. A report published by the CPS in 2013 found that over the seventeen-month period under review there were only 35 prosecutions for making false allegations of rape, as compared to 5,651 prosecutions for rape. Yet despite the evidence, the spectre of a woman willing to falsely accuse looms disproportionately large in the collective male psyche and receives similarly disproportionately prominent coverage in the media. And yet there is no question that women rape complainants often struggle to get the police to take their allegations seriously. Those who retract their claims, under police pressure or the emotional strain of the investigative process, risk prosecution for making false rape allegations under laws which are enforced much more aggressively in the UK than in comparable legal systems.

Lawyers are past masters in the art of subtle discrimination. In 1976 Judge Sutcliffe, when discussing the corroboration rule, gave the game away by reminding a jury that 'it is well known that women in particular and small boys are liable to be untruthful and invent stories'. It was interesting to speculate about when exactly the moment of transition takes place, and lying little boys become truthful male adults. Judges would never make such a comment now but defence lawyers still plant the suspicion that women aren't upfront about their willingness to lead men on.

Of course, there are women who lie. There are a few misguided or malicious women who make false allegations of rape, and it is essential that the strong protections for defendants which exist within our system should be jealously maintained. There are also women whose mental state may be fragile and who may feel abused in the aftermath of intimacy to which they seemed to consent. While these cases are rare, a fair and due process means evidence has to be tested and proof has to be of a high standard if someone is at risk of losing their liberty. These processes and standards protect women, too. I often have to debate with women who want the standard of proof to be lowered in rape cases to secure more convictions, or who suggest that the burden of proof should be passed to the accused, meaning that the man should have to prove beyond reasonable doubt that he secured consent – a total reversal of how our legal system works. It has even been suggested that we make sex without consent an absolute offence with an automatic acceptance of the woman's word that she did not want the sex. To do any of this would inevitably open the doors to serious injustice and we have to guard high standards with all our energy if we want to live in a free society.

In 2017, Jemma Beale was jailed for 10 years for making a series of false rape and sexual assault claims against 15 men, one of whom was sentenced to seven years in prison following a wrongful conviction for rape which was based on her false testimony. In my view, the courts are right to imprison women for making deliberate and calculated false allegations of rape. If women campaign for rape to be taken seriously, then on those rare occasions when a woman does make a false complaint she must bear the consequences.

But because of the myth that women frequently invented allegations of sexual impropriety by men, the law used to require corroboration in rape cases to support the woman's testimony. Her word alone was insufficient. A ludicrous situation arose in a case where a man broke into a woman's house, burgled the premises and then raped her. The judge had the task of explaining to the jury that it could be dangerous to convict on the uncorroborated evidence of the woman in respect of the rape, but not dangerous so far as the burglary was concerned. An overhaul of the rules on corroboration has put an end to the judicial warning to juries that women can be untrustworthy except in Scotland where the rule still stands. The judge's direction in the rest of the UK has now been reformulated, putting the emphasis on the jury's right to convict should they believe the woman's evidence and reminding them that all women are still entitled to say 'no'. What is still not emphasised enough is that a woman may consent to sex but she is entitled to say 'no' if a man introduces acts or activity to which she does not consent. She may be content to have vaginal intercourse but only with a condom. She may agree to vaginal intercourse but not want to be penetrated anally. And while she may want to be with one man, she may not be willing to have sex with all his teammates at the same time. At each stage of intimacy a man should be saying 'is this OK?' If it isn't OK, it's rape.

The credibility issue at the heart of the rape case is worth examining. Many of the decisions juries make daily in our courtrooms when they assess witnesses and facts are based on credibility. Are rape cases rendered special by the sexual component? Is rape different from other offences of violence because of the profound emotions and complicated psychological responses that men and women have to sex? Yes, it is different, but not so different as to invite a completely separate set of values. In most cases juries can spot false from reliable evidence without judges or defence counsel wading in with half-baked theories about sexual neurosis and female fantasies and the need to approach a woman's evidence with special caution.

Juries gauge the truthfulness of witnesses in the way that we all do – by watching their demeanour and listening to their account, especially when it is being tested under cross-examination. Sometimes inconsistency counts against someone, though it may be utterly explicable given normal failure of memory or the trauma of events. Sometimes people lie about insignificant issues because of a misguided notion that the truth will count against them. There are times when this is fatal to a case, because juries then worry about what part of a witness's evidence they can believe. At other times the quality of detail and the sheer certainty with which the witness testifies on the crucial aspects of a case leave them in no doubt as to where the truth lies. Additional evidence from an independent source does make the task easier. Convictions inevitably follow more readily if there is supportive evidence, and the police have to be trained to be more proactive in securing it.

Yet the very nature of rape tends to locate the crime in the privacy of a closed room, in dimly lit streets, in the shadow of darkness. There are rarely eyewitnesses. Forensic evidence may prove that intercourse took place or, with the new genetic testing of semen, confirm the identity of the assailant. But in the majority of cases the defendant is not denying that he performed the sexual act. The issue is whether the woman consented. Judges and juries are more convinced if they can see torn knickers and proof that the victim was beaten, but even the signs of resistance have to be more than the odd bruise, which defendants explain away as the result of vigorous sex-play and playful pinching. The paradox is that the requirement to show that they put up a fight flies in the face of everything we are told about self-protection. As one victim said when interviewed about her experience, 'Everything I did right to save my life is exactly wrong in terms of proving I was telling the truth.'

Most rape-prevention education advises women not to invite greater harm by fighting the assailant, who may have a weapon. The extensive reporting of cases where women have been raped and then killed confirms that the violence may not stop at the act of rape, and it may be better not to antagonise the attacker. The persistent cross-examination ploy of defence counsel is to deny that fear might paralyse the victim and to insist that a woman guarding her virtue would fight like a lioness. We are still haunted by powerful cultural images of what good women do in the face of ravishment. In a long literary tradition which begins with Livy and Ovid, Lucretia fights off her attacker and refuses to yield to his threats. The deed done, she takes her own life. In Lorenzo Lotto's famous painting in the National Gallery, there is a note on the table by the victim's side which declares: 'NEC ULLA IMPUDICA LUCRETIA EXEMPLO VIVET' (We would have no immoral women if Lucretia's example were followed).

What all this means is that, if there is little independent evidence of the complainant's account, it is one person's word against another, and judges and juries are thrown back on the impression made by the victim in the witness box. It is as though she were the person on trial. Indeed, in one case a Canadian judge repeatedly referred to the complainant in a rape case as 'the accused'. He also asked the complainant – who alleged that she had been raped while sitting on a basin – why she did not just prevent the rape by sinking lower into the basin, or closing her knees together. At one point, he responded to her evidence that the rape had caused her pain by saying 'sex and pain sometimes go together – that's not necessarily a bad thing'. The judge was found guilty of serious misconduct and has since retired.

Navigating these issues requires a judge who truly understands the offence of rape. The *Equal Treatment Bench Book* is a guide that is distributed to all judges. It now contains a section which expressly debunks a number of the most potent rape myths, including the mistaken belief that rape victims should put up a fight and show signs of injuries, or that stranger rape is invariably more traumatic than rape by an acquaintance. To combat the theory that consent can be assumed from dress, flirting or boozing, judges are encouraged to tell juries that if a man flashed his bulging wallet around in a pub and then had it stolen, no one would say that the person who stole it was not really a thief.

Another common myth is that genuine victims report rape immediately. Judges are now entitled to tell the jury that 'experience shows that people react differently to the trauma of a serious sexual assault. There is no one classic response ... You may think that some people may complain immediately to the first person they see, whilst others may feel shame and shock and not complain for some time. A late complaint does not necessarily mean it is a false complaint.' The evident truth of this statement is made even plainer by the steady flow of people only just now coming forward to say they were victims of historical sexual abuse. It is crucial that judges use their summings-up to give directions to the jury which combat the misconceptions about rape that eddy and swirl around the courtroom.

In 2002, the House of Lords decided that a woman could be cross-examined about her sexual history if the purpose was to support a man's claim that he honestly believed she consented. As long ago as 1991 I advocated that when a man claimed that he honestly thought a woman was consenting even if she was not, there should be an objective test – would a reasonable person have thought she was consenting (if she was saying 'no' or was asleep or was drugged)? In the Sexual Offences Act 2003 the government changed the law to embrace my suggestion. The change remains very controversial and raises the question as to whether such a divergence from the normal criminal rules is justifiable. I think it is and should be strengthened. In the debate of that legislation in the House of Lords, Viscount Bledisloe chose an unfortunate but telling example to define the normal rules: 'If I am accused of stealing your property, it is a defence if I show an honest belief that I had a claim of right to that property. That is the general test of the criminal law.'

In a case of theft, it is enough that a defendant genuinely thought that the item had been abandoned even if most normal people would think it unlikely that someone would abandon a ladder or bicycle or a rundown cottage in the country. The jury would simply decide whether to believe the accused. With the new objective test in the rape case the jury would have to decide whether it was reasonable for the accused to think the woman was consenting. It would not be enough for the accused to say 'yes she was saying no very loudly but I still think she really wanted me'. Or 'yes she was crying and began to bleed vaginally but I just thought she was menstruating.' Would a reasonable person believe she was consenting?

The question is whether the protection of human beings, not property, from a profoundly damaging experience might justify higher expectations of behaviour, a greater care and respect for the humanity of others, than is seen in other areas of the law. In the same debate one of our retired judges Lord Lloyd, speaking about rape, very sensitively enunciated its kernel: 'the forcible penetration of the vagina is a corruption of the deepest and tenderest of emotions of which human beings are capable'. Gay men and lesbians do not feel any differently even if the form of intimacy is different. Forcing intercourse or sexual acts upon someone, securing their engagement in sexual activity through fear, is a corruption of lovemaking and good sex. Yes, sometimes people do it casually and without any reference to love, but that does not negate the fact that it is the way we have found to express that profound emotion. That is why sexual offences are so lasting in the damage they do to lives, contaminating what is precious. It is why sexual offences are different, involving an 'abuse of intimacy', and it is why we may deal with them differently.

That does not mean reversing burdens of proof, forcing the accused to prove their innocence, but it does mean prohibiting negligent disregard for the other. If human rights mean anything we are here walking on human rights terrain. The law now spells out a range of circumstances, not exhaustive, in which it will be presumed there is no consent. One example is if the woman is asleep, unconscious or too affected by alcohol or drugs to give agreement. Some men claim that the reforms place an impossible burden on them to show that the woman agreed to sex if she had a few drinks beforehand. But this is wrong. It will not be for the man to show that the woman consented. The prosecution will still have to show that she didn't. Nor has it created a new hazard for women. The rule that a woman cannot agree to sex if she is too drunk is already well established in law and dates back to a case in 1845. It is a statement of the obvious. Rape is a denial of personal autonomy and a woman who is asleep, unconscious or in a state of extreme intoxication is in no position to say 'no'. An unreasonable belief that she consented must not provide a defence and judges should be emphasising this when summing up the law.

Suggestions that 'real rape' should be distinguished from 'date rape' are often floated, with proposals that a subcategory of the offence should be created with a less odious name, to encompass forced intercourse between acquaintances – as though it were inherently different. In 2011 Ken Clarke – about one week into his tenure as Justice Secretary – gave a radio interview in which he appeared to distinguish between date rape and 'serious' rape. These sentiments reflect not only a distrust of women but a misappreciation of the crime. There are indeed degrees of seriousness in rape, but that does not alter the elements of the offence. Differentiating the degree of seriousness should happen at the point of sentencing, and it should be done by assessing each case individually, within a sensible sentencing framework which recognises that rape psychologically damages its victims. Sentencing guidelines were revised in 2002 so that rape by a known defendant should be treated as seriously as rape by a stranger, because all the psychological research showed that it was often just as traumatising.

Rape campaigners have tried to shift the perception of rape as being a crime about sex towards an understanding of it as an offence of violence and power. However, for many men violence equals force, a male threat which they understand. They fail to appreciate that there are many other, less explicit, ways in which men can cause women to fear them. It is the absence of actual force which often persuades people that something less than 'real rape' has taken place. Yet as Baroness Stern noted in her 2010 review into the handling of rape complaints: '[the law] says that one person having sex with another when that person has not agreed to it is rape. The law does not say force has to be used for it to be defined as rape. Violence is not part of the definition. The absence of consent is the defining factor.'

Again, there are calls for a total ban on cross-examining about sexual relations with persons other than the accused. I am not in favour of total bans as life has taught me that there is invariably a case where one would want to see an exception made. Over and above the question of consent, some discretion has to be left with judges as to when questions about a complainant's previous sexual activity may be relevant. I have myself acted in a case where a 13-year-old girl accused her stepfather of rape. She had been having sex with a stepbrother whom she loved and she feared would be prosecuted if their relationship came to light. After she had a miscarriage she was questioned about who had made her pregnant and named her stepfather. She may have been telling the truth about her stepfather's abuse but she may also have been covering for the stepbrother. The jury was entitled to know the full facts.

An application under section 41 of the Youth Justice and Criminal Evidence Act 1999 must be made to cross-examine about sexual history. If the only object of such cross-examination is to show that this is the kind of woman who consents, it is not supposed to be allowed. Because a woman has consented to sex either with the accused or with anyone else in the past does not mean she should be denied the right to be believed about her allegation.

The fact that a woman has gone on websites like Tinder and Bumble to meet potential sexual partners in what seems to be an indiscriminate way is invariably problematic even if it has nothing to do with the rape allegation before the court. The very notion that a woman is prepared to have casual sex with a stranger still weighs heavily against her despite her claims that she would only actually have sex with someone to whom she was attracted. Judicial warnings will be given but they rarely expunge the bias that will already have been created. If the case in point emanated from a contact made through a hook-up website, there would be little hope of a conviction.

Unfortunately, applications to ask such questions are not being made early enough in the proceedings so that the Crown and the judge can carefully evaluate the relevance of such evidence. Sometimes, they are not made at all but the judge allows the questions anyway. Sometimes defence lawyers just chance their luck and ask a question which is then stopped but by then it is too late. The judge too often lets matters proceed, all too aware of the costs already incurred in having the trial. The evidence should not be admitted if its only purpose is to impugn the credibility of the complainant, but it is often hard to separate out relevance from prejudice. The decision to quash the original conviction in the Ched

Evans appeal has further blurred the lines. The Court of Appeal judges decided that evidence from two other men who had had sex with the complainant should have been received as it suggested that the complainant had a predilection for unusual sex. The claim was that the complainant had had sex on all fours with vaginal penetration from behind and had said 'Fuck me harder.' Leaving aside the question of whether the evidence was truthful, the fact that judges in their sixties thought that this was unusual sexual behaviour said a lot about their own sexual experience and their lack of familiarity with contemporary pornography in which this behaviour is standard. As a result of this decision judges are now even more inclined to allow sexual history to be adduced in evidence.

Research conducted in Newcastle throughout 2017, commissioned by Vera Baird QC, the Police Commissioner there, exposed the wholesale failings of the current rules on excluding sexual history in rape trials. Such observations of actual trials are the only form of research that sheds light because if a man is acquitted of rape there is no review of why this was the result in a case where the evidence was strong. There is no analysis of judges consenting to cross-examination on the women's sexual life and why. There clearly needs to be stricter guidance to judges on how to handle rape cases and better training. There has to be a *presumption* to exclude any cross-examination on sexual history, save in the most exceptional circumstances. If necessary, this presumption should be enshrined in new law.

In *Facts of Rape*, Barbara Toner quotes a police officer: 'A good witness relives the experience in court. She doesn't hold back her emotions. If she wants to cry, she bloody well cries. If she wants a drink of water, she asks. She re-experiences the feelings she had at the time. A bad witness will frustrate the court.'

Of course, women who have been raped use different coping devices just to live with themselves after the assault, and some are able to draw upon reserves of composure and poise which can work against them with the judge and jury. Others manifest signs of rape trauma syndrome, including a strange distancing from the event, which makes them seem cool and unemotional. The very resources a woman uses to assuage the horror of the experience can be held against her by police officers, lawyers and judges at her trial.

Often the one thing a victim cannot bring herself to do is to relive the event before a courtroom of strangers. The reason for a rape victim's inability to 'emote' may be nothing to do with her credibility but a direct result of the rape itself. Again, this is something a good judge should be able to explain to a jury.

Women frequently describe their trauma in the courtroom as a further abuse. This may sound hysterical and exaggerated, but part of the problem is that a woman's powerlessness in the trial evokes all the feelings of powerlessness that were experienced in the original rape. In 2003 Ms M. told the Fawcett Commission on Women and the Criminal Justice System, 'Six months ago I could not understand why a woman would not wish to bring her attacker to court. My own experience has taught me otherwise.' This is partly because the woman complainant has no lawyer. She is no more than a witness being called by the Crown, subject to the same constraints as any other witness. American films like *The Accused* mislead British women into thinking they will have their own barrister who will talk them through the issues. In reality, counsel for the prosecution is constrained from spending too much time talking with a complainant under the Bar's professional rules. It used to be forbidden altogether but now counsel can introduce herself and explain the procedure; however, care has to be taken to avoid any question of coaching. The process seems remote and unconcerned with the woman's feelings.

Taking on a rape case is a complex proposition and not just because of the pitfalls of the process. The professional code of conduct of the Bar requires that you accept any brief that comes your way. This is known as the 'cab-rank' principle. Every barrister is asked regularly by perplexed lay people how they feel about representing someone they know to be guilty. For my own part, representing clients who are probably guilty is rarely a problem; it is representing those you think are innocent which induces sleepless nights. However, the polite answer we all give is that it is not our role to judge guilt or innocence; we concentrate instead on evaluating and testing the evidence and putting our clients' cases as they would themselves if they were representing themselves. If every lawyer refused to act for those whose conduct is reprehensible, many unpopular people might go unrepresented or be represented by a limited section of the profession. And there is another important consideration. If a barrister were able to pick and choose his or her clients, endorsement would follow from having a certain counsel and, conversely, failing to secure eminent counsel would emit a damning message.

Yet many female barristers declare an instinctive ambivalence about rape cases. It is never our function as defence counsel to judge the guilt or innocence of our clients, and as women at the Bar we adhere to that principle just as men do. In practice, some women rely upon the goodwill of the solicitors who brief them, and hope that rape cases will go somewhere else. Otherwise they grit their teeth and get on with the job, trying to conduct the case without the use of sexist innuendo. Others have no problem, because they will not entertain considerations of sexual politics. As in any other case, they see it as their duty to use every legitimate tactic to undermine the other side, and if that means reducing the witness's moral value in the eyes of the jury, that is the course to be taken.

The debate has engaged me as a woman and as a lawyer for many years. I have defended men charged with rape and secured their acquittal. I have felt ashamed as women I am cross-examining flash angry eyes at me for betraying them. Rape separates the girls from the boys. The fundamental difference in the way that men and women perceive rape has affected the conduct of cases, the nature of admissible evidence, and the pattern of sentencing by judges. If the criminal justice system were more even-handed in the way that rape is investigated and tried, women lawyers would feel less compromised by the role they are expected to play. Women should conduct rape cases, prosecuting and defending, because we should be setting the standards as to how cases should be conducted. I was sacked by a client in a sexual assault case because I said it was irrelevant that the complainant had on some previous occasion stood on a bar stool and performed a striptease. The accused was not even present at the time and had only heard about the incident after his arrest. I have no doubt that some other lawyer would have tried to find a way to get this piece of extraneous prejudice in by the back door but ask that same lawyer whether he thinks it is acceptable to use material to play on racial prejudice and he is unlikely to agree.

The prison sentences passed on convicted rapists have greatly increased in the past twenty years. There has been growing acceptance of the profound psychological damage caused by sex crimes and this is reflected in the sentences. Sentencing guidelines make it clear that lengthy jail terms should be the norm for rape. Yet cases of poor charging practices in the first instance and then early release or early parole in cases of serial rape call into question the assessment of risk posed to women by rapists as they come back into the community.

The controversy surrounding John Worboys's parole is a vivid case in point. It is estimated that in total Worboys drugged and raped over 100 women and yet he was only prosecuted on 12 sample charges. He was convicted of just one rape charge and five assaults after a trial which forced some of his victims to testify against him. He was given an indeterminate sentence with a minimum of eight years and his victims assumed that the indeterminate nature of his term was to reflect the multiplicity of his crimes. Subsequent to his being charged many more women came forward giving very similar accounts of assault and rape. At no time during his trial did he accept responsibility for his crimes, and when some of the women took civil actions against him after his convictions, he still maintained his innocence. None of this suggested a man who had acknowledged his offending behaviour. Yet in January 2018 the Parole Board announced that he would be released imminently as he 'no longer posed a risk'. His victims were given no forewarning. When demands were made by MPs to explain the rationale for his early parole they were told that the Parole Board does not give reasons for its decisions. The lack of transparency left profound concern as to the quality of the evaluation of Worboys as a risk to women. Carefully plotted rapes and assaults on such a scale with such a level of cunning and ability to deceive would seem to indicate a serious pathological disorder and deep misogyny. The presumption of a need to detain would be high. The puzzle is what persuaded the board to consider him suitable for release if not their own shared view that the offences were not so grievous and that he had miraculously mended his ways. A number of his victims secured the right to challenge his early release on the grounds that the assessment of risk by the Parole Board may have been flawed.

As a result of public pressure, some of the cases which were never pursued are being re-opened, and legal reform is going ahead, requiring reasons be given for Parole Board decisions. A good move. Women are entitled to know why the decision was made that Worboys posed no risk. However, we are not entitled to say he should never come out. The right to fundamental justice has to be there for men as well as women. Because women have been so badly failed by law does not mean we should lock men up on lower standards of proof or automatically assume the credibility of all women. Campaigning groups have a tendency to forget that we cannot be choosy about whose human rights matter. They should by definition be available to all, even those we suspect have committed egregious wrongs. A fair trial is the only way to deal with serious malfeasance.

Now, there is controversy once again about whether defendants in rape cases should be identified before they are convicted. Defendants were briefly granted anonymity by legislation which was introduced in the mid-seventies only to be repealed ten years later. The issue rocketed back onto the agenda in 2010, when the coalition government pledged to extend anonymity to men accused of rape. The pledge was subsequently dropped, but the debate rumbles on. One argument in favour of defendant anonymity is that the stigma associated with rape is such as to cause lasting damage to the accused's reputation, even where no formal charge or conviction results; this is the 'no smoke without fire' rationale. Another argument is that since rape complainants are allowed to remain anonymous, it is unfair to require defendants to be named.

I accept that there are some problems with negative publicity in rape cases, particularly where a person is investigated by police in respect of a rape claim but never charged. However, I cannot agree that defendants should be entitled to anonymity once they have been charged. The public naming of a person charged with serious sexual offences is crucial because it enables other victims, who may not originally have gone to the police, to come forward. We are seeing this almost every week in relation to some or other case of historical sex abuse. The argument for equality with rape victims is also misguided. The law allows complainants to remain anonymous because we know that rape remains an overwhelmingly under-reported crime with nowhere near as many convictions as rapes. Anonymity helps women to deal with the fear, shame or embarrassment which they may feel at coming forward. Indeed, granting anonymity to defendants in rape cases, but not in trials for theft, burglary or attempted murder, risks reinforcing the myth that women are more likely to lie about rape than about other crimes. This is another example where there is a false equivalence between men and women in the name of equality.

In the rape debate it is very easy for the arguments to become so polarised that eyes are closed to the problems on both sides. In the early days of campaigning for fairer procedures I offered myself as a volunteer adviser to a group involved with the issue. My services were turned down because it was known that I defended men on rape charges and would not accept a rule against defending in such cases. As a lawyer concerned with civil liberties, you have only to be familiar with the travesties which took place in the American South, with the regular framing of black men for the rape of white women, to appreciate the problems in a society filled with competing prejudices. Class also plays its role in rape; a middle-class woman making an allegation against a working-class man is more likely to be believed, and the tables are turned for a middle-class male accused if the woman is less socially acceptable.

Once, after I spoke at a conference, a senior police officer sympathetically pointed out that there was anxiety about publishing a racial breakdown of conviction statistics in rape cases, because so many offenders were black. Such figures, however, reflect more upon the

145

underlying attitudes which prevail in police stations and courtrooms than upon any particular tendency of black males to rape. On racial grounds, black men probably lose much of the male solidarity which surrounds rape, especially if the complainant is white. Black men too have to deal with the weight of mythology about their sexual appetite, their lack of control, the size of their equipment and their desire to punish white men by taking their women, all of which tells against them in the courtroom. In the morass of prejudice, black women have the hardest time being heard and securing the protection of the courts. Black victims face both the rape myths that confront all women, and stereotypes of black women as more likely to consent to sex, more sexually experienced and less likely to be psychologically damaged.

When I ask women magistrates and lawyers who know the system what they would do if they were raped by an acquaintance, many say that they would think twice before exposing themselves to the legal process. Men in the law express the same reservations for their wives and daughters.

Yet progress is being made. All police forces now have officers specially trained to deal with rape, and most have specialist sexual offences units. Many forces now have sexual assault referral centres, which give victims access to women doctors, counsellors and specialist non-uniformed officers. There is no compulsion to prosecute but attending the centre enables the securing of forensic examination for any future trial should the complainant decide to proceed. These centres should exist in every city and one per police force is not enough. The Crown Prosecution Service has established a network of specialist prosecutors who are trained to prosecute rape cases and who share knowledge and experience among themselves. Independent Sexual Violence Advisors provide long-term emotional and practical support for rape complainants throughout the investigative and court process.

The Stern Review found that ISVAs do sterling work in helping complainants to cope with the trauma of making a rape allegation. However, as with so many other public services, the ISVA network is vulnerable to uncertain funding and budget cuts.

Discussions about rape unearth profound feelings once you move beyond the trite condemnations. This chapter has focused on those rapes which are perpetrated on women by men. But it is important to recognise that rape can take many other forms. Men also suffer rape at the hands of other men, and contrary to popular myth, this is true whether they are gay or straight. While the legal definition of rape requires penetration with a penis, there are rare instances of women sexually assaulting men with dildos or other foreign objects. Men who are abused in these ways have to deal with the enormous societal prejudice that their victimhood somehow makes them weak or emasculated, or springs from their effeminacy. There is growing awareness that sexual abuse can happen within lesbian relationships, and one day the law may sufficiently evolve so as to categorise such abuse as rape rather than mere sexual assault.

All of these offences can be devastating for their victims, and any modern discussion about rape must acknowledge that it is a more complex and multifaceted crime than has ever been appreciated. At the same time, it remains true that the vast majority of rapes are an exercise in male power over women. The subject is complicated because of the confusion with genuine intimacy which invades the emotions of everyone in the courtroom. It is never going to be simple, and women are often just as confused as men are. The singularity of the law of rape stems mainly from a deep distrust of the female accuser and from the fact that sexual relations are seen from a male perspective. Male lawyers and judges to this day say that rape is an easy allegation to make and a difficult one to defend. In my experience the reverse is true; the charge is hard to bring, but it is still too easy for a guilty defendant to avoid justice.

It is important to acknowledge that 'asking for it' responses do not just arise in relation to rape. Half of all female murder victims are killed by a current or former husband or lover. Under the old common-law rules, the male defendants in these cases were permitted to mount a defence of provocation, claiming that it was the conduct of their wives or partners that drove them to kill.

Within the male stronghold of the court it was all too easy to create the feeling that a woman had it coming to her. Pictures of nagging, reproachful, bitter termagants who turn domestic life into hell on earth were painted before the jury. Man-haters skilled in the art of cruelty were summoned up to haunt the trials of men pushed to their limits. In one case, a man was freed by the court after killing his wife because her snoring had driven him over the edge. One dead wife who became known as the Lady in the Lake was described by defence counsel as 'an aberrant piece of humanity'. He meant that she had committed adultery and did not make the beds.

Other defendants also secured lesser sentences by invoking their wives' infidelity. Described in the old cases as the highest possible invasion of a man's property, adultery came to be seen as severe provocation which justified the cuckold in killing his wife, and often her lover as well. Rather than questioning the deeply gendered and possessive attitudes which drove husbands to commit so-called 'crimes of passion', the courts often simply accepted that the red mist of marital betrayal rendered men less responsible for their actions.

These attitudes were the common currency of our criminal courts until disturbingly recently. On 3 December 2002 a number of cases were reconsidered by the Court of Appeal at the behest of the then Solicitor General, Harriet Harman, who argued that the sentences had been too low in the circumstances.

Mark Paul Wilkinson and his partner had been in a relationship for approximately eight years and had two children. According to the victim's family, Mark was suspicious and jealous throughout their time together and had been violent to her. They separated, and shortly afterwards Mark lured his former partner to his flat on the pretext that they would be meeting a counsellor. Within half an hour of arriving the victim had been suffocated. According to the accused she told him that she wanted to settle with a new boyfriend and would like him to adopt the children. Mark saw red and pressed the life out of her. He was sentenced to four years' imprisonment for manslaughter on the grounds of provocation. Darren Suratan was sentenced to three years and six months for killing his partner, who died of a subdural haemorrhage after being repeatedly punched about the head. His story was that she kept falling over because of her drinking. Leslie Humes, a solicitor, stabbed and killed his wife Madeleine during the course of an argument at their family home. She had just told him that she had feelings for another man, with whom she intended to have a sexual relationship. He was given seven years after his plea to manslaughter was accepted without any resort to a trial. None of the sentences were changed, and many of us criticised the Court of Appeal for failing to affirm the irrelevance of sexual jealousy to considerations of criminal culpability.

In 2009, the Coroners and Justice Act abolished the old common-law defence of provocation, and in its place introduced a new statutory defence of loss of self-control. Today, a defendant must show that a qualifying 'trigger' caused a loss of self-control which resulted in the killing, and that a person of the defendant's sex and age, with a normal degree of tolerance and self-restraint, would have reacted similarly in the circumstances. One of the key aims of this legislation was to get rid of the courts' leniency towards husbands in adultery cases. The 2009 Act therefore expressly provided that the defence could not be 'triggered' by the victim's sexual infidelity. The idea was that a murderous husband would no longer be able to point to his wife's adultery as evidence that she had 'brought it on herself'.

The Lord Chief Justice at the time, Lord Phillips, caused controversy when he publicly expressed misgivings about doing away with a sexual infidelity defence altogether. But His Lordship need not have worried. The legislation has since been interpreted in a way that allows evidence of the wife's adultery in by the back door. In 2010, Jon-Jacques Clinton noticed posts on his wife Dawn's Facebook page that made him suspicious that she was having an affair. When he confronted his wife about the suspected infidelity, she told him that she had had sex with five different men. She also went on to taunt him about not having the 'bollocks' to commit suicide, and said that she expected him to look after their children in future. Clinton then beat and strangled his wife to death. At trial, the judge held that the 2009 Act required the court to disregard Dawn Clinton's infidelity, and that her other jeers had been insufficient to trigger the defence of loss of self-control. The Court of Appeal disagreed. While sexual infidelity could not on its own suffice to trigger the defence, it still formed part of the relevant context which the court could consider in deciding whether the defence was established. Evaluating the impact of Dawn Clinton's verbal taunts in the context of her infidelity, the Court of Appeal concluded that her husband was entitled to plead loss of self-control. On the first day of his retrial, Clinton pleaded guilty to murdering his wife. He was later sentenced to life imprisonment.

The Clinton case shows that despite the good intentions of Parliament, the law continues to measure a man's criminal culpability by reference to the character or infidelity of the woman he kills. Wives and girlfriends are expected to be faithful, loyal and obedient, and women who transgress these standards are viewed as partially culpable in their own murder. Of course, it is almost inevitable in murder trials, regardless of sex, that the conduct of the deceased is called into question. But attacks upon the character of women victims often have a particular quality, and it is no longer acceptable to evaluate a woman's conduct, directly or indirectly, by reference to outdated standards of morality. Wifely obligations of fidelity were originally based on the need to secure the succession, and ensure that those carrying a family's name were entitled to do so. This was all before scientific advances meant that DNA could conclusively prove paternity. These are also less pressing concerns in a society which is more relaxed than ever before about casual relationships and unmarried partners.

The fact that a murdered woman can never present her own side of the story makes it particularly important to confront any bias in the way she is portrayed in court. I have known families and friends of the victim to listen in horror from the public galleries to descriptions of those they know and love that bear no relation to reality. A sexual liaison described by defending counsel as the height of betrayal might, viewed through an alternative lens, simply be a natural consequence of the breakdown in the relationship between the defendant and the victim. Media portrayals of murder cases can be equally problematic; a recent report by Femicide Census highlighted the sympathetic write-up which perpetrators often receive in the press. Twenty-six years on from the publication of the first edition of this book, it is depressing to have to type these paragraphs. But it remains apparently necessary to repeat that women who nag, cheat or lie, or those who drink, enjoy sex or dress as they choose, deserve the law's protection just as much as anyone else.

5

THE WHORE

The law has always had problems with sex. People bring so much baggage to the courtroom about how men and women should behave – and what happens in bed. With the sexual revolution in the sixties came the freedom of women to explore their own sexuality, and yet the double standard is still present in our courts. Promiscuous behaviour by heterosexual men brings down little condemnation. When it comes to homosexual men, however, promiscuous conduct is still frowned upon. We may have gay marriage but gay sex has to be rendered as wholesome as possible to gain acceptance, and the idea that women are autonomous sexual beings with sexual needs and desires is still too often a source of negative judgement. The double standard simmers beneath the surface in divorce, child custody and in every legal arena that women enter.

What has altered the terrain of the law dramatically is the Internet. Now there is rarely a case of any kind where email and text communications are not part of the evidence. The first thing the police look for is the mobile phone or the computer or tablet. In civil litigation and divorce, emails can be a litigant's downfall. People condemn themselves with their ill-considered outpourings, their tweets and their sexting and their porn collections and their saved YouTube favourites. Facebook photographs are there to expose women as the flaunting sex bait that defendants say they are. Throwaway comments and jokes take on very serious meaning in the cold light of the courtroom. Every online search you have ever made can be used to show you have enquired about sex aids or bought Viagra or looked up dating sites or shown an interest in material which will be relied upon to show your guilt or your complicity or that you are not a worthy victim or a credible witness.

With the growth of the Internet and social media, the nature of intimate relationships is transforming. Interacting socially online is second nature to most people and while online dating is incredibly popular, it can also pose significant danger. Today, not only can you communicate with strangers who live across the globe you can also connect with strangers in your neighbourhood for sex. Police are increasingly caught up in cases involving the hazards of online dating. With tag lines like 'Interested in sexual liberation at your fingertips? Well, of course there's an app for that', individuals are being pulled into a dangerous game of 'Guess Who?' As many of the sites are limited to a picture and a few lines of personal description, men and women are meeting complete strangers online and agreeing to meet up for a sexual relationship or just casual sex. While this is heralded as a sign of technology simply coming to terms with the sexual liberation of modern society, the use of such apps can lead to dangerous situations, including a wide variety of exploitation from child grooming to human trafficking and cases of rape. The conviction in June 2017 of Gayle Newland, who pretended to be a man and had sex using a prosthetic penis with a young woman while she was blindfolded, has been one of the most publicised accounts. The pair met via Tinder, with Gayle Newland using a male identity. The allegation was that having developed an intimate online friendship, she procured sex under false pretences because she persuaded her new friend to cover her eyes with a blindfold when they met as she was disfigured and did not want to be seen. This is just one of many cases where women have been lured into sexual situations where there have been unintended consequences, not least threats of blackmail.

The NSPCC has reported an increase in teenagers contacting the charity's helpline with bad experiences after downloading 'hook-up' apps such as Grindr and Blendr, both developed by the same company. The app designers say users need to confirm their age (usually that they are above 17). However, stories appear in the media like that of the 13-year-old boy who was groomed by a 24-year-old man after using the app to meet up.

Grooming is where someone builds an emotional connection with a young or vulnerable person in order to win their trust and then sexually abuse them. It can happen on social network sites, gaming sites or in chat rooms and can also lead to face-to-face meetings between an adult and a child.

The MP Diane Abbott has also shed light on a trend that has been spreading internationally over recent years, and that is the rise of cyber-bullying of a sexual nature throughout social media. She drew attention to her own experience of sexual and racist abuse by anonymous trolls and expressed the view that this comes from our 'Hypersexualised

British culture in which women are objectified, objectify one another, and are encouraged to objectify themselves'.

Children are introduced to ideas of being sexy from a very young age through clothing and even dance videos on television. Sexual imagery is all-present. Schoolboys watch porn films openly on their phones and share them with classmates. As a result, girls as young as 10 and 12 say that their first introduction to sex is through being shown online clips of sex acts and being asked to perform oral sex on boys. Fellatio is now commonplace among adolescents and the idea of sexual reciprocity is never considered. The pleasuring of the girls does not figure in these transactions. The recording of a sexual activity means that it lives on to haunt girls as they grow older; such recordings are often used in courts to undermine the credibility of girls and demean them in the eyes of a jury.

The trend of sending sexual pictures has got politicians into trouble but they are not the only ones. Kids at school are doing the same without considering the consequences when shots of intimate body parts are shown around the class or neighbourhood. As are people, usually boys and men, who circulate intimate photographs of their girlfriends or wives after the break-up of relationships. In Canada, a judge was forced to step down from her position when her husband shared embarrassing sexual pictures of her with other men online without her consent. She was undoubtedly angry and distressed but did not divorce or leave her husband. She is still suspended, unable to sit as a judge because the court authorities feel she has lost her judicial esteem and would be a source of public scorn.

There are now over 30,000 sites dedicated to such postings. Revenge porn has become a significant problem in a culture where 18% of students have reported sending nude pictures to others. The effect on women is humiliation, breakdown, ruined lives and in some cases suicide. A wide range of people have been on the receiving end – from the 'girl next door' to actors and actresses. It should be accepted that revenge porn is one more example of coercive control, producing significant psychological harm. The impact on victims can be as violent and shaming as stalking, domestic violence and other forms of abuse. It has at times led to blackmail, exploitation and coercion of the victim to keep the images out of the public domain. As a result, revenge porn is now an offence under section 127 of the Communications Act 2003. Any Internet providers, search engines or websites publishing revenge pornography could be party to an offence. The charging criteria are whether any prosecutions are in the public interest and whether there exists a strong likelihood of conviction. There have been no prosecutions of Internet providers.

Beyond the act of putting out images without consent is the deeper issue of how porn culture pressurises women and girls to conform to male expectations set by their exposure to porn. It brings an acceptance of degrading behaviour and of levels of violence that should not be taken for granted. We should be teaching boys to ask at every turn 'is this OK with you?' but you never hear that in porn films. And it is never part of the accounts you hear in court. Not only are girls feeling the pressure, but boys too are pressed to lose their virginity at earlier and earlier ages to prove their manhood. They are made to believe that this stuff is what women want. The deleterious impact of the casualisation of sex and rape works to the detriment of both men and women.

Freedom of speech and freedom to publish is very important in a democracy and I am concerned about the calls for the banning of pornography. As a lawyer I am all too aware how hard it is to draft legislation that does not exceed its purpose and for this reason I have never been keen on criminalising pornography other than that which is extreme. The debate still rages over whether porn makes men rape.

What I do know is that the repertoire in rape cases has now changed since I first started in practice. It is increasingly rare for women not to be penetrated anally as well as vaginally and orally in the rape cases that appear before the courts and that is undoubtedly from exposure to the prevalence of such acts in pornography. There is not much to see in missionary-position sex, which is why the whole panoply of filmed activity has to include rear penetration. While mainstream pop culture grows increasingly pornographic, the porn industry goes on to produce harder-core porn and explicit material which is more overtly cruel towards women and more widely accepted than ever. You only have to turn on the television or flick through a magazine or look at billboards to see that porn has become the blueprint for how the media represents women's bodies. To understand the impact of pornography you only have to look at the numbers. The sex industry is the largest and most profitable industry in the world – its revenues are higher than the top tech companies' put together. It includes street prostitution, brothels, massage parlours, strip clubs, human trafficking for sexual purposes, phone sex, child and adult pornography, mail-order brides and sex tourism – just to mention the most common examples. In this marketplace, women and children are commodities. It rarely comes before the courts. Extreme pornography, which means portrayals of sex that threaten a person's life or are likely to cause serious harm, has now been made an offence in England and Wales under section 63 of the Criminal Justice and Immigration Act 2008. However, catching the producers of pornography in the net of the law is almost impossible.

According to research organisation Our Culture is Porn Culture, in 2010 13% of global web searches were for sexual content. Pornhub, which is the YouTube for pornography, receives over 1.68 million hits per hour. Internet porn in the UK receives more traffic than social networks, and more than sites for shopping, news, email, finance, gaming or travel combined. Porn films make more money than Hollywood, which is not surprising since a new porn movie is made every 39 minutes. And the sad fact is that the fastest growing consumer group for Internet porn is boys between the ages of 12 and 17. By their own accounts, they start by using it to obtain information about real-life sex. Ten per cent of adult men now admit to having an addiction to pornography.

What this tells us is that boys need help in working out how to have mutually satisfying sexual relationships. Porn is not the way. It serves up dominance and submission. And unfortunately it can create an appetite for ever stronger material. Our current porn culture shapes ideas about sexuality, relationships, masculinity, femininity and intimacy, and it feeds into popular imagery and culture in a way that in turn produces misogyny. Real-life women are not going to be able to fulfil the demands and fantasies created by pornography and so men turn to prostitution to act out their desires. Their inner life still categorises women as madonnas or whores, separating women who do the dirty stuff from the ones who don't.

The explosion of porn and social media may be relatively new, but of course prostitution is anything but. In the past the declared aim of laws against prostitution was the 'preservation of public decency', curbing the nuisance of soliciting on the streets and protecting the prostitute herself from violence and exploitation. Contracting to provide sex for money is still not in itself unlawful. It's the market, for heaven's sake. This leaves women involved in prostitution in an ambiguous legal position. According to the famous Wolfenden Report in 1957: 'The simple fact is that prostitutes do parade themselves more habitually and openly than their prospective customers, and do by their continual presence affront the sense of decency of the ordinary citizen. In doing so they create a nuisance which in our view the law is entitled to recognise and deal with.'

This seemed to justify making life difficult for the women involved in the business but not for the men who bought their services. The Street Offences Act was therefore introduced in 1959 criminalising a woman's loitering or soliciting for the purposes of prostitution. Hence the law was invoked only to criminalise concomitant, 'nuisance' activity. This has helped sustain the fiction that the law is not concerned with morality. However, moral opprobrium is always present. Prostitution has been tolerated because of two sustaining concepts: the protection of the private sphere from the hand of the law and an acceptance of male promiscuity, which is not afforded women.

The double standard is all too evident. Eventually, legislation was introduced in 1985 and further refined in 2001 to make the male behaviour of kerb-crawling a crime, but only because 'respectable women' who were not prostitutes had to be protected from persistent propositioning by strange men. Very few are in fact prosecuted. It really has to be persistent before the police will act and now they often use an ASBO, or anti-social behaviour order, as a way of frightening the driver who can then be arrested for breach if found driving around in the area again.

The harm which society sought to regulate in the laws around prostitution all largely revolved around the nuisance effects on the public. However, as a result of women's campaigns in the last 20 years, there has been growing recognition of the harm to the women them-selves. Wolfenden asserted that 'the association between prostitutes and ponces is voluntary and operates to their mutual advantage'. He was wrong. Men often force women into prostitution using coercion and violence, and in the current acceleration of sex trafficking there is little voluntarism by the women. Women's groups have argued powerfully that prostitution is rarely a victimless crime but one which victimises women, children, families and communities. By 2003 the problem of prostitution had been reconstituted from one of private morality to one of victimisation. The activism of these groups had refocused the argument. As a result, the Sexual Offences Act of 2003 recognised that while some women choose prostitution wilfully, most are forced into it by necessity, manipulation or intimidation. Sections of the legislation deal with trafficking and child prostitution. But the main thrust of the Act was to establish ways of diverting prostitutes into the hands of social services and away from the criminal justice system. Its drafters recognised that certain vulnerable groups of girls and women are more likely to become involved in prostitution, particularly those who have suffered physical or sexual violence or neglect. They may be further marginalised by experiences that include running away from abusive situations, being taken into local authority care, being involved in crime and drug addiction and being excluded from education. Vulnerable and desperate, these girls and women are then 'facilitated' into prostitution as a result of grooming by pimps or other procurers who often start out treating them as girlfriends. Three-quarters of those involved in prostitution in Britain entered street prostitution before their 18th birthday. As the Court of Appeal noted in *Regina* v. *Massey* (2007), these 'are often vulnerable young women with disturbed backgrounds, who have never known a stable relationship or respect from others and are therefore prey to pimps. It is all too easy for such a person to fall under the influence of a dominant male, who exploits that vulnerability for financial gain.' The research of Dr Susan Edwards, an eminent feminist academic, has shown the alarming increase in the number of women forced into prostitution by hardship in Britain today. A significant proportion of these women are also feeding a drug habit.

Both national and international studies indicate that many women, men and children involved in prostitution experience physical, mental and sexual violence. Research carried out on the harm caused by prostitution to women involved in it found that 71% of those interviewed had experienced physical assault; 63% had been raped; 68% met the criteria for post-traumatic stress disorder. The danger prostitutes face is unimaginable. They are both wanted and reviled, so as well as being viciously attacked and raped by pimps they are frequently beaten by clients too but the women do not report the assaults to the police. Street workers often take their clients to isolated places where they are less likely to be interrupted but this also makes them more vulnerable. Off-street sex workers usually operate from massage parlours or saunas or in accommodation where there are other women, or a 'maid' who keeps an eye out for oddballs and acts as a doorkeeper. Many 'maids' are women who were themselves at one time 'toms', as the police call prostitutes. Off-street sex is much less risky but unfortunately the Sexual Offences Act of 2003 criminalised the role of maid, making life for sex workers far less safe; it is also increasingly the venue for paid sex because arrangements are made on the Internet.

Since *Eve Was Framed* the calls for the law to direct its attention to the men who use prostitutes rather than the women supplying the sex have grown louder. Many campaigners want the purchase of sex to be criminalised and this is the official policy of the Women's Equality Party. This has been done in Sweden and recently in Northern Ireland. The jury is still out on whether it works or whether it simply drives the sale of sex underground with consequent higher risks for the women. Until there is better evidence from the places where this change has operated for a number of years, I remain very sceptical about the criminalisation of the male purchasers. I foresee sex workers being coerced by the police to testify against clients and threatened with prosecution for drug offences or other crimes if they do not. I see payment being arranged in other forms, such as the supply of drugs or the gifting of items which can then be sold on. Women have always been engaged in transactional sex. It just hasn't always been called prostitution.

The legal treatment of prostitution reveals another prejudice – that of class. The British are famous for institutionalising social and moral hypocrisies. The well-bred unemployed are referred to as socialites; the poor on the dole are spongers. The upper-class divorcee is rarely included in the term single parent. The prostitute who can afford the title call girl and who has a flat in an expensive part of town does not face the indignities of the courts and runs few of the risks faced by her poorer sister, who works on the street. The laws against brothel-keeping still prevent two or three women sharing a flat for their work, which would reduce the risks of assault and provide companionship.

There was a great deal of media excitement in October 2003 when Margaret MacDonald, a British woman, was tried in France for running a high-class ring of more than 500 prostitutes and found guilty. She was sentenced to four years' imprisonment and given a substantial fine. What intrigued the public was that this was a highly educated, convent-schooled woman, who spoke French, Spanish, Italian, Arabic, Japanese and Greek, had worked for Médecins Sans Frontières in El Salvador and also for a refugee agency in Nicaragua and who had then entered the world of business and marketing. She put the experience to use by setting up an agency 'run by women, for women'. She had started working as an escort herself when she had run up some debts and then spotted a niche market. 'It is the same skill, whether you sell computers or something else' she told the judges. She charged up to

5,000 euros for an introduction and took 40% for herself, but explained that she produced the brochures and paid for upmarket advertising in journals and the *International Herald Tribune.*

There are women, operating on a less grand scale, who would vociferously endorse Margaret MacDonald's description of their activities as 'work' and they are quite indignant that all sex work is classed as exploitation. There are women who would rather be sex workers than cleaners or care workers, as they earn much more money doing it, and until women's work is better paid, they want to carry on without interference. They want middle-class feminists off their backs. When in high spirits, they also tell you they have been forced to have bad sex all their lives, so why not at least get paid; that sexual relations in the comfort of marital beds is often just as transactional, but that is not subject to state interference. They do not want to be drawn into the all-embracing straitjacket of women as victims. This is difficult territory, as legal scholars have pointed out. There is always a tendency to avoid defining exploitation because vast tracts of the labour market might be deemed inherently exploitative. There are also sex workers who have as their clients men with disabilities who have sexual desires but no opportunity to establish relationships with women. Or they have clients who have wives they love but who are seriously ill. The women are not judgemental about the needs of the men who pay for their services and they are often quite moving in describing their ability to provide friendship within purchased intimacy. These women feel they are doing something valuable for other human beings and are indignant about the revulsion they face and feel it is fed by a puritanical strand of feminism.

We should always be leery about a rush to legislation as the automatic cure for ills. Some working women claim that as soon as you make the purchase of sex illegal and criminalise the purchaser, women will be coerced by police to testify against the 'consumers'. They will be used as agents provocateur when the police want to go after certain men. Women will be accused of luring men into criminality because as sellers of sex they will not be at risk whereas the buyer is. The purchase of sex will be driven further underground, they say, and this will inevitably make life more risky for the women involved. Some see the business of prostitution being commercialised by bigger crime businesses with no money changing hands between woman and customer but a salary for working casino tables, providing massage in sports clubs, waiting tables in restaurants, with the understanding that sex is part of the service. The prevalence of casual sex makes it hard to unveil the transactional nature of the interactions. I have very conflicted views on the issues of criminalisation and think the moral arguments are complicated. I also think that there is real confusion for many young women about what liberation means. Hooking up just for sex with the varnish that the woman is as much in control is illusory. To me, it is also corrosive of real sexual empowerment. I come at it as a feminist lawyer and would want to see evidence from a reliable source about the Swedish experiment and those in other jurisdictions to see if criminalising the purchase of sex actually works.

We must always look carefully at how law can be misused. The government's antisocial behaviour orders are now being used to bar women from working certain streets or from associating with each other, although the original public rationale for the orders was about protecting the public from gangs of boys or bad neighbours creating a nuisance. Breach of an order can attract a maximum sentence of five years which means the reintroduction of imprisonment for prostitutes which had been removed in the Criminal Justice Act 1982. So while the rhetoric is all about helping women, England and Wales are fast becoming the most punitive countries in Europe for prostitutes.

Further legislation to address prostitution was introduced in the Policing and Crime Act 2009. This removed from the statute books the term 'common prostitute' which was offensive and unnecessary, but importantly it replaced the kerb-crawling offence with an offence of soliciting a person in a street or public place for the purpose of obtaining sexual services from them as a prostitute. It was addressed at the men who went out to buy sex in public. The previous legislation concerning kerb-crawling had required persistent behaviour which meant the police had to see more than one attempt to procure a woman, but this new law made that persistence unnecessary.

Who are these men who pay for sex? At the higher end of the scale are businessmen, playing away. But according to police, the ordinary trade is maintained by the fellow next door. There is no shortage of custom, and in our entrepreneurial times many women are taking to the streets, selling the one commodity they have which they know is in demand. Even more women are now advertising themselves online. If a man's work is sorting out computer systems for organisations and it takes him to Land's End or John O'Groats, he only has to go online and find out if there is a sex worker in the vicinity and book an appointment, along with selecting his preferred sexual practice. The women even have reviews by previous customers. Men who use prostitutes may raise sniggers in court, but that's about all. When the Duke of Devonshire appeared at the Old Bailey in the early nineties to give evidence in a cheque-fraud case it came to light that he had been using the services of a call girl and paying with cheques. Everyone smiled benignly and just thought how daft he was. There was no question of his not being able to show his face in the club. Likewise when Allan Green, the Director of Public Prosecutions, resigned in 1991 having been seen round the back of King's Cross, allegedly looking for a prostitute, the sympathy for him was shared by most of us in the profession. He had been the fairest of prosecutors in his days at the Bar and was an exceptional director, of unquestioned integrity and courage, who had the unenviable task of dealing with the Irish miscarriages of justice. Using prostitutes was not seen as a bar to lawyering.

I'm not sure that, as a woman, being a prostitute in my spare time would have gone down so well in the profession, though. Attitudes were very different indeed to prostitutes themselves. In her 1989 book *Misogynies*, Joan Smith highlighted the prejudice against prostitutes in the investigation of the Yorkshire Ripper killings. She recalls the words of a senior police officer at a press conference before Peter Sutcliffe was caught:

> He has made it clear that he hates prostitutes. Many people do. We, as a police force, will continue to arrest prostitutes. But the Ripper is now killing innocent girls. That indicates your mental state and that you are in urgent need of medical attention. Give yourself up before another innocent woman dies.

This distinction, between respectable women and the others, whose lives seem to have a different value, was made repeatedly in the press, by the police and in court. One of the most prevalent kinds of serial murder is indeed that of the prostitute; she especially represents the myth of Eve, of woman as responsible for male concupiscence and carnality. So entrenched is the idea that prostitutes have it coming to them that, in order to allay speculations and emphasise the seriousness of the risk to real women, the police often feel obliged to stipulate that female victims are not prostitutes. Since the Yorkshire Ripper, we have had several other horror stories involving the serial killing of sex workers. There was the Ipswich murders of five prostitutes by Steve Wright in 2006, and, in 2009, the gruesome case of the Crossbow

Cannibal, Stephen Griffiths, who picked up a crossbow and turned it on his neighbourhood's prostitutes. He killed three women and dismembered their bodies with power tools and a samurai sword in a bathtub, dumping their chopped-up bodies afterwards in the River Aire – except for the bits he ate, mostly cooked but some raw.

In June 1990, a notorious pimp called Colin Gayle stood trial at the Old Bailey on 18 counts of rape, threats to kill, actual bodily harm and living off immoral earnings. The victims of his appalling assaults were the young prostitutes who became involved with him and who supplied him with money to pay for his cocaine habit. The evidence of brutal beatings with a metal rod and hammer sat uncomfortably with the love letters the women had written to him. Why would women beaten, bruised and disfigured return to their tormentor? Love poems were written to Gayle by one young woman who had received terrible injuries at his hands, resulting in damage to her kidneys as well as extensive cuts and bruising, because he did not think she showed enough respect. Some women have suffered so much in their lives, and their self-image and self-respect is so low, that they are grateful for any expressions of interest.

Among the prosecution evidence were letters written by Gayle promising that he would stop the relentless beatings; it was probably those careless pieces of self-incrimination which secured his conviction. Even so, he was acquitted of the charges in relation to one of the prostitutes because her evidence was so confused and, in the view of police, unsympathetic to the jury because of her swearing and filthy mouth.

The prosecution has a problem in cases where prostitutes are witnesses because the women are terrified of the consequences of giving evidence against their controller. The fear of reprisals from the accused or his friends is enormous and the women also know that they will be cross-examined in detail about their lifestyles in a way that will reinforce hostile views towards them. These women are often angry at the comparatively short sentences which are passed because the pimps are so soon back on the streets seeking revenge.

Prostitutes have come to expect poor treatment in the criminal courts, but they have problems in the civil courts too, particularly concerning the welfare of their children. Many prostitutes who appear before the courts say they do this work because it fits in well with their childcare arrangements; they can work during school hours or in the evenings, when they have a babysitter. Many are women living alone with children, with little prospect of any other kind of employment.

Charges of living off immoral earnings were introduced to reach the pimps who exploited women and forced them into sexual misery. However, many women complain that in fact they make their own choices about how they earn a living, and the law is frequently used against boyfriends and husbands or family members who exercise no control over them at all. The effect is to prevent these women having any semblance of a home life. Taxi drivers, particularly minicab drivers, are sometimes charged with living off immoral earnings if they provide a regular service for prostitutes and facilitate their work. The same is true for landlords and massage-parlour and sauna owners if the police take against them.

There is no specific offence for placing advertisements promoting prostitution in newspapers. However, the Newspaper Society has always advised publishers not to place advertisements for brothels and other illegal establishments, and there is now a law prohibiting the placing of adverts in telephone booths (which are almost redundant in any case). So far Internet websites and platforms seem to be immune. Google has a website called Backpage where prostitutes advertise and where victims of human trafficking are sold for sex. Backpage is

169

involved in 73% of cases of suspected child sex trafficking in the USA. Efforts in the US to introduce cross-party legislation to target human trafficking with a Stop Enabling Traffickers Act is being scuppered by lobbyists working for the Internet behemoth, which takes the position that there should be no assault on freedom of the Internet.

In 2011 I chaired an Inquiry for the Equality and Human Rights Commission into Trafficking in Scotland. At that point there had been no prosecutions of traffickers in Scotland, but there was growing evidence of the problem there. Often police were raiding premises using drugs or arms warrants for men suspected of organised crime, and coming across women from abroad who did not have their own passports. While they recognised there was prostitution, the common practice was to hand the women over to the immigration authorities for assessment and deportation, making it an issue of immigration rather than crime.

Being the head of that inquiry gave me a very close view of the horror of the trafficking we know less about – the trafficking for cheap labour or domestic servitude. The gangmasters who bring over migrant labour claim the workers are self-employed when in fact many are like indentured labourers – doing back-breaking agricultural jobs or cockle picking or poultry cleaning and packing, living in inhumane conditions and being paid well below the minimum wage. Domestic servitude is even more shocking. The first cases which came to light in the UK involved diplomats bringing servants here, and ill-treating them but making it impossible for them to leave or complain because they had removed their passports. It came as a surprise to find that in some parts of the UK settled immigrant families often brought people from their home countries, then treated them like slaves, paying tiny wages to their relatives in villages back home. Many slept on mats in kitchens and worked all hours without any money to spend here.

But worst of all was the evidence of women and children who had been trafficked for sexual purposes. Sometimes it started as domestic slavery but became predatory and sexual with time. I thought I had heard about most inhumanity through my years of practice both nationally and internationally, but the stories of these trafficked victims were heart-wrenching. One of the things we have learned about our world is that cataclysmic events like wars and social unrest create terrifying risks for women and children. The end of the Cold War and the collapse of the Soviet Union, the disturbances in the Balkans, the unrest in the Middle East as well as upheavals across whole tracts of Africa have all created vacuums in which organised crime has flourished. The under-belly of globalisation and free markets in legitimate commodities is that the same developments which allow lawful trade to flourish also facilitate the trade in drugs, arms and human beings. Prostitution and people trafficking is now considered the world's third most lucrative black-market activity, just behind arms and drugs. Global estimates by Interpol and UNICEF range from $19 to $32 billion in yearly profits. Thousands of women and children are spirited into Britain every year to work against their will as prostitutes, domestic slaves or exploited agricultural labour.

Sex trafficking preys on the most vulnerable and is a heinous sustained violation of human rights. There are many hundreds of flats, massage parlours and saunas selling sex in London alone, with 81% of the women in them from overseas. Research has concluded that a growing proportion of women 'on the game' were being coerced into prostitution through violence, repetitive rape and entrapment, and those conducting the research found evidence of trafficking rings operating in all parts of Britain, from Cornwall to Glasgow. The most common sources of women are Eastern Europe, South-East Asia, West Africa and China. The collaborative work made possible by the existence of

Eurojust (the European Justice System agency) and the European Arrest Warrant for arresting traffickers in other parts of Europe and bringing them speedily to courts here or there is invaluable for the police. The Sex Offences Act 2003 introduced wide-ranging laws to tackle trafficking for sexual exploitation, but as the full extent of the problem became exposed, the government took further steps. In 2009 the National Referral Mechanism was set up as a process for identifying and supporting victims of trafficking. It is also the process for capturing data on potential human trafficking victims in the UK. But research by the UK Human Trafficking Centre in 2012 suggested 54% of victims were not recorded on the NRM in 2011. While greater numbers are coming to light it is believed that we still only have part of the picture. Of those referred, a third were children and most of them girls.

The government introduced the Modern Slavery Act in 2015 to give further powers to police and other authorities to confront the issue. In 2003 it had been made unlawful to traffic people, but the Modern Slavery Act increased the sentences, established a legal duty to report potential victims of trafficking to the National Crime Agency to build a clearer picture of this hidden crime, and created a new Anti-Slavery Commissioner role to galvanise law enforcement's efforts to tackle modern slavery. In 2009 the Police and Crime Act made it an offence for someone to pay for sexual services from a prostitute who has been subjected to force, threats or any other form of coercion or deception to induce them into prostitution. This means it is a crime to have sex with a trafficked woman or girl. There is a similar law in Scotland where the legal system is different. It is not a defence for an accused to say that he did not know that the prostitute had been subjected to force or coercion. It is that rare thing, a strict liability crime. It is also a specific crime to pay for sexual services from a child, which means any young person under 18, and there are extremely heavy penalties.

It is clear that the law has to be accompanied by better measures to protect and support trafficked people. They need to be recognised as victims and not the perpetrators of crime. Some are anxious to return to their families, but others could be in danger in their home countries, particularly if they inform on organised criminals. The stories are heartbreaking and invariably describe being lured to Britain with the promise of legitimate work as a route out of poverty. Women find themselves trapped in a cycle of vice, imprisonment, abuse and the threat of violence to their families back home if they try to break free. The real way to stop trafficking is to address the problems women face in their home countries, where deprivation is usually rife and political systems are corrupt. Overseas aid plays a crucial role. But we also have to deal with this crime by cross-border collaboration, working with organisations like Eurojust and Europol (the European Police Agency) and using tools like the European Arrest Warrant to extradite gangmasters and the heads of crime syndicates to bring them to justice. It can never be solved by one country acting alone. The plan to leave the European Union never bore any of these vital considerations in mind.

In recent years I have represented several trafficked sex workers. Incapable of stepping out of the shadows, they are utterly controlled by their pimps. Ill health and fear of pregnancy stalk them and they are forced to have illegal abortions because they are too frightened to go near doctors. This is the sort of inhumanity we collude in when we take away legitimate routes out and systems of support.

In one case I defended a young Croatian woman who became a pawn in a turf war between pimps, arguing over ownership of different women. She was present when a pimp was murdered, her fingerprints found in the seedy hotel room that was the scene of his violent death. A terrible story of sexual grooming from the age of 14 came to light and a background of such horrifying cruelty that the court was stupefied. Even after she was given her freedom and the murderer was imprisoned, she was frightened out of her wits that he would have her killed.

At last some of the traffickers are coming before the courts. In 2013, seven members of a sex-grooming ring in Oxford were convicted of crimes including rape, arranging child prostitution and trafficking between 2004 and 2012. The six girls who were brave enough to testify suffered the abuse between the ages of 11 and 15. Twenty-five criminals were convicted and jailed in August of 2014, all of whom had been involved in Eastern European trafficking gangs. A Hungarian gang led by a man called Vishal Chaudhary trafficked at least 120 women into London where they were raped, beaten and forced to work in brothels across the capital. These gangs include women who provide a legiti-mate-looking front in persuading girls to come for straight employ-ment. Tatiana Shmyrova, a Russian madam who ran a high-class escort agency in London, was convicted in May 2014 of luring a young woman who had been a successful athlete with the prospect of a job as a tour guide, only to find herself in the hands of a violent trafficking gang.

Child trafficking is a singular horror story.

Poverty and war and lack of opportunities present the perfect oppor-tunity for traffickers to promise parents in poor countries a better life for their child in stable Western countries. Equally, a failure to uphold children's rights, a lack of robust child protection services and living in abusive or neglectful circumstances make it all too easy for traffickers to target children for grooming. As we have seen in the refugee camps, as well as the temporary camps like Calais, refugee children can be particularly vulnerable to being trafficked because they are easily manipulated and physically controlled.

A better understanding of child abuse has led to intensive govern-ment action on child prostitution. It should be emphasised again that a person is a child under our law until they are 18. The children's charity Barnardo's led the front when it came to redefining child prostitution as sexual abuse: 'There can be no such thing as a punter, or a customer or a kerb-crawler when discussing children ... a man who winds down his window and asks for sexual services from a child or girl who is underage is a child sexual abuser.' The way in which child abuse can lead to adult prostitution has also entered the official bloodstream:

> The prostitute is a commonly vilified figure. This is often based on a general assumption that those involved are in control of their situation. However, the evidence is clear that this can be far from true. High levels of childhood abuse, homelessness, problematic drug use and poverty experienced by those involved strongly suggest survival to be the overriding motivation. (Home Office, 2004.)

In recognition of the high levels of coercion involved in prostitution, the government has adopted a two-pronged approach by using charities and other welfare-based organisations to deliver 'soft law' or social policy responses to divert women and children from prostitution, while reserving the full power of the criminal law for two categories of people: those who persistently return to prostitution and those who exploit individuals in prostitution.

The approach is at first glance a huge leap in the right direction. However, a very persuasive book by Joanna Phoenix and Sarah Oerton called *Illegal and Illicit: Sex Regulation and Social Control* analyses the hidden currents operating beneath the surface to the detriment of some women and girls. They point out that those who face the full rigour of the new law are women who choose prostitution voluntarily or for economic reasons, women who are poor and who have few options, or women who are forced into the netherworld of sex work and find it very hard to abandon it when a new demand for rent or electricity payment arrives. The Home Office consultation paper *Paying the Price* neatly demarcates the problem of prostitution into two categories: the problem of 'victims' and the problem of 'offenders'. Victim status is only conferred under specific conditions – there has to be a third-party coercer and the 'victim' must never return to prostitution after being offered help. Women who stay on the game after social work interventions therefore move beyond the pale. They must cooperate with the NGOs and the authorities and behave like good women or they are sacrificed to the criminal justice system.

On an initial reading of *Paying the Price*, the striking argument is the overwhelming level of victimisation experienced by women and children in prostitution and their need for support in their struggle with drug addiction and debt. It seems we are now living in a society where the prevailing thinking is that poverty is largely the fault of the impoverished. If they do not pull themselves up by their bootstraps, and the help of 'back to work' initiatives, they are making a lifestyle choice. Talk of poverty as a driver of human behaviours is out of favour. Victimisation is recognised as a valid excuse for prostitution but poverty is not. Poverty is seen as a lifestyle choice.

Even when women have been groomed into prostitution through abusive relationships, they have been forced to reveal past convictions for soliciting or loitering under the Street Offences Act when applying for jobs and visas or even for volunteering at their children's schools under DBS (Disclosure and Barring Service) checks. It did not matter that they had been forced into sex work as teenagers. It meant that abused women could never move on from their pasts. A great victory was won in March 2018 in the High Court by a brave woman called Fiona Proudfoot and two other determined women who chose to remain anonymous. They fought a case against this stigmatisation and won a ruling that forcing women to reveal past convictions for prostitution was unlawful. They described to the court the cost to them not just in employment opportunities but in humiliation and mental anguish.

There are compelling arguments for and against the decriminalisation of street offences and the legalisation of brothels. Although some of the arguments are articulated on the grounds of keeping neighbourhoods decent and avoiding insult to citizens, the core argument is about the symbolic importance of punishing deviant sexuality. It would be quite possible to divert the police vice squads on to more pressing crime problems by abolishing the soliciting laws and using in their place, where it is occasionally necessary, offensive behaviour legislation. Where any passer-by is seriously affronted, public order charges of insulting words and behaviour can still be laid. At the same time, provisions protecting children from sexual exploitation and adults from coercion and fraud could be strengthened. It is interesting to look closely at the reforms in the Australian state of Victoria and in Holland. The creation of legalised brothels in both places has not removed all street soliciting but has greatly reduced the numbers. Brothels are not run by the state but have to maintain health standards for permits to be obtained, and their location is controlled by town-planning laws. Local residents can make objections at planning hearings if nuisance is a serious problem – all of which shifts some of the problems associated with prostitution away from the criminal courts. Failure to have a permit or planning permission means premises are closed down. Inevitably, advertising has to be permitted for a legalised brothel system to work, and strict codes are established regulating where such information can appear.

Police claim that 'respectable clients' who use street prostitutes would never risk entering a brothel for fear of being seen, and that likewise some women with children who work on a casual basis would not want to chance being discovered. However, risk is half the excitement for many of the men, and since danger of criminal prosecution has not dampened enthusiasm it is unlikely that entering a brothel would. The majority of women on the street would welcome decriminalisation and might feel differently if they realised a brothel scheme would not be run by the government.

There might even be tax benefits for the Treasury if the law was reformed. Lindy St Clair, a prostitute who lost her High Court challenge to the Inland Revenue's taxation of her earnings from prostitution, wittily accused the government of living off immoral earnings. The outlawing of prostitution and then the application of fiscal regulations as if it were any old job is an indication of the double-think involved in the whole issue. The income from prostitution would probably write off the national debt if properly audited, but, as it stands, only women on the low end of the scale are 'taxed', in the form of regular fining. Women appearing in the central London courts describe the fine as their licence fee and get straight back on the job to pay it.

Saving women from prostitution must also mean removing sexual and economic inequalities, providing job opportunities, training and equal pay – in other words, by recognising the economic realities which drive most women to the streets. Unfortunately, economic realities do escape some members of the bench and the chasm of class misunderstanding still exists.

The power inequality of sex, and its transactional nature, plays out in other working environments too. Sex is a potent force in many workplaces. Hardly a woman exists who has not had to deal with unwelcome sexual attention, requests for sexual favours. Yet the subject is met with collective denial by many men, who think sexual harassment is about po-faced women having no fun. It was just a bit of playfulness, they say. It's women who are the problem.

Of course, sexual attraction is a component in a lot of the relationships which compose our daily round. The gentle flirtation of our social commerce is a harmless and pleasant aspect of life, irrespective of gender. The positive exchange of sexual energy can be as creative at work as elsewhere, but sexual harassment is of a different order and both men and women know the difference. One involves a mutuality and the other is unwelcome. It is not the product of the fevered feminist imagination. Most women can give plentiful accounts of dealing with groping and risqué remarks, and some women with a quick wit can handle anything. However, the majority feel humiliated and demeaned by the experience. There is a sense in which women who complain are considered to be whingers who have let it happen – what has been described as an extension of the 'good girls do not get raped' theory. Men groan that things have got so politically correct that they are not able to enter the office and say, 'That's a nice dress, Doris,' without letting loose the furies. It is disingenuous nonsense but is designed to marginalise women's complaints.

The combination of sex and power is a particularly destructive one. All things are not equal when someone in a superior position within an organisation presses attentions or constantly comments in a very suggestive way about the appearance or clothing of a more junior member of staff, or insists on talking about sex, or engineers intimate interludes.

Sexual harassment is defined as unwanted behaviour of a sexual nature which violates your dignity; makes you feel intimidated, degraded or humiliated; or creates a hostile or offensive environment. The conduct can include sexual comments or jokes; physical behaviour, including unwelcome sexual advances; touching; and sending texts or emails with a sexual content. In the workplace it can involve displaying sexual imagery such as Page 3 calendars or leaving porn around. It is a form of unlawful discrimination under the Equality Act 2010 and a victim could sue the perpetrator or bring a case before an employment tribunal. The problem is that legal aid is not available and court costs make it a prohibitive exercise for most women, though these are now being reviewed for that reason. Most large workplaces have established routes for complaint about colleagues who make a person's life a misery, such as going to the human resources team or a manager or a trade union. However, most women take no action. Two out of five female barristers in a 2016 survey by the Bar Standards Board reported suffering sexual harassment.

It is hard to find a woman who does not have war stories to tell of dealing with gropers, touchers, strokers, squeezers, pressers, voyeurs and dirty talkers. It has been our lives since girlhood. It is miserable and depressing but women do not take action because they learn early on that there will be an even greater price to pay for speaking out. Why would a woman take a case to court to sue for assault or discriminatory conduct when she knows that she will be roundly attacked as Kate Maltby was when she described the conduct of the deputy prime minister, Damien Green? She faced a two-page spread of vitriol in the *Daily Mail*. Women know the consequences of speaking out. We have been warned.

Harvey Weinstein was one of the dominant figures in the film industry. By all accounts he was a horrible bully to men and women both, but in his relations with women he was a serial and serious predator. However, men just like him have got away with it forever because people would be too fearful to take them on. Think back to what happened to the lawyer Anita Hill in the United States. When Clarence Thomas, the right-wing black jurist, was proposed for the Supreme Court, she stepped forward to say that he was not an appropriate person to fill such a position of authority as he had systematically sexually harassed and abused her when she was his junior. She testified before a congressional committee, was accused of malicious falsehood and was taken apart by misogynistic male politicians who could not stomach a woman undermining their candidate. Why would a young black woman lawyer make such a claim against another African American and be able to describe in such detail the indignities to which he subjected her? She has since pointed out that she had no clout, and that it was over 20 years ago when women were less confident and powerful. I suspect that this is wishful thinking when it comes to the majority of women in ordinary workplaces. In the case of Donald Trump many women came forward during his campaign for the presidency to describe his assaults and harassment but were traduced in the media and beyond. What changed the narrative in Weinstein's case is that a new generation of women are saying 'enough already' and our current celebrity culture has elevated some female film stars to new heights of fame and financial success, which has empowered them to challenge his abusive conduct without being attacked for daring to do so. As one woman said, it was just a pity that Donald Trump did not grope Angelina Jolie. If he had, he might not have become the president of the United States.

But even in Weinstein's case, before the complaints turned into an avalanche, some women were saying 'Why would you go to a man's hotel room? What did they expect?' Predatory sexual behaviour had become so normal that blaming the victim was the default position. The young actresses were invited to the hotel room of one of the most powerful figures in film-making ostensibly for business conversations about potential movie parts, often initially accompanied by women who worked for Weinstein, thus providing cover, but who subsequently made themselves scarce. Then the actresses would be subjected to violation, often starting with requests for massages or conversation as he lay in the bath and thereafter they would be jumped on for sex. The accounts revolted the world because they were so vivid, so corroborative of each other and because they were being related by beautiful film stars. That is what changed the weather. Even so, those actresses who said that out of fear they allowed him to abuse them were 'slut-shamed' by many as having put their ambition at the service of a man of influence.

What followed the scandal though was the brilliant use of the Internet with the #MeToo campaign encouraging women around the globe to give their own accounts of abuse, mainly in their working lives.

Predatory sexual behaviour has enjoyed 'social proof' for a long time. Social proof is conduct which becomes mimicked by people in a social group until it gains acceptance and finally becomes behaviourally normal. It has been shockingly 'normal' for certain men in certain situations to predate on women, but now it is suddenly sounding as though it may become un-normal.

Some of the behaviour complained about is of a really serious criminal nature while other accounts are of miserable overstepping of the mark. But if you want to change a culture, you have to deal with less significant transgressions too. Making complaints about the gropings, invasive behaviour and sex-talk does not minimise or take away from the urgency of dealing with allegations of rape. Calling an assistant 'sugar tits', asking an employee to purchase on your behalf sex toys, asking young women about their sex lives, taking a young woman's hand and placing it on your flies, offering avuncular career advice and then being sexually suggestive; none of it is OK. A hand on the knee is made to sound utterly trivial. It is claimed it might just be a comforting pat in a friendly manner. Sure. But men and women know the difference between that and the creepy under-the-table stroking. The fleeting communication that means 'I want more'. Its secret and slight nature is part of the turn-on for many men, especially if others in the vicinity – even their own wife – are oblivious. It is a covert signal. Another is stroking a woman's palm when shaking hands.

Of course, the world over, women have learned pest-avoidance techniques. As we get older we become more adept at the off-the-cuff put-down and body swerve. However, it is tough when you are young. Young women are filled with self-doubt and wondering why this aged Lothario thought it was OK to come on to them. What have they done to deserve it? It is the classic self-blaming that women have been socialised to do and they are not helped when other women are dismissive or find fault with them for failing to handle it with a slap or cutting remark. We are all different and how we are able to handle these situations depends on so many factors about our own history and make-up. Women always have to make a calculation about what effect making a fuss might have. To be saddled with the reputation of being 'that girl who got old Charlie the sack' or simply as a trouble-maker or complainer can narrow a woman's career options.

It is particularly disturbing when someone seems to be offering to mentor you and you find it is actually transactional and that person who is the same age as your father wants something in return. It feels grossly invasive and sickening but also undermining. It is important for men to know how it feels to young women. I mentor many young women in the law and I still hear stories close to my own experience when I was a pupil, when I had to escape the clutches of a senior member of the Bar. I once referred to this when asked about sexual harassment in a media interview and it drew down the rage of a senior prosecutor in the Old Bailey Bar Mess who asked who would want to harass me, an abusive insult that received much braying laughter among his cronies. I felt humiliated even though I was a confident, successful woman in my mid-thirties. This is still the kind of male riposte you often get for daring to mention sexual harassment.

There are few walks of life where this conduct does not take place. Having male approval is an important part of getting on. That is why women who succeed are often totally averse to any kind of boat-rocking. The law is a highly competitive world and those entering it are vulnerable because there are many people who might seek their favours in return for opportunities and advancement. At the Bar, women face this conduct from solicitors dangling tantalising briefs in important cases. It is incumbent on us to root it out of key institutions like the law and Parliament, otherwise what hope is there for women on the shop floors of factories or stores or offices around our country? The request to come to the basement to stock-take, where you are expected to perform fellatio on the boss if you want overtime or a raise or time off for a sick child, is all part of the same continuum.

If a woman is raped or physically assaulted at work, or in a work-related situation, a crime has taken place and she can go to the police. But for all the reasons already rehearsed many women have profound reservations about this course. If the conduct falls short of rape, attempted rape or assault, and would amount to sexual harassment a woman's remedy is through her trade union or her employer's HR department and warnings can be given. But in many smaller workplaces these support structures do not exist. If complaining does not get results she can take her employer to an industrial tribunal but legal aid is not available and free legal advice and advocacy hard to come by, unless the woman is in a union but fewer are now because of the assault by government over decades on trade unionism.

In 2013 the government introduced tribunal fees of £1,200, causing the number of discrimination cases to drop by 71%. It was forced to reverse the move after the Supreme Court ruled it was inconsistent with access to justice. The government also scrapped the legal requirement for employers to protect workers from abuse from third parties such as clients or customers, and removed the equality questionnaire which allowed claimants who said they had been sexually harassed to enquire whether other complaints of a similar nature had ever been made. As a result few women bring cases. The Deregulation Act 2015 removed the power of tribunals to make recommendations for the benefit of the wider workforce. None of this points towards a growing desire by the powers that be to see equality law enforced.

A woman may not have an employer as such. She may be part of the gig economy where she is deemed self-employed, getting a pittance on zero-hour contracts. What is her remedy then? The whole legal framework fails these women. In the United States the film stars who allege they were sexually abused by Weinstein are suing him but a woman seeking to do that here would need serious financial resource as there is no legal aid for civil litigation. The American stars are creating a fund through donations to help ordinary women there bring cases against their abusers.

When women are brave enough to complain and threaten to sue their employer for sexual harassment they are frequently paid off in an out-of-court settlement, but subject to a confidentiality clause so that no one gets to hear about the misconduct and abuse. Breach of a non-disclosure agreement will carry serious financial penalties. Gag orders and confidentiality clauses are the 'get out of jail card' for rich men. It is yet another way in which women are silenced. Harvey

Weinstein used such clauses repeatedly. Young women are frequently paid off, encouraged by their lawyers to take the money and run rather than expose themselves to the full ruthless force of a disputed case where she will be branded a liar. Weinstein's staff had such confidentiality clauses written into their employment contracts. These clauses are commonplace in the UK too but must be outlawed when they are covering up crime. This is an issue of public policy as it is against the public interest that contractual law should be used to silence women about criminal acts. The West expresses horror that in some cultures women are raped but her rapist may pay her family compensation or marry her to redress his crime, yet we are guilty of allowing similar conduct – the pay-off and gagging order to silence women.

To change behaviour, the threat of litigation and exposure has to be real. At the moment in the UK it is not. Legal aid has to be made available so that people subjected to sexual harassment and workplace discrimination – employed or self-employed – can get legal advice and representation and ultimately a remedy. Executives in companies come lawyered up with teams of experienced litigators to outgun the complainant. It is no wonder women agree to a secret pay-off rather than go through with a court case.

From time to time I have adjudicated in internal hearings within organisations on allegations of sexual harassment. Dispute resolution is a sensitive business and both parties have to feel the justice of the outcome. In each case the male party has accepted that he perhaps 'went too far' and has with hindsight recognised the issue of power imbalance. In these cases the most important lesson for the man is an understanding of the responsibilities that go with power, and the recognition that it is an abuse of his position to leave a woman uncertain about her right to say 'no' to his advances without fear of it jeopardising her career.

But sexual harassment is not just taking place in the workplace. It happens in clubs and pubs, in public spaces and on public transport. Women are touched and groped by strangers, subjected to comment and scuzzy insult. One new form of harassment is photographing up women's skirts or down their blouses.

Sexual assault and harassment are usually assertions of power and abuse of it, but sometimes it is about men hating their own feelings of powerlessness. A perfect example of the debasement of women was the recent exposure that the journalist Toby Young frequently comments on the cleavage and breasts of female politicians in a prurient and disgusting way. Without feeling in the least inhibited, he responded to a comment about a photograph, in which he had been pushed into the back row behind the beautiful actress Padma Lakshmi, with the tweet: 'Yes but I had my dick up her arse.' Many other gross tweets about women had poured from his prolific Twitter account over the years until quickly deleted in the face of opprobrium. This was a man who was appointed to become an education regulator and who was defended as suitable by his political friends. It was pressure from women which forced him to step down. I suspect Young's insults to women are about feelings of inadequacy and absence of power. For many men who have little power, watching women being successful and instrumental is a source of impotent rage, which finds expression in non-physical abuse.

The industrial scale of sexual harassment both in the workplace and elsewhere means that clear steps need to be available for women to seek redress. There should be a new government-supported advice line so that women can be talked through their options. Harassment is repeated unwanted contact which causes alarm or distress and it includes harassment by text or phone. It is both a criminal offence and a civil cause of action so that a person can take a case in either a criminal or civil court. The police should be much more active in dealing with women's complaints but it will need resourcing as currently the police feel it is low on their list of priorities. The industrial tribunal system should also be streamlined and made more responsive to these cases so that women can take this route if it is one they prefer.

Abuse of women does not just happen at the hands of individuals. Sometimes the state plays a part, which makes it even more egregious. Nowhere is this clearer than in the scandal of undercover police officers entering into long-term relationships with women for intelligence-gathering purposes. Sometimes these Special Branch policemen met the parents of the women, proposed marriage, fathered children and then after years of intimate involvement simply disappeared, leaving behind distraught, confused and grieving partners who feared their man had committed suicide or had a fatal accident or rejected them for someone else. The long-term emotional damage is hard to fathom. Eight of the women brought legal actions against the Metropolitan Police and the Association of Chief Police Officers, and in November 2015 as part of a settlement the Met published an unreserved apology to the women and agreed that the conduct constituted abuse and gross violation with severely harmful effects.

A public inquiry under a senior judge was ordered.

The infiltration of left-wing groups by secret police to spy on political activity is nothing new to me. I was involved in political cases in the seventies and eighties where it came to light that MI5 had an agent embedded, and acted in Irish cases arising out of the Troubles where there were often informants and agents around and about. However, these women were used in the most callous way simply to gather information about environmental activism and anti-globalisation; none of them were suspected of terrorism or planned the overthrow of the state or the blowing up of Parliament and nor did their friends. One of the questions for any public inquiry is whether such police conduct can suborn the rights of individual women in order to pursue a police operation. New rules for undercover work have been created, but it remains to be seen to what extent this behaviour had become permissable, even institutionalised, the sexual exploitation of women seemingly of little consequence to police.

The judge appointed to preside over the inquiry, Mr Justice Mitting, was formerly the main judge in the Special Immigration Appeal Court (SIAC), which often sits in secret, dealing with intelligence in cases allegedly linked to terrorism. The women's legal team, led by Philippa Kauffman QC, applied for the judge to sit with a panel of people with more diverse experience of gender and race discrimination, suspecting – not unreasonably – that he would prioritise protection of the intelligence services and the police, but Mr Justice Mitting turned the application down. He also ruled that there should be no disclosure of the identity of the managers and supervisors of the undercover police and expressed the view that it was unlikely that one particular officer would have had intimate relations while undercover because he had been married for many years. When the court gasped at this utterance he suggested that maybe he was naive and old-fashioned but that was his view.

The heroic Philippa Kauffman unloaded full barrels of powerful advocacy on the judge, saying that she, her team and her clients had no confidence in the prospect of his inquiry being properly probing or of his understanding the evidence. This was why she had applied for a panel; the precedent was the Stephen Lawrence Inquiry where Lord Macpherson was assisted in assessing whether there was institutional racism by having a multiracial panel of advisers including the black Archbishop of York, John Sentamu. Her challenge went like this:

The presence of our clients is pure window dressing, lacking all substance, lacking all meaning, and [will] achieve absolutely nothing other than lending the process the legitimacy it doesn't have and doesn't deserve. I'm sorry to say this but we have the usual white, upper middle class, elderly gentleman, whose life experiences are a million miles away from those who were being spied upon. And the very narrow ambit of your experience is not something I'm simply creating out of thin air. It has been exemplified already in the way you have approached these applications.

She then withdrew from the court together with her entire legal team until the issues she had raised were considered. The crass folly of the authorities in appointing such an ill-equipped judge to preside over such a sensitive case, which required emotional intelligence and a full understanding of what such abuse would do to a woman, is astounding and shows we still have a long way to go in creating a judiciary fit for the 21st century.

6

THE 'OTHER' WOMAN

Law is produced by the most powerful in any society and inevitably it reflects their concerns and interests and is the product of their world view. Of course, decent parliamentarians from both left and right, and judges too, create or develop law with an eye to societal cohesion. They are not oblivious to the ways in which law is an important instrument in creating normative behaviour, and know that exclusionary law can lead to social disruption. The system is therefore constantly tweaked and rearranged to ameliorate some of its worst failings, but at the core of its failures is its ownership. The experience of the legal system by those who are the brokers of power is of a very different order from those of the working class to whom it has never given much comfort. However, there is a double burden for 'the other', those who diverge from the norm in terms of race, sexuality, religion or other status which places them at the margins of the page, making them different. People who are black, Asian or of other minority ethnic background, foreign nationals, refugees, gays, lesbians, people who are transgender – too often such people experience the law as particularly oppressive and punitive.

The brutal murder of Stephen Lawrence in 1993 was an iconic event. His killing by a group of white thugs and the bungled investigation by the police sparked off a long period of soul-searching in British society. Stephen's mother Doreen Lawrence has been the keeper of the public conscience, constantly reminding the nation that in a civilised society there must be justice for all. The subsequent inquiry into the death of Stephen was led by a retired judge, Sir William Macpherson, and the Macpherson Report in 1999 found that the police were institutionally racist. It was a moment of hope for black people and the government pledged to stamp out racism in the criminal justice system. Subsequent legislation – most recently the Equality Act 2010 – places a positive duty on public services to promote equality in every area of work, although immigration is noticeably excluded from its scope.

Despite this genuine commitment to racial equality, the government often loses a sense of what the implications of new policy agendas will be for racial minorities and race relations. For all the rhetoric of anti-racism, immigration and asylum policies feed into hostile views about those who are seen as 'other'. The effect has been particularly acute in recent years, with large numbers of people forced to migrate to escape war, persecution and conflict, and politicians of all stripes willing to exploit public prejudice towards migrants. The erosion of civil liberties invariably also has a disproportionate effect on minority communities. Leaders of black, Asian and minority ethnic communities, male and female, know that changes in legal protections and lowering of standards will have the greatest impact on the most vulnerable. They know that BAME people will take the biggest hit. Public debates about racism implicitly refer to black or Asian men while similar debates about gender discrimination have white middle-class women in mind. The inability of policymakers to see the simultaneous interaction of multiple discriminations is a continuing problem for BAME women.

The issue of race is highly contentious in legal circles. Incredibly, most judges still do not accept that the colour of a person's skin in any way affects their judgments, even if it is suggested that attitudes and biases may be unconscious or that discrimination can be indirect. Many see racial disadvantage as rooted in society, requiring a political resolution, and as outside the province of the courts. They describe their function in a mechanistic way as the application of 'the law', an impartial set of rules, without fear or favour and regardless of sex, colour or creed.

In September 2017, David Lammy MP published a review of how the criminal justice system treats people from BAME backgrounds. It found that although BAME people constitute approximately 14% of the population, they make up 25% of the prison population. Over 40% of young people in custody are from BAME backgrounds. Black women are significantly more likely to be arrested than white women. The number of Muslims in prison has increased by nearly 50% in the last decade.

There are still those who choose to interpret the statistics as proof of a particular propensity to criminality among BAME people. Such crude views defy contradiction or rational debate. Ever since the early 1990s, when Roger Hood of the Cambridge Institute of Criminology for the Commission for Racial Equality conducted his seminal study into race and sentencing, the idea that there is no sentencing differential between defendants of different races has been totally debunked. Yet there has always been resistance to any suggestion of racial bias in the system. Home Office research in the same period claimed little difference in outcomes for white and black accused, but when white Irish were taken out of the frame the picture changed. The prejudice faced by the Irish community, particularly in the wake of Irish terrorism, distorted any simple comparison by race and created a more favourable impression than was the truth. Minus the Irish, the differences between what happened to black offenders and white offenders became quite stark.

The unwillingness to admit that the problem exists arises because those involved in the administration of justice know the courts must be above reproach – the one area of society which should be beyond doubt. The legal establishment can accept that people may be discriminated against in education or employment because of their colour, but insist that in court the problem is in the minds of defendants (which they consider unsurprising since recipients are rarely satisfied with the justice of their deserts).

For many years, the lack of concrete data on the law's disproportionately severe treatment of BAME people also proved a formidable obstacle to getting the issue recognised. It was thought that if something could not be measured in empirical terms it did not exist. If there was no actual proof of discrimination, it must have followed that the courts were colour-blind. Then again, one of the problems with conducting quantitative research is that different responses may be obtained in different regions and before different courts. The outcomes can vary depending on the race of the researcher. It has also been shown that surface examination of the offence and the sentence may show no discernible difference in approach, because in such an assessment no account is taken of the complicated process which has gone before.

When I started practice at the Bar I spent a large part of my time in courts representing young black men charged with being a 'suspected person'. The accused did not have to commit an offence; it was enough that the police saw him behaving in a way that led them to believe that he was up to no good. There was no right to jury trial. In court, the standard case involved two police officers corroborating each other, using their identical notes made back at the police station. They would describe seeing the suspect behaving suspiciously, looking around him to see if there were observers and then trying a car door handle or pushing against a gate or reaching into a shoulder bag. There were never any fingerprints or independent witnesses or stolen items. Large numbers of young black men acquired criminal convictions on this kind of evidence, with magistrates nodding the cases through. The scandal of discriminatory police practice around the 'sus' laws led to legal reform, but 'stop and search' has become the new litmus test of police attitudes.

Home Office figures released in October 2017 show that the number of stop and searches conducted by the police fell across all ethnicities in the period 2015–16. However, the number of white people stopped and searched decreased at almost double the rate of the number of BAME people. Those from BAME backgrounds were three times more likely to be stopped and searched than those who were white. This statistic rose to six times more likely for those who were black. In London, the disparity is even more pronounced.

As Home Secretary, Theresa May tried unsuccessfully to reform the police's power to stop and search. Today, the Metropolitan Police Commissioner Cressida Dick argues that stop and search is critical in the battle to reduce knife crime. I have no doubt that, as the Macpherson Report found nearly 20 years ago, stop and search can be a useful operational tool. But it must not be used to discriminatory effect. The disproportionate use of stop and search against BAME communities is the most alienating policing tool in contemporary use. It corrodes trust in the police. Black and Asian men rightly suspect that they are being targeted simply because of the colour of their skin. Darcus Howe, the late broadcaster and journalist, described being stopped and searched 10 times over a 20-year period. Once in the West End of London, an officer lied through his teeth and claimed he had seen him dipping into women's handbags with intent to steal. Even Neville Lawrence, the father of Stephen Lawrence, whose face was so familiar from television appearances, was stopped and searched after his son's death. As indeed was Archbishop Sentamu, one of the commissioners on the Macpherson Inquiry. The same story can be repeated by almost every black male, no matter how prominent. It is unacceptable. No matter what views linger in unpleasant crevices of the police psyche, being black in public is not a crime.

BAME people are also more likely to be arrested. In 2017 the government conducted a Race Disparity Audit, which collected a large amount of statistical information about the differences in the way white people and BAME people are treated. The audit found that black men are three and a half times more likely to be arrested than white men. A natural sense of injustice can result in greater confrontation with police and consequent accusations by the police that they have been disorderly or violent. In their understandable distrust of the frequently all-white bench of magistrates, BAME defendants elect trial by jury in the Crown court more often than their white counterparts. This means longer sentences on conviction because higher courts have greater sentencing powers. According to the Lammy Review of BAME treatment in the justice system, BAME men are also more than one and a half times more likely to enter a not-guilty plea than their white counterparts. Their fundamental lack of trust in the system leads to a sense that it is not safe to cooperate with the police, or trust the duty solicitor's advice. Again, the result is a much harsher sentence if convicted. It is also noteworthy that a greater number of BAME defendants are ultimately acquitted at trial, suggesting that the original arrests may well have been unwarranted or that there was overcharging. The whole process confirms a sense of unfairness.

The contact of BAME communities with the police is so often negative that it spills over into the courtroom. However, when some judges see part of their role as validating a pressurised police force, they are faced with an unpalatable choice and either side with the police or avoid criticising them in the way that an aggrieved defendant feels an impartial judge should. The judge's attitude may not actually affect sentencing, but it will affect the way the court process is experienced by BAME defendants.

These defendants face all the usual problems: fear, worry, confusion and concern for their families – but they also have especially low expectations of how they will be treated, often anticipating hostility from court staff and the bench. Authority is white, and the courtroom reinforces that message. The great majority of lawyers are white. While BAME representation is at record levels among judges under 40 in lower courts, the latest judicial diversity statistics show that overall just 4% of circuit judges, and 2% of High Court judges, come from a BAME background. Eleven per cent of magistrates are black, but this statistic is somewhat skewed by the relatively high number of BAME magistrates currently sitting in London. For all other regions bar the Midlands, the proportion of BAME magistrates is well under 10%. The Society of Black Lawyers has stated that 'the poor image which black people have of the courts leads to the sense that if one is black in court one has to prove one's innocence rather than the court prove one's guilt'. In 2017, Agenda and Women in Prison conducted a series of focus groups aimed at understanding the experiences of BAME women within the criminal justice system. Many of the participants felt their ethnicity and gender had affected their sentence. The report concluded: 'either sentences are unfair or the reasoning behind them is not properly understood. Either way this lack of trust in the system is a problem.'

While black, Asian and other ethnic minority people are often grouped together for the purposes of statistical analysis, it is important to avoid the assumption that all BAME defendants experience the criminal justice system in the same way. Different groups are subject to distinct forms of racial stereotyping. Asian defendants are often considered industrious and family-minded. This means, for example, that they are more likely to obtain bail than black defendants. However, they are also seen as more dishonest and lacking in credibility than other BAME defendants. The special burden carried by West Indians is that for some reason they are often assumed to be more violent. The ultimate albatross for all black men is that they are believed to be sexually insatiable. This is reflected in the fact that prosecution rates for rape are significantly higher for black men than for white men.

For black women, the racism of police attitudes is often compounded by sexism. Sometimes, women need to use the police to investigate domestic violence and sexual assault but in those negotiations are distrustful because they have witnessed the abuse of police authority in relation to the men in their communities.

I remember once visiting Holloway Prison to talk to women about separation from their children. I was surprised at the numbers of black women and questioned the probation staff on the size of the ethnic population in the prison. That week the number of black women in Holloway had passed the 50% mark (counting both unconvicted prisoners awaiting trial on remand and those already sentenced). At the time, that was 10 times the ratio of black to white in the population at large. I knew that Holloway presented a very different picture from other prisons because of its wider catchment area and because it covered the metropolis and the major ports of entry. But the visual impact of so many black women kept incarcerated by so many white women and men in uniform (few of the officers were from ethnic minorities, and even today only 6% of prison officers are BAME) was shocking.

Why should black women be deserving of prison sentences or refusal of bail where white women are not? I am convinced that black women are penalised for failing to conform to 'appropriate' notions of womanhood. To some judges and policemen the lifestyles of many black women in Britain today seem unorthodox. The set-up is often matriarchal, lacking the 'restraining male influence' for which judges tend to look. The fact that the family unit of four is no longer an accurate reflection of social organisation among the white population, and that the percentage of single-parent families is high regardless of race, does not help black women, because we are now also seeing a moral and political crusade against the 'lone parent'. According to the Lammy Review, black children are more than twice as likely to grow up in a lone-parent family than white children. The courts still see single motherhood as a signal of an unstable background, regardless of family structure.

The higher prevalence of single-parent families among the black community has a different impact on young black fathers. A recurring theme is that of young black men refused bail on the basis that they have insufficient roots in the community to guarantee their staying around to stand trial. The fact that they may have children seems to count for very little when the kids are living separately with their mother. The men are often just as deeply involved with their children as any white father, and the likelihood of their absconding is no greater than that of most, but the courts minimise their family attachment by reference to the difference in lifestyle.

For black women there is a general assumption that they will disappear into a subculture which will be difficult for the police to penetrate. Another objection to bail frequently raised by the police is that they consider it likely that the accused will commit further offences. This objection, usually based on the existence of previous convictions, communicates the view that the woman is so undisciplined that appearing in court operates as no constraint on her behaviour. If the court sees a young woman who is affecting lack of concern they read her demeanour as supporting the police view, and off she goes into custody.

This is problematic because black working-class women are often less submissive in the face of the legal system than their white counterparts. This is not to say they are unafraid of courts – they are as much in terror of them as any woman – but I do not think that they see any reason for colluding in a system which discriminates against them. Many of the black women that I have represented arrived at court angry. Their anger was rarely understood; it was taken for aggression, and as an unwillingness to show deference. Even if they themselves had not gone through criminal proceedings before, they had often learned from the experience of male family members and friends not to have high expectations. The collective experience went into court with them.

Being seen as 'lippy' is a particular problem for young black women. Afro-Caribbean girls are often given independence at an earlier age than white girls and are allowed to be responsible for their own lives. They are assertive in a way that is not accepted in the dominant culture. The writer Ann Oakley has pointed out that the dividing line between what is masculine and what is criminal is at times a thin one; assertiveness and independence are seen as exclusively male characteristics, and when displayed by young black women are seen as indicative of 'trouble'.

For many BAME people the court appearance is their last stand. The whole process has been humiliating. Direct racist abuse of defendants by the police is thankfully less common today but often there is a sense of unfair treatment in other, less perceptible ways. For example, by the time they arrive at the trial, black defendants are more likely to have been remanded into custody than white defendants. Women talk of feeling dirty, like scum; the relative calm of the courtroom is their last chance to say: I am not going to be crushed.

A classic story of a black woman's road to crime was told to me by a young woman who was first convicted at the age of 14. The family was celebrating her brother's marriage, and the wedding party was in full swing when the police raided the house, suspecting that drugs were being consumed. The festive spirit was immediately spoiled and the house was turned upside down in the presence of all the guests. No drugs were found, but the girl became involved in a struggle with the police and was arrested. Despite all the claims that girls are treated lightly and are cautioned for first offences, she was brought to court and given a two-year conditional discharge as well as a fine and compensation to the officer for a torn epaulette amounting to £82.

It took the schoolgirl a long time to pay off the money, and her deep sense of the unfairness of what happened lives on. The conviction counted against her when she left school and tried to get a job, and offences of dishonesty started to accumulate. In interview, this woman made the important point that even as a girl she had the physical appearance of a mature woman, and she was dealt with as such. She felt that this assumption was often made about black girls if they were physically well developed.

Another problem for black women is that police consider their colour before their gender, and in situations of arrest they are often dealt with quite aggressively. The police assume, as they do with black men, that black women will be violent, and that perception informs the way they handle a situation. In turn, any altercation with the police is dealt with seriously by the courts; defendants on charges of assaulting police are invariably sent to prison. Assumptions about the sexuality of black women are also insidious. They are deemed to be inherently promiscuous, happy not only to have sex with anyone but to do so with rampant regularity and abandon. This belief is habitually subtly present in courtroom exchanges and social inquiry reports, and affects the way they are sentenced.

In rape cases in particular, the black experience seems to represent an amplified version of the disadvantages facing women generally. When black women are raped they have problems having their allegations heard, because all the myths about women generally merge with those about black sexuality and aggression. In the eyes of many jurors, black women are not readily seen as fragile creatures in need of protection, but as well able to look after themselves. It is hard to get statistics on the rape of black women as separate figures are not kept by all of our 43 police forces but 20% of those using the services of the Rape Crisis Centres are black (when only 3% of the general population is black).

Black women's organisations also campaign vociferously about the neglect of black women's complaints when they are subjected to battering. They say there is an assumption that they can give as good as they get and the police avoid getting involved. In the trial of a Ugandan woman for grievous bodily harm to her husband by pouring hot cooking fat over him, it came to light that, although she had called the police repeatedly, her violent husband had never been arrested. Indeed, it was suggested to her that she was not telling the truth when she said in interview to the criminal investigation department that she had made many previous complaints; there was no record of such complaints and the claim that she was exaggerating her husband's brutality was put to her again at her trial by prosecuting counsel. It was a prosecution witness, a neighbour, who inadvertently came to her aid. He complained in the witness box about the number of times he had been awakened, first by her screams and then by police mistakenly ringing his doorbell when they came in answer to her calls.

It's not just the disproportionate use of stop and search against black men that makes BAME feel that there is an accepted belief that they are dishonest, criminal and possibly terrorist. BAME people are much more likely to be apprehended on the street than white people. A colleague of mine represented a black hospital sister who was arrested at the Chelsea Flower Show. Not many black faces are to be seen at the Flower Show, a quintessentially English, middle-class affair, but the woman in question was in fact both English and middle class, and also a lover of gardens and horticulture. To her amazement, she was pulled out of a group of women who were queuing to use the ladies' lavatory by two young police officers who maintained that they had seen her put her hand into the handbags of other women. She was aghast. No stolen article was found on her and no person in the queue had complained, but she was charged with attempted theft and trailed through the nightmare of a Crown court trial before being acquitted.

Black mothers often feel that their bond with their children is perceived as less significant and that their views on a child's welfare are deemed less valuable. One mother, sentenced to two months in prison for refusing access to her daughter's father, felt that she was viewed as bloody-minded and obstructive, when in fact she was trying to express deep concern for her child's well-being. Her ex-boyfriend was a drug user and the little girl returned from visits describing in detail his use of drugs and drug involvement with others. The mother feared that the influence of drugs would affect his ability to care for the child when she was with him, and wanted any access to be supervised. In court, her concerns were ignored. She explained:

> The judge thought I was a stubborn, determined person who was going out of my way to break a court order. I think had I not had two children by different fathers they would have viewed me as a different type of person. I think the judge was trying to say, 'You can't have your children and do what you like with them.' I think the colour factor comes into it, but it's something that can never be proved.

The heroism of 'mother figures' who bring up families in the face of hardship and poverty is part of the received wisdom. While young black women are often underestimated as committed mothers, older black women are almost invariably seen as overcommitted matriarchs, who indulge their sons and protect them from the forces of law and order. The Brixton riots in 1985 were fired by the shooting of Cherry Groce when the police were looking for her son, Michael. The race riots which took place in Tottenham later that year were sparked off by the death of a black mother, Cynthia Jarrett, who suffered a heart attack while her home was being raided by police.

Although a lot of water has gone under the bridge since these events, they are part of the collective memory of the black community, cited with the Stephen Lawrence case as reflective of policing that is cavalier about the rights of black people.

The Black Lives Matter campaign in the United States is confronting racism in law enforcement, the shooting of black suspects and the mass incarceration of black people, but it has also stimulated blogs and articles about the raising of black children, and not only is the absence of black fathers being put under the microscope but also the parenting by single black women, who are left to bring up their children alone or largely unsupported. There is nothing new or race specific in the blaming of mothers for the behaviour of their children but unspoken accusations of failure or over indulgence hover around black families.

To most people living in the 21st century such stereotypes seem ridiculous. They are, but we should not let the fact that some parts of society have become more enlightened blind us to the bigoted beliefs still held by many. In most circles it is no longer acceptable to air such toxic views aloud, but that does not mean that they do not lurk, unarticulated, in the furthest recesses of the courtroom.

The racism experienced by many BAME women cannot be disconnected from what they see happening daily to their fathers, brothers and sons. When you unpack the stop-and-search figures, they disclose disproportionate suspicion of young black men and boys and a greatly increased interest in young Asian men (including men from the Middle East), in the aftermath of 9/11. In airports, Asian men are overwhelmingly more likely to be stopped for additional security checks, especially if they are Muslim. The British Pakistani actor Riz Ahmed has written powerfully about the many times he has been 'randomly' stopped in airports, both in the UK and the United States. He describes being shown into a holding pen and seeing 20 slight variations of his own face looking back at him. Americans would call this racial profiling. As well as alienating men, it feeds negative feelings among women and undermines confidence in the authorities as a source of help when women need them.

Unsurprisingly, many Asian communities feel beleaguered, sensing a growing hostility and Islamophobia not just from the authorities but also from their neighbours. Baroness Lola Young conducted an independent inquiry into criminal justice and race which spelt out the over-representation of young Muslim and black prisoners in the British justice system. She found that only 1% of offences by Muslims related to terrorism yet the community was viewed with suspicion of insurrection by the authorities. Terror attacks by men who claimed to be acting in the name of Islam have led to huge surges in hate crimes against Muslims. There have been instances of pigs' heads being left near Islamic community centres or thrown through people's living-room windows. A van was driven into worshippers as they left evening prayers at Finsbury Park Mosque. One man died at the scene and at least eight others were injured. The increasing sense of 'them' and 'us' has serious repercussions for women. Women's groups working with minorities feel that the community solidarity created to deal with this perceived targeting and Islamophobia make it impossible for women who are being abused or forced into marriages to turn to the authorities for help.

Asian women's experience of the courts is frequently different from that of other racial minority women. There is a greater willingness to believe that they are not acting through their own agency and quite often that is true. An interesting paradox was presented to the courts during the Grunwick dispute back in 1977, when assertive, politically organised Asian women picketed their place of work and were arrested for offences arising out of the dispute. Jayaben Desai, the union leader, was charged a number of times and defended the cases successfully, and with great dignity, discarding the submissive stereotype and earning herself an individualised hearing.

The more recent challenge to the idea of the submissive Asian woman has arisen in relation to terrorism. Women have appeared in the dock in a number of cases where their complicity in plans to cause explosions or to commit other terrorist offences has been proven, defying the idea of passive wife or sister. I have acted several times for the wives of jihadists or bomb plotters and the assumption is that the women know what their husbands are planning and are supportive, which is not always true by any means. They are usually charged with failing to report their husbands to the authorities.

Bouchra el-Hor was charged with urging her husband to fight 'jihad' and failing to report his plans to the police. She was arrested with him and their baby son at Luton airport, and in his computer were incriminating extremist videos and information about how to construct pipe bombs. In her suitcase was a journal which contained notes and prayers as well as domestic lists and pieces of writing, all of which indicated her love of her husband and her anxiety about his love for her. One was a very elaborate letter describing a battle and which invoked the idea of a husband's death and his going to paradise where she would eventually join him. It was a reference to a well-known Arabic love story, like that of Lancelot and Guinevere, but was automatically interpreted by the police and their Pakistani expert as incriminating. At her trial at the Old Bailey in 2007, el-Hor was able to show that she was in despair about her marriage and often wrote emotional pieces, drawing inspiration from mythology or hadith or history. Her husband was convicted and jailed for three and a half years but the jury acquitted Bouchra el-Hor, much to the disdain of some of the press.

Cossor Ali was the wife of the transatlantic bomb plotter-in-chief, Abdulla Ahmed Ali. He was convicted in September 2009 of planning to cause explosions using liquid bombs on planes crossing to North America. He, with others, was sentenced to life imprisonment with the order that he serve a minimum of 35 years. Cossor Ali was charged with failing to pass on information that would have been useful in preventing an act of terrorism. The prosecution argued that she knew her husband was planning mass murder by targeting passenger jets but failed to tell the police. They insisted that she must have known as they lived together in a one-bedroom flat where extremist books were found and where notes Abdulla Ahmed Ali had made while listening to lectures on jihad bore her fingerprints. She described her lonely and emotionally distant life from her abusive husband. She had had a moderate religious upbringing in Walthamstow but after her marriage she felt her identity being erased by her husband and his strict religious family. She told the jury that he once hit her so hard that imprints of his fingers were left on her face for days. She had phoned her father who had driven her to the police station to report it. Although she had later under pressure withdrawn the complaint, the record of the incident was found which supported the account she and her father gave. She was forced by her husband to wear a veil and he had bitten her face to remind her to wear it. She was never to be in any room where men were present and was not allowed to watch TV, read or listen to music. She spent her days caring for their baby, cleaning and praying. When she was acquitted, her father told reporters that they had suffered as a family for over three years waiting for her case to be heard 'because of some individuals with whom we have nothing in common'. He and his wife were registered foster-parents who were suspended from their jobs while the case was outstanding. Family association carries grievous risk where terrorism is involved.

Sometimes, Asian women on trial have language difficulties and an interpreter has to be used. Conducting a defence through the medium of a translator is never satisfactory because the usual methods of measuring truthfulness are greatly reduced; questions and answers become mechanical and bland, and the emotion and subtlety in a person's intonation are lost. The delay before the answer is treated with suspicion; jurors imagine the witness understands more than she is letting on, and that she is using the time to consider her response. It is true that if you try to conduct cross-examinations in poor English, the risk of misunderstanding is considerable, but the accused is not as 'real' when she is distanced by language from those who try her and she suffers the consequences. The ultimate linguistic failure happened in the case of Iqbal Begum, a battered wife who pleaded guilty to the murder of her husband at Birmingham Crown Court in April 1981 without understanding the language spoken to her by her lawyers or the court clerk.

Wearing a niqab or burka presents real problems for juries in evaluating the credibility of a defendant or a witness. I would be very anxious about a witness giving evidence against my client if I could not see her face when I was asking a question or see her facial expression when she was answering. I would object to the evidence. I think it is also problematic for a defendant to sit in the dock through a case with her face covered. Juries watch defendants throughout a trial and see their facial responses when witnesses testify. It is the whole process that assists in their decision-making, not simply the giving of testimony, and they feel cheated of that opportunity to assess a defendant. I have persuaded clients like Bouchra el-Hor to remove face veils for this reason. Human rights often involve balancing rights which are in contest. I have discussed this issue of facial covering in courts with Muslim female friends and they largely agree that requesting removal is not unreasonable in the interests of a fair trial. In these instances religious freedom is in contest with justice and in my view justice has to take precedence.

Women in minority communities are particularly vulnerable to the effects of cultural relativism, where non-intervention is justified because certain behaviours are assumed to be cultural norms. 'They're not like us and we have to tread with care or we will be accused of racism by their community leaders,' was one of the explanations I was given by a prosecutor. Needless to say, most of the community leaders are men. Repeatedly, Asian women report that if the police do turn up they are often too distressed to be very coherent, and little effort is made to discover what they have suffered, and if the wife has poor English, the police tend to rely on the story being told by the men around. One Asian woman testifying to the Fawcett Commission on Women and the Criminal Justice System described being taken to the doctor's by her husband who had caused her injuries. He did the talking. 'The GP, who was an Asian friend of the family, did not pick up on the violence.' Another said that after 10 years of domestic violence and reporting it to the police, the first real help came when she saw a domestic violence coordinator who took on all her cultural concerns. 'Until then the response of the police was very poor.'

It is true that the pressures on women in some minority communities are great, because it is considered an insult to the honour of the man's family if his wife should leave. The notion of honour is used to control women. A shocking number of Asian women have been killed by their husbands or a member of their husband's family because they have attempted to leave or seek help from the criminal justice system and been fobbed off. Balwant Kaur was killed by her husband inside Brent Asian Women's Refuge. Other women are killed by their own families for bringing shame on them. Culture does have a bearing in terms of the strategies available for Asian women to escape violence. But there is a precarious tightrope to walk. While not wanting to construct Asian and particularly Muslim culture as some monolithic and static phenomenon, problematic and pathological, it has to be spelt out how women can be constrained by their families and communities.

In June 1995 Tasleem Begum was killed by her brother-in-law, Shabir Hussein. He ran her over with his car, reversed over her body and sped forward once more, crushing her three times. She had been married to an older cousin who lived in Pakistan and did not visit her for four years. In his absence, she fell in love with a married Asian man at work, an action which dishonoured the family in Hussein's eyes. He was sentenced to life imprisonment for murder but appealed and was eventually convicted of manslaughter on the grounds of provocation, receiving six and a half years. The result was attacked by women's groups, including Southall Black Sisters. Hannana Siddiqui, the coordinator, stated:

> For us, the concept of honour is being used as a justification or mitigation for violence. It can often be used to judge women's sexual conduct or just general behaviour like refusing to be obedient, regardless of the reasons why they might be refusing. The consequences for women can be anything from social ostracism and harassment to violence and, in a few cases, murder ... Cultural defences which use notions of honour to justify murder or other offences of domestic violence have been accepted by the courts, which has led to differential treatment of black and minority women and a system colluding with that justification.

Over the past 20 years the courts have had increasingly less truck with the plea that cultural difference can explain away murderous behaviour. In 1999, 19-year-old Rukhsana Naz was strangled by her mother and brother after she refused to have an abortion. When she was 15, Rukhsana had been forced into a marriage. Her husband lived in Pakistan and she had only seen him twice. Her family was incensed on discovering that Rukhsana was expecting an illegitimate child by a young man called Imran whom she had secretly dated since she was 12. He too had been forced into a marriage he did not want. Rukhsana's body was found five days after her death when a farmer stumbled across it in his field. She was eventually identified because scrawled on her hand was Imran's pager number. Both her mother and brother were sentenced to life imprisonment but some members of the community believed that strangling was too good for an adulteress and she deserved to be stoned to death (see *From Homebreakers to Jailbreakers*, edited by Rahila Gupta, 2003).

Heshu Yones, who was 16 and a student from west London, had her throat cut by her father in October 2002, after she was discovered dating a man from outside the Kurdish Muslim culture. Abdalla Yones had become so 'disgusted and distressed' by his daughter's westernised ways that he stabbed her 11 times and left her to bleed to death before trying to kill himself. He was convicted of murder and sentenced to life.

Faqir Mohammed stabbed his daughter 20 times when he found her with a boyfriend at their family home in 2001. In September 2002 Badshu Miah suspected his estranged wife was having numerous affairs, including with white women, so he used a machete and a kitchen knife to slay her and her four-year-old daughter and her disabled brother. Sahjda Bibi was stabbed 22 times on her wedding day in 2003 by her cousins Rafaqat and Tafarak Hussain because she dared to marry a man of her own choice, a divorcee and non-blood relative. The men got life.

Shafilea Ahmed was just 17 years old when she was killed by her parents in 2003. The Warrington teenager had apparently brought shame on the family through her westernised behaviour. After months of attempting to keep her in line through bullying and violence, Shafilea was drugged and taken to Pakistan. She drank bleach in an attempt to escape a forced marriage and was brought back to the UK, where her parents suffocated her in front of their other children. Her body was dumped in undergrowth on a riverbank. Both parents were sentenced to 25 years in prison.

In 2010, the cousins of Banaz Mahmood, an Iraqi Kurd from south London, were sentenced to life imprisonment for her murder, having strangled her and buried her body in a suitcase. Her father and uncle had earlier been sentenced to life for ordering her death because she had left her violent husband and begun another relationship. Banaz had previously thrown herself through the window at her grand-mother's house when she realised her family wanted her dead. She had given a recorded interview to the police who dismissed her fears as fantasy and wanted to charge her with criminal damage.

The police continue to insist that gathering evidence is rendered almost impossible in many of these cases because the value systems in some communities still legitimise domestic violence. They point to how families and groups close ranks to protect their menfolk. Communities are not always the cosy havens of warmth, security and comfort romanticised by politicians. Sometimes they are places with secrets and hierarchies and practices like female genital mutilation.

Women can be just as brutal as men, as seen in the cases of Rukhsana Naz and Shafilea Ahmed. Women in minority cultures are socialised to accept male constructed morality and concepts like honour. In 1998, Surjit Athwal travelled to India for a family wedding. She never came back. It later emerged that her mother-in-law, outraged by the news that Surjit had been having an affair and wanted a divorce, had organ-ised for her to be murdered during the trip. Almost a decade later, Surjit's husband and mother-in-law were jailed for life for arranging her killing. A number of other British women have died in suspicious circumstances while visiting family abroad. In July 2016 Bradford-born

Samia Shahid was strangled in Pakistan by her first husband whom she had dared to divorce. The deaths are sometimes explained away as 'sudden heart attacks'. Murder is hard to prove across continents. More than 11,000 incidences of honour crime were recorded by UK police forces during 2010–14, ranging from forced marriage to FGM, while there were 18 recorded cases of honour killings in the UK in the same period.

Southall Black Sisters has been constant in challenging the underlying racism and sexism in official decision-making for over 20 years. Standing at the intersection of race, gender and class, these women have changed the landscape of feminist activism and their doggedness has paid off. The Home Office, in conjunction with the Foreign Office, is now actively tackling the issue of forced marriages, providing support and return flights when young women are taken abroad, ostensibly on a family holiday but forced to marry while there. In 2016, the government's Forced Marriage Unit dealt with 1,428 possible cases of forced marriage, the vast majority of which involved female victims and had an overseas element. The charity Karma Nirvana advises girls who suspect they are being taken abroad for a forced marriage to hide a metal spoon in their underwear when going through airport security. The idea is that the spoon will set off the metal detector, and the girl will be taken to one side, making it easier for her to ask for help.

Since 2014, it has also been a crime to use violence, threats or any other form of coercion to force someone into marriage. For a period this was resisted by some of the Asian women's groups because it was felt that too few women want their fathers or other family members prosecuted and possibly jailed; it was believed that criminalising would prevent their seeking help. Civil injunctions were pursued as the initial remedy but they seemed to have little impact and it was recognised that a stronger response was needed. The new process involves an application for a forced marriage protection order and it can be ordered at the behest of an individual or a local authority or the police. The order can forbid marriage and engagement anywhere in the world and in appropriate cases can forbid parents and relatives from attempting to locate the victim. Breach of the order carries up to five years' imprisonment. The penalty is not intended as an assault on the custom of arranged marriages but is to prevent marriage where a party does not consent or only consents under duress. The traditional offences of assault or kidnapping had often proved woefully inadequate in forced marriage cases, especially when a woman was tricked into making a visit overseas. The first successful prosecution for forced marriage took place in 2015. The perpetrator had repeatedly sexually and physically abused his victim, playing on her shame to blackmail her into silence. He forced her to marry him by threatening to kill her parents if she refused. He was jailed for 16 years.

These are welcome developments, but there is still room for improvement. Until recently, the Foreign Office required victims of forced marriages taking place abroad to pay the costs of their own repatriation to the UK. In some cases, the woman's passport was confiscated until she was able to pay back the 'loan'. The policy, which applied even when the victim was under 18, was roundly condemned by women's groups when it came to light, and rightly so. Not only was the policy liable to deter women from seeking help, but making survivors pay the price of their own salvation is a cruel affront to the dignity of these women. However, the increased focus on forced marriage does risk the further stigmatisation of certain minority groups. Southall Black Sisters argues that the government has used forced marriage cynically as a justification for pushing a restrictive immigration agenda. While I am in favour of criminalising forced marriage, it must not be exploited as a tool for entrenching old prejudices. Forced marriage can and does occur in a wide range of communities and not just among Muslims.

Women's organisations also say that the police are still insufficiently responsive to early signs that a woman is at risk. The escalating suicide rate among young South Asian women is one of the darkest secrets in our society. Unsuccessful attempts at suicide often go unheeded. The tension of living in a Western developed nation, where the relationships between men and women are in the process of great change, and reconciling that reality with the mores and customs of another cultural tradition can be unbearable. The pressure to conform, combined with high expectations, can cause massive strain on young women, who are taught to hide any problems that bring shame on the family. This is not an experience confined to the Asian community. Domestic violence and pressures to marry people from the same background have operated in Catholic, Jewish and other communities too. Speaking publicly about the behaviour of your own people is seen as an act of betrayal because minority communities feel that such exposure will further stigmatise them in the eyes of the majority. On the one hand are those who want the lid taken off the secrecy and call for a clear denouncement of unacceptable practices; others fear that focusing on 'honour and shame' may lead to the Asian community being stigmatised and even more stereotyped. But activists like Hannana Siddiqui are anxious that multicultural sensitivity may lead to moral blindness and feel the government is still wary about taking on the leaders of ethnic minority communities over cultural traditions.

The case of Zoora Shah has long been a cause célèbre among women campaigners, for it threw into stark relief the failings of the courts to understand women who challenge cultural stereotypes. In the 1970s Zoora came to Bradford from Mirpur in rural Pakistan following an arranged marriage. Her husband, who had subjected her to violence, abandoned her and her young children when she was pregnant with her third child. She was totally destitute and isolated when she was befriended by Mohammed Azam, a drug dealer from the criminal underworld of Bradford. He helped her acquire a house and because of her indebtedness to him he began to make sexual demands. This sealed her reputation as a 'prostitute'. In the years that followed she became enslaved to him, used for sex as and when he pleased, and was threatened and tyrannised so that her home became a prison. She suffered from periods of depression and illness which were confirmed in medical records. Her efforts to get help from community leaders fell on deaf ears or they would themselves exploit her sexually. Eventually Zoora poisoned her persecutor when she thought he had sexual designs on her daughter and might ruin her life too.

At her trial Zoora Shah refused to give evidence. She was ashamed of what she had become in the eyes of the community and could not bring herself to reveal the full details of her debasement in public. Bound by all the powerful notions of honour and shame, she therefore chose to remain silent in the hope of saving the honour of her daughters. She was found guilty and sentenced to life with a tariff of 20 years. Her subsequent appeal also failed. In the words of her lawyer, Pragna Patel, 'she did not lead a "normal", "passive" existence as a "victim" of violence but tried to retain control in an impoverished world inhabited by male predators'. The psychiatrist for the Crown had no experience of gender issues within Asian communities. He presented Zoora as a cold and calculating woman, especially because she chose to stay silent at her trial, acted in contradictory ways and had an ambivalent relationship with her abuser.

As Pragna Patel points out: 'There was a complete absence of awareness of the intertwined issues of culture, gender and power within minority communities ... Women face very real consequences when they find themselves transgressing the norms of their community and it is important for those sitting in judgment to understand why cultural values keep a woman silent and close down her options.' The sustained efforts of Southall Black Sisters meant that Zoora Shah's tariff was reduced to 12 years in 2000. She was finally released in 2006 after spending 13 years in prison.

Southall Black Sisters raise the important issue that many immigrant women, who originally acquired entry to Britain through their marital status, feel obliged to stay in violent marriages because to leave may jeopardise their right to remain in this country. Such fears make women diffident about calling in the police or, if they do, about answering all their questions, which in turn is perceived as deceit. The One Year Rule in immigration law means that if a marriage fails within a year, a party who has come from abroad will lose their right to stay. Following campaigns by Southall Black Sisters, concessions to the rule have now been made for spouses and partners who are victims of domestic violence.

The abuse and violation of women is a human rights issue and there can be no hierarchies of human rights. Women from ethnic minorities deserve the same legal protections as any other women, and women deserve the same protection as men. As my friend Claire L'Heureux-Dubé, a former Canadian Supreme Court judge, has said, context is everything. But this is a lesson still to be learned here, and until it is, equality at the hands of the law and before the law will not be secured.

It is not just the ethnic minority communities who suffer racial prejudice. Today, around 12% of women in prison are foreign nationals. While there are still significant numbers of Jamaican and Nigerian women in this group, Eastern European women are now being imprisoned in the UK in increasing numbers. According to the Bromley

Briefing Prison Factfile 2015, one in three imprisoned foreign national women are serving sentences for drug offences, compared to 12% of British women. We are in addition seeing a rising number of women arrested for immigration-related offences, charged with the deception of the authorities over their immigration status, or the use of false documentation to enter or leave the UK, obtain work or access benefits. Irregular immigration status, and the resulting fear of being imprisoned or deported, also makes many migrant women particularly vulnerable to coercion. Agents who traffic women to the UK to work in the sex trade, cannabis production industry or as domestic servants use the threat of a report to the authorities to keep their victims in line. Those who do not hold British passports have similar experiences.

The noughties saw a spike in the number of women from overseas being imprisoned for drug offences, usually importation, mainly from Nigeria, Ghana and Jamaica but also from India and Pakistan or Latin America. In 2003, these women made up around 20% of the female prison population in England and Wales. The conviction rate for these offences was high because, even where the women claimed they had been duped or pressured into carrying drugs, judges and juries were sceptical. The worlds they heard about were so alien that the accounts often seemed fantastic. A woman from Colombia, sentenced to nine years, said that her trial judge suggested to her that she had read too many books about the Mafia or watched too many films. There was no real appreciation of her terror at what could be done to her family back home.

To people leading impoverished lives, the financial rewards for importing and distributing drugs are considerable, though they often bear very little relation to the value of the drugs themselves. The use of women as couriers, or 'mules', is frequent and intentional. A steady supply of extremely poor women can be persuaded to earn cash which will see their children through school, pay for medical bills or just secure their family's existence for the foreseeable future. For many, coercion has played a part in their decision to act as a courier. Sometimes, drug dealers will offer a struggling woman a loan. Carrying drugs is the price exacted as repayment. Other women have drugs planted on them, and have no idea that they are carrying. Either way, they are the pawns of the drug gangs and they become the forgotten prisoners within our system. Few of the women are aware of the sentences they are likely to face, or of British sentencing policy. According to a 2012 briefing paper produced by the Prison Reform Trust, a common theme is women being told: 'The worst that can happen is that you will be sent back.'

Thankfully, the number of foreign women being arrested for drug importation appears to be slowly declining, but the number of immigrant women under legal scrutiny is increasing. Those who go through the criminal justice system rarely have much voice, but immigrants are one of the most silent groups. Few prisoners have a vote, and no foreign men and women charged with crime do. They are the most vulnerable of all the adults who appear in our courts.

Between July 2016 and June 2017, over 4,000 women were detained for immigration control purposes, either before being deported or while waiting to see if they are given permission to enter the UK. An order of the court is not necessary to detain these women; it can be done on the say-so of a Home Office official. Many women in immigration detention have committed no crime; the Home Office can detain them in order to establish their identity, or if there is a risk they will abscond if released. Others have committed crimes which render them liable to deportation, and once their prison sentence is complete, are transferred to immigration detention while a decision is taken on whether to deport them or not.

The majority of women in immigration detention are held at Yarl's Wood, an immigration removal centre in Bedfordshire equipped to hold around 450 women. It has long been a magnet for controversy. Many women detained there have physical and mental health-care needs which mean they need ready access to doctors and medication, but are faced with long waits for appointments, delayed prescriptions and inadequate support. Allegations of sexual abuse have been rife, and in 2013 two male staff members were fired for having sex with a detainee. In another incident a few years previously, a detainee became pregnant by an officer. Privacy is effectively non-existent. Research conducted in 2015 by the charity Women for Refugee Women found that almost all the women they interviewed said that men watched them in intimate situations, including while naked, in the shower, or on the toilet. The threat of coercion is omnipresent.

There is no limit on the length of time that people can be held in immigration detention. Both men and women are sometimes held for very considerable periods of time, and in extreme cases for several years. This is striking when contrasted with the position of most other European countries; the UK is one of the very few not to impose an upper time limit. In most, detention is for a month or, at a maximum, a few months. An analysis of five main European countries found that the UK takes fewer refugees, offers less generous financial support, provides housing that is often substandard and does not give asylum seekers the right to work. The UK has been known to punish those refugees who do voluntary work and routinely forces people into destitution and even homelessness, driving them into shoplifting or other crime. The position may be particularly acute when a foreign national has been to prison and is then trans-ferred to immigration detention to await deportation, so that an indeterminate stay in a removal centre is tacked on to the end of their custodial sentence. The uncertainty this causes has a serious impact on the mental health of detainees who have no idea when they are going to be let go – to say nothing of the moral dubiousness and financial inefficiency of detaining people who do not need to be locked up. In 2015, an All-Party Parliamentary Group recommended the introduction of a limit of 28 days as the maximum length of time anyone can be held in detention. That recommendation was not implemented by the government, although the system has recently been changed so that pregnant women cannot be detained for longer than 72 hours.

Charities and campaigning organisations continue to fight for a time limit on immigration detention, or better yet, for its abolition altogether. Yet the arguments used by campaigners can be twisted and used as a justification for making the system tougher, not fairer. A good example was the 'detained fast track' asylum procedure which was used to process asylum claims until it was declared unlawful by the High Court in 2015. Under this speeded-up process, asylum decisions were made, and appeals disposed of, within a matter of weeks. Ostensibly aimed at curbing excessive stays in detention, in reality the extremely tight time limits often operated to deny asylum seekers the right to a fair appeal hearing. Another example is the introduction of strict limitations on the amount of time that children can be detained in immigration detention. This is obviously a good thing; there can be no justification whatsoever for detaining a child. But it does mean that the use of immigration detention for those with families now involves splitting up children from their parents. This has the same disproportionate impact on mothers as it does in the prison context. There is an obvious answer to this, which is not to detain the parents in the first place, but this is not the approach which has been adopted by the government.

Women who end up in immigration detention are often vulnerable. Many are asylum seekers, fleeing persecution or violence at home. They may well have suffered sexual and physical abuse. Many of them have committed no crime; those that have are much more likely to have played ancillary roles, or also to be victims of crime themselves. The anxiety and fear experienced by women in immigration detention is magnified through the lens of previous abuse. At the same time, it is important not to deny the personhood of these women by viewing them solely as victims. Just as in prison, there are some women in immigration detention who are there because they freely choose to do bad things. Others, who are there because of circumstance, abuse or because they are in reality the victims of crime, have individual personalities as well, and experiences and stories to tell.

In an increasingly punitive climate there is a temptation to pander to the expectations and prejudices of judges and juries in ways which will secure a favourable outcome. (It is an approach to which we have all succumbed, lawyers and probation officers alike. We have all experienced the fear that our client will turn up with a Mohican haircut, or with her tattoos showing, or with a ring in her nose, especially when the judge really is a conformist and is likely to draw adverse inferences.)

The Probation Service is now actively addressing the issue of racism and sexism, and their studies have identified stereotyping as a particular problem. The accepted image is an easy shorthand to fall back on when there is little time. When I was making a television programme on a similar subject I interviewed the BBC's head of comedy, who told me that reliance upon stereotypes in sitcoms was partly due to the need to impart information quickly and to create shared laughter in shared values. The problem is that these values, wherever they are used or appear, are then reinforced, allowing prejudice to creep in. In the courtroom their use prevents important distinctions being made between each case and each person. Basic information is provided, responses are triggered, and the individual who is encased in this envelope of assumptions is never allowed to surface. For BAME women, emerging as special and different is especially tough.

BAME women lawyers complain that the problems of being taken seriously are exacerbated for them. They have well-tuned antennae and empathise with the problems faced by women clients of their race. As the late barrister Tanoo Mylvaganam said, 'You cannot be a woman lawyer, experiencing discriminatory practice yourself as a professional, without being alerted to the way that the same attitudes affect women who do not even have our class advantage.'

One black woman barrister, a rising criminal practitioner, described defending a black client who was one of several defendants; the other lawyers were all white. She had the strong feeling that the trial judge, who was renowned for his rudeness, was particularly dismissive of her legal arguments. At one stage, when she sat down, he sent her a note asking her whether her accent was English, and if so where she had been to school. She ignored the note, uncertain what it meant, but felt very undermined, as though her fluency and education were being questioned. After this barrister had made her final speech to the jury, the judge summed up to the all-white jury with this remark: 'Members of the jury, we are British and this is a British court and British standards of behaviour are being protected.' She thought the comment diminished her own address to the jury, as coming from someone with a different and less valid value system.

Elizabeth James, a British barrister of Nigerian descent, was defending a Nigerian woman charged with credit-card fraud when the judge opined that 'this type of crime is far too prevalent amongst the Nigerian community'. There is absolutely no support for his view, and she had the courage to challenge him in court and to say that she took personal exception to the remark.

The negative experiences and social injustice encountered by these different communities comes to a head in our courts. This takes us to a sensitive issue: the potential racial imbalance of juries in cases with a racial component. In London it would be rare to have a jury that was not multiracial. However, even in the metropolis it can happen that a jury is overwhelmingly white and if the accused is black it may create the feeling that white justice is being delivered on black people. The removal of the right of the defence to challenge jurors without cause has happened by salami-slicing the entitlements of those who stand accused. When I first came to the Bar it was possible to challenge up to seven jurors on behalf of each individual client. This right was reduced under a Labour administration to three challenges per defendant, and was finally removed altogether in 1988 because it was claimed that anyone who carried the *Daily Telegraph* or who looked as though he or she had half a brain was being dismissed by manipulative defence lawyers.

There was no doubt that efforts were made to second-guess the type of juror from all sorts of aspects of their appearance, a lot of the time to little avail. (I myself, for example, had a sneaking aversion to men who had badges on brass-buttoned blazers and women who looked like my old headmistress.) But there were occasions when the challenge had a valid and important use. In cases involving aspects of child-rearing, such as cases of baby-battering, it is helpful to have people who have not forgotten the demands of a newborn. Equally, age can be important in cases involving youths, where their lifestyles may be incomprehensible to jurors of an exclusively older generation.

However, it is particularly worrying that in cases of a racial nature we can have all-white juries trying BAME defendants. Successive studies have now shown that jury verdicts are not generally affected by ethnicity. But it is also important to consider how the process looks from the point of view of the person in the dock. A predominantly white and male jury may well not feel fair to a black or Asian female defendant. As one of the participants in the Agenda and Women in Prison focus groups commented: 'I had a pretty old jury and I was thinking well I'm young and I'm black, hmm ... what are my chances?'

Some positive developments are taking place. Judges are consciously endeavouring to remove the spectre of cultural ignorance from the courts. It is thankfully unheard of now for generalised statements about racial groups to be made in the courtroom. But before reaching the position where racism is completely ousted there has to be recognition that people do not start equal – that the old British playing field is not level. The baggage which comes with the defendant or complainant to the courtroom must be thrown into the scales. All the experiences of BAME people at the hands of the law have been absorbed into the collective consciousness of their communities: the black taxi driver badly beaten for no reason by off-duty policemen; the middle-aged woman who suffered a dislocated shoulder when her £20 note was automatically suspect and she was wrongfully arrested with force by a detective; the young man whose head was stamped on in a police station; the Asian families burned out of their homes because the police failed to take seriously the threats being made by racist neighbours.

When the subject of racial and sexual awareness training was first raised in the legal profession it used to be greeted with sneers, but judges now speak of the benefits of learning about cultural difference and recognise that judicial training has played an important role in securing confidence in the system. But the learning does not run deep enough. Until there is a clear appreciation of racism and the social factors which bring BAME people before the courts, as well as an understanding of the subtle dynamics which work in the courts to discriminate against them, those from ethnic minority communities will continue to be among the sections of the community least well served by the law.

The idea of 'the other' is of course not restricted to the colour of people's skin or their cultural background. One of the effects of the change in women's status in society has been the greater confidence it has given them to express their sexuality freely, a factor which has highlighted so many of the dichotomies in the law. The new confidence has enabled gay women openly to declare their sexuality. The fact of lesbianism has never even been acknowledged in the criminal law, which is an extreme expression of the way the law denies the existence of active female sexuality.

In a divorce case reported on 21 May 1954 in *The Times*, the judge was so wedded to Queen Victoria's disbelief in the very existence of lesbianism that he refused to grant the divorce. In his judgment he said:

At the highest the wife and Miss Purdon were seen hand in hand, used to call each other darling, kissed on the lips, spent a good number of holidays together, were constantly alone in the wife's bedroom at the vicarage and on two or three occasions occupied the same bedroom at night ... It was a very odd business, two grown women spending all this time together often

227

in the same room and often in bed together, but the court is quite satisfied that that is perfectly innocent.

There are laws which can be used against lesbians such as 'Behaviour likely to cause a Breach of the Peace' or 'Indecent Assault on a Woman', but the law puts much more emphasis on protecting women from vaginal penetration by an unsanctioned male and on protecting men from homosexuality.

Sexuality matters because human beings do not thrive when cut off from desire or sexual expression. Although male homosexuality was decriminalised in 1967 it was still vilified and evoked disgust; gay men were subject to harassment and prosecution for gross indecency by the police for many years thereafter. It was not about equality of sexual orientation or any questioning of patriarchy. Occasionally in the seventies and eighties, publicans tried to expel gay women from their bars if they kissed or embraced, and consequent 'sit-ins' by lesbian groups led to arrest for breach of the peace but the forces of law and order were largely uninterested in gay women.

In 1988 the Thatcher government passed into law Clause 28 of the Local Government Act making it an offence to promote homosexuality in schools. This was interpreted to mean that teachers could not be positive about any sexual identity other than straight and if pupils came to them about bullying or depression, in need of advice or counselling, they could not say it was fine to be gay. Teachers knew they put themselves at risk of contravening the law just by expressions of support and kindness.

However, because lesbianism poses an implicit challenge to heterosexuality and a world ordered to suit men, when a woman's lesbianism is put before the court as part of the general evidence in a case unrelated to her sexuality, it can still be manipulated against her. Lesbians can disrupt the idea of passive femaleness so strongly that the law is used symbolically for public condemnation. In one case, the wounding of her lesbian lover led to a woman being imprisoned for seven years in circumstances where corresponding heterosexual domestic violence would have had a much less severe result.

Another scandal of the penal and justice systems is the inappropriate detention of people in prisons and special hospitals. This is partly because of the devastation of psychiatric facilities in ordinary hospitals through lack of funding. However, many women are made the subject of Mental Health Act sections who should not be sectioned at all. They are left to spend indeterminate periods in places like Broadmoor and Rampton, largely because they have been aggressive and angry or generally acted inappropriately for their sex.

To get into these places, patients have to be diagnosed as mentally ill and deemed to be a danger to society or themselves. For women it is very often the latter, because their desperation is so often turned inwards. Many of the female patients in Broadmoor are there for comparatively ordinary crimes, whereas the detained men have committed sex offences or sexually motivated murders.

Prue Stevenson of Women in Secure Hospitals (WISH) described in lectures the attack on identity and sense of self that women, especially lesbians, experienced in places like Broadmoor, where they are put under pressure to wear make-up and feminine clothing, grow their hair and have tattoos removed. Behave like a proper woman was the message. Most women complied, since to refuse could go against them in assessing their readiness for discharge. However, the process of making women conform starts much earlier in the criminal justice process, and young gay women have felt they are partially punished for non-compliance.

Lesbians experience the criminal justice system, from policing onwards, as hostile. As the victims of crime they are at a profound disadvantage, and have difficulty persuading the police to pursue complaints of sexual harassment, verbal abuse and assault by men. It is a particularly courageous gay woman who will brave the attack upon her character she knows will attend any trial such as rape. Some attacks are not confined to cases where gay women have been sexually assaulted. In almost any case the fact of her sexuality can be used against her in subtle ways. A gay policewoman told me that she has always had to be prepared for an attack in the witness box on the basis that her arrest of a male accused was based on bias against men.

The failure of the law to provide adequate protection for transgender people is now getting more attention.

In 1996 I fought the first transgender case before the European Court of Justice, where my client had been constructively dismissed from her job because she was embarking upon transition and the employer did not want her on the 'front of house' workforce. It was in fact a global first on transgender rights. Having lost in the courts in the UK, we won in Europe and the case started the slow process of legal reforms. However, transgender men and women still suffer greatly in the legal system, especially in our prison system, which too often locks up transgender prisoners according to their genitalia rather than their chosen gender identity and often with tragic consequences.

One of the most distressing cases I ever conducted was defending a young transgender woman who had been raped and vaginally damaged by a former partner. She had gone to the police and reported the violation only to be greeted with ridiculing asides and suppressed laughter. The case pre-dated the Human Rights Act and reforms in rape law and the Equality Act. Her experience at the hands of the police was so wretched that she decided to withdraw the allegation whereupon the police charged her with perverting the course of justice. I tried to persuade the court to drop the case but only succeeded in having her charge reduced to wasting police time and a conditional discharge by way of sentence. I like to think this could not happen today as so much legal change has taken place and there is greater public understanding of transgender issues and the abuse suffered by transitioning people who have gone on the tough journey to assert their gender identity. The courts and prosecution service are mindful of the human rights issues at stake as are the police and prison service.

Since the Gender Recognition Act 2004 came into force transgender people have been able to have their acquired gender recognised by going through a detailed legal process which, if satisfied, allows a new birth certificate to be issued. For legal purposes the person is then identified in their new gender. While this has been a valuable step towards recognising gender autonomy it has created a hierarchy for trans people that has permeated the legal and penal systems. Anyone with no gender recognition certificate has been placed in the prison estate that reflects their birth gender. This was in line with the national guidance. Between 2015 and 2017 three openly transgender women took their own lives in custody in English prisons: Vikki Thompson, Joanne Latham and Jenny Swift. None had the right certification and were in male prisons.

The discrimination, verbal, physical and sexual abuse experienced by trans people in and out of prison can take people over the edge of despair. Self-harming among trans prisoners is frequent. New prison policy was published at the end of 2016 on transgender prisoners, which stipulates that prisons must recognise gender-fluid and non-binary inmates and if a transgender person is sufficiently advanced in their gender reassignment process they may be placed in the estate of their acquired gender. It improves the procedures for making prison-allocation decisions but still leaves a lot to the discretion of governors and prison boards, who will have to decide whether incarcerating a trans prisoner in the prison of their own choosing might put their well-being or security at risk or the security of other inmates. Tara Hudson, a transgender woman who was held in a male prison, was moved to a female facility after her complaints of sexual harassment received sufficient public attention. She had lived all her adult life as a woman and had undergone gender reconstruction surgery but had not acquired the certification. She was female in all but law.

The convictions of Gayle Newland and Justine McNally for sexual offences that involved deceiving others about their gender show how complicated it can be if someone self-identifies as a trans person but is not legally transitioned. Both were recognised as suffering from gender confusion and had sought psychiatric help for anxiety and self-harming but neither had medically or legally transitioned. By misrepresenting their legal gender they were deemed to have prevented their victims from making informed decisions about consent – even though they may have self-identified as male at the time of the offences. Changes to the way we see gender, as more fluid or as crossing a spectrum, are going to present real challenges to the system. If either Gayle Newland or Justine McNally had legally transitioned, could their victims have claimed that they were deceived and would not have consented in the knowledge of that transition?

If certification is essentially the passport required by institutions and by law, will such a certificate be more readily obtainable? And what if non-binary people do not want to be saddled with a fixed gender or want to have surgery or want to choose which side of the divide they prefer? How can they be protected from molestation and abuse in or out of prison?

It has become clear that the Gender Recognition Act needs amendment to take account of these many and varied aspects of gender identity. I greatly regret that the transgender issue has divided some women. For any of us who have worked with those transgender people who have been raped and abused, sacked from employment or rejected by family and friends, who have lived from childhood with the emotional pain of having the wrong identity, we know these are questions of human rights and compassion.

To be different and 'other' tests the legal system, which is created around norms and rules that have been formulated with very traditional ideas about citizenship and belonging and indeed what it means to be fully human. The woman who is an outsider has an even harder time fulfilling the system's demands and in consequence justice for her can become more of a lottery.

7

MAN-SLAUGHTER

The idea of woman as a killer challenges popular beliefs about femininity. Women kill infrequently but the rarity of the occurrence often fuels the repugnance. There is still a shock value in women, the begetters of life, taking a life.

Murder is usually committed by men. Analysis of crime figures over the years show that children are more likely to be killed by men, and women are more likely to be killed by men. Statistics vary from year to year but taking an average over the three years leading up to 2015, 97% of female domestic violence homicide victims were killed by a male suspect. Women are far more likely to be killed by a partner or ex-partner than men are. In the year ending March 2016 50% of female murder victims aged over 16 – 77 women – were killed by their partner or former partner. This is part of a slow downward trend but no cause for putting out flags. Yet, only 7% of men who are murdered are killed by a partner or former partner. Here in Britain, because of our strict gun laws, only 5% of homicide victims are killed by shooting; the most common method of killing is a knife or other sharp instrument, though women are often strangled or suffocated. The Femicide Census profiles the cases of women killed by men and it makes harrowing reading.

Women keep their killing within the family. Usually they kill their children, mainly babies (40–45% of women convicted of killing fall into this group) and usually they are mentally ill at the time, usually suffering from post-natal depression. About 35% of those convicted of homicide have killed their partner. However, the overall numbers of women killing men is tiny. In 2015, 14 women were convicted of murder and only five of the victims were men.

It is instructive to look in some detail at a key historical case when examining the attitude of the law to women who kill. The trial of Ruth Ellis, the last woman to be hanged in Britain, was over in one and a half days, a feat which would no doubt win the acclaim of many judges today, who bemoan the long duration of trials. A murder trial, which involves exploring the psychological state of a defendant against a complicated background of emotion, violence, insecurity and abandonment, inevitably takes a good deal of time and is built upon a very full knowledge of the person represented.

Ruth Ellis's leading counsel, Mr Melford Stevenson, later became a High Court judge and the scourge of the Old Bailey. When Stevenson represented her he was relatively inexperienced in the criminal courts; he was mainly a divorce practitioner, and had done few major criminal trials. He had none of the instinctive feel which the good jury advocate needs to overcome the unspoken prejudices which lie beneath the surface in any criminal case. Nor did he have the empathy which might have helped Ruth Ellis tell her story in a more compelling way.

Mr Christmas Humphreys, who must be the only Buddhist to sit on the bench, opened the case for the Crown on 21 June 1955. Ruth Ellis stood alone in the dock charged with the murder of David Blakely. Humphreys laid emphasis on the fact that Ellis was conducting simultaneous love affairs with two men: with David Blakely, whom she killed, and with Desmond Cussen. What was never explored was the true nature of her relationship with Cussen, whom she leaned on for emotional support but never considered seriously as a lover; it later transpired that their sexual liaison lasted only a matter of weeks, in June 1954. Humphreys told the jury that Blakely was trying to break off the association and that Ellis was angry about this, even though she had another lover at the time. He described how she took a gun, found David, and shot him dead by emptying that revolver at him, four bullets going into his body, one hitting a bystander in the thumb and the sixth disappearing completely. After the shooting outside a public house in South Hill Park, Hampstead, Ellis was questioned by a police officer who told her that he had seen the body of David Blakely and understood she knew something about it. Her reply was: 'I am guilty, I am rather confused.' She then made a written statement to the police describing how, after putting her child to bed, she had picked up a revolver that had been given to her by a man as security for a loan three years ago, and had put it in her handbag. She had gone out, she said, with the intention of finding Blakely and shooting him.

Christmas Humphreys called only a few witnesses to provide evidence in support of the history of the relationship between Ruth Ellis and David Blakely and the events surrounding the killing. After each person completed their testimony, Melford Stevenson rose briefly to his feet to announce that he had no questions. The case for the Crown was over within the morning.

In his opening speech to the jury, Stevenson made great play of the fact that the defence did not challenge any part of the prosecution's version of what had taken place. The jury was informed that the defence would call an eminent psychiatrist who would tell them that 'the effect of jealousy upon the feminine mind, upon all feminine minds, can so work as to unseat the reason and can operate to a degree in which in a male mind it is quite incapable of operating'. The two feminine minds on the jury must have loved this description of their frailty.

The defence tactic of keeping clear of the prosecution case may well have been based on the idea that the less said about Ruth Ellis's lifestyle the better, and that what was said should come from her, carefully circumscribed by her own counsel. But juries have a sixth sense when they are not hearing the full story, and their conjectures about what they are not hearing can sometimes be more damaging than the real thing. Sometimes it is better to reveal the defence hand completely. It is as much in those subtle displays of judgement as in fine advocacy that you find great lawyering.

The defence must have realised that Ruth Ellis could appear rather hard-faced because of the way she described the events. Even when there is no challenge to the evidence of prosecution witnesses, they can be the source of crucial material which sheds light on a case and provides corroboration for the defence. Melford Stevenson was unlikely to secure anything very useful from the evidence of personal friends of Blakely, who gave evidence for the prosecution. But among the witnesses for the Crown was someone who knew intimately the suffering experienced by Ruth Ellis. Desmond Cussen, her 'alternative lover', was the only real friend Ruth Ellis had, and his love for her was unquestioned. He undoubtedly hoped that in time she would get Blakely out of her system and look upon him with more favour. Cussen knew that Blakely was happy to exploit Ruth Ellis sexually and financially.

Unlike Ruth Ellis, a daughter of the lower classes, David Blakely came from a well-to-do family. His father was a doctor of sufficient means to provide his son with a small private income. At 25, Blakely had no steady job but hung around the edges of the motor-racing world. He seems to have been intoxicated with the fast life as well as with hard liquor. When he first met Ellis, who was the managing hostess of a run-down nightclub in Belgravia, he was engaged to a 'suitable' young woman from his own background. No doubt Ellis provided an earthy sexual diversion, but the relationship developed into a compulsive affair in which she was regularly beaten and humiliated. She obviously had hopes that this was the relationship which would provide her with social acceptability and a real partner, a delusion which was somehow never dispelled even when Blakely had affairs with other women, refused to involve her in some parts of his life and made it clear to her that she was despised by some of his own circle.

Ruth Ellis gave evidence on her own behalf. Whenever a defendant walks from the dock to the witness box to give their own account there is always a strong sense of anticipation; you can almost feel it, especially in a murder trial. For the defending counsel this is the moment to turn the case round and view it from a different perspective. Taking a defendant through the evidence may seem like a straightforward process to the onlooker, but there is a special skill involved in choreographing a defendant's account so that, while coherent, it also gives the jury a sense of the misery and turmoil that can lead to behaviour that would normally never even be contemplated. The counsel's task is to enable the client to communicate their sense of desperation, or whatever other aspects of their emotional state figured in the offence.

It should be like watching a *pas de deux*. Defendants have to be drawn out so that they describe exactly how they were feeling at the time, the things that were running through their heads, their emotional state in the weeks and days before the crime was committed. Expressing such emotion in a court of law, particularly Court I at the Old Bailey, is a daunting prospect and is usually only possible if the person on trial has established a degree of trust and understanding with their counsel.

Any reading of Ruth Ellis's testimony makes it clear that Melford Stevenson had little point of contact with the woman he was representing. At best she was an enigma to him; more likely he saw her as a woman of little virtue. She responded to his questions methodically and briefly; expansion was rarely sought. Even when she was dealing with the violence and rejection which would form the basis of any defence of provocation, weak answers to Stevenson's own questions were left unpursued. She was never asked to explain a bit further when she said Blakely 'only hit me with his fists and hands', even though she was clearly subjected to regular beatings, causing bruising, black eyes and treatment at the Middlesex Hospital, and even though Cussen could have confirmed this. Like many battered women before and since, her underplaying his violence was probably a coping mechanism, and it also displayed the complicated emotions that go with loving someone who treats you like a dog. Her feelings of rejection and humiliation when Blakely finally dumped her, aided and abetted by his circle of friends, were never fully explored, nor was there any probing of the intensity of emotion that she must have experienced during her long vigil outside the public house, in which she could hear him laughing and socialising. Every sense of herself as an outsider, beyond the pale of his social class, must have been reinforced, and her head must have been buzzing with visions of Blakely with another woman. None of this reached across the courtroom to the jury. Her irrationality was explained as jealousy, the fury of the woman scorned, rather than as the response of someone who had been systematically abused, exploited and demeaned.

Counsel for the prosecution asked only one question in cross-examination. 'When you fired that revolver at close range into the body of David Blakely, what did you intend to do?'

It was not even a leading question. Ruth Ellis replied: 'It is obvious. When I shot him I intended to kill him.'

I can almost hear the silence in the courtroom when she gave that answer, and the gloom it must have invoked in her lawyers. Yet no attempt was made to recoup in re-examination. No doubt she did intend to kill him at that moment, but the real issue was whether she had been provoked beyond endurance, whether her action was that of someone out of control, a product of desperation in intolerable circumstances. When he came out of the public house, did he see her and ignore her, and did that final act of rejection cause her to snap? It was a case which had to engage the sympathies of the judge and jury in order to surmount the obstacles presented by the law as it then stood.

Where her lawyers had their hardest task was in dealing with Ruth Ellis's decision to take a gun with her when she went to the address in Hampstead where she suspected her lover would be. From such a deliberate action the jury would reasonably assume, in the first instance, that this was a premeditated act of revenge. The immediacy or 'heat of the moment' principle is an important aspect of provocation, and it was bound to fail in this case unless Ruth Ellis had some explanation of how her intentions varied at different times, and how the unexpected sight of him led to a sudden temporary loss of self-control. The questions put to her did not seem designed to elicit such an account, if one existed or had ever been explored with Ruth Ellis in the preparation of her case. It has since transpired that her solicitor knew that Cussens had given her the gun but she had asked him not to tell anyone so had not passed that information to counsel.

The evidence was completed and the rest of the day was spent (in the absence of the jury) presenting the legal arguments to Mr Justice Havers. There were then muddled exchanges about the effect of infidelity, jealousy and 'new law'. No mention that she was battered by him and that he had induced a miscarriage by his blows. Finally the judge gave Melford Stevenson the opportunity to clarify the defence position. 'Does your proposition come to this?' he asked. 'If a man associates with a woman and he then leaves her suddenly and does not communicate with her and she is a jealous woman, emotionally disturbed, and goes out and shoots him, that is sufficient ground for the jury to reduce the crime of murder to manslaughter?' No mention whatsoever was made of Blakely's violence, nor of his psychological abuse. Apparently Melford Stevenson was unable to answer Mr Justice Havers's question.

The following morning the trial judge addressed the court before the jury returned. He ruled that there was not sufficient material to support a verdict of manslaughter on the grounds of provocation and that as a matter of law he would so direct the jury. The death sentence was more or less passed at this point. Stevenson made no comment, and indicated that in the circumstances he accepted that he could not make a closing speech to the jury. The judge then summed up, telling the jury that it was not possible to bring in a verdict of manslaughter. The jury retired for 14 minutes before returning with their verdict of guilty. The ritual of the black cap and the grisly formula that she would be taken to a place where she would be hanged by the neck was pronounced. Ruth Ellis was led away.

Despite the uproar at a woman going to the gallows, and many efforts to obtain a reprieve, the execution took place three weeks after the trial, with the traditional crowd gathered outside the prison awaiting the publication of the death notice on the gate. Victor Mishcon, a brilliant solicitor who became a Labour peer, was brought in at the end to see if he could persuade the Home Secretary that the death penalty was excessive in the circumstances of this case. He, by then, knew from Ellis that she had been given the gun shortly before the shooting by a not disinterested party, namely Cussens.

Given the state of the law of homicide at the time, the same result might well have followed whoever the judge and counsel. What ensued, however, was a public debate over whether a distinction should be made between a killing of this kind and a cold-blooded murder. The important postscripts to the Ellis case are that it lent fuel to the powerful campaign to abolish the death penalty, affected the development of a psychiatric defence to murder which fell short of insanity, and helped to codify the provocation law.

Ruth Ellis's case would have been conducted differently today and would very likely have led to her acquittal of murder. This is largely because of the changes in the law, which have introduced a number of fresh concepts to homicide trials. Parliament thought it was being thoroughly modern when it introduced the Homicide Act in 1957 because it established two statutory defences to murder, reducing the offence to manslaughter (a) where the accused was suffering from a mental disorder which diminished his or her criminal responsibility, or (b) where the killing was a response to provocation by words as well as deeds.

Provocation was available as a defence prior to the enactment, but because of concern that vengeful behaviour would escape just punishment, which for murder meant the death penalty at that time, it had been narrowly interpreted in the case law. Provocation was interpreted for juries by the judges as conduct immediately preceding the killing. The archetypal case was that of the betrayed husband finding his faithless wife and her lover in flagrante and killing one or the other, or both, on the spot. There could be no pause for premeditation. Words, for example, could not amount to provocation prior to the 1957 Homicide Act.

As for diminished responsibility, until the Act, the only debate about mental states was whether a defendant was sane or insane according to the 'M'Naghton rules'. There it had to be clearly proved that at the time of committing the alleged offence the party accused was labouring under such a defect of reason or disease of the mind that he did not know the nature and quality of the act he was doing, or that he did not know it was wrong. The defendant had to be so demented that he would think he was squeezing an orange when he was throttling his victim. The test derived from the case in the 1840s of a Scotsman who felt he was being persecuted by the Conservatives because he refused to vote for them; in delusion he murdered a Tory agent. (I used to wonder whether anyone who refused to vote Conservative in those days was readily considered mad by members of the judiciary.) By the 1950s the test had become seriously discredited as a method of determining the mental state of an accused. The verdict of not guilty to murder by reason of diminished responsibility, reducing an unlawful killing to manslaughter, does not require that someone is certifiably insane, just that he or she has a definable degree of mental disorder. The defence can include a difficulty in controlling one's actions, provided this arises from an abnormality of mind. A psychiatrist has to assist the court.

Even today, the issue of whether someone suffers from some abnormality of mind which diminished their responsibility for a killing is one which taxes juries. It used to be said that juries were reluctant to convict people of murder when they faced the death penalty, but even without the ultimate sanction there seems to be an unwillingness in jurors to declare someone guilty of wilful murder when they were in the grip of crushing emotional turmoil at the time. Equally, juries are reluctant to let a person who takes a life escape all sanction, which is why self-defence is rarely successful in murder. The moral conviction that the taking of a life cannot go unmarked is present in the court and there needs to be an overwhelming sense of justification – that one's own life was under immediate threat – before a jury will allow an accused to walk free with no conviction whatsoever. However, the willingness to accept manslaughter as the appropriate plea often depends on the sympathies evoked by the defendant. In mercy killings, where family members bring to an end the misery or pain of a terminally ill relative, judges and juries alike are usually prepared to stretch the definition of diminished responsibility.

There seems little doubt that the outcome of Ruth Ellis's trial in 1955 was affected by a moral evaluation of her way of life – as a sexually active divorcee, a mother of an illegitimate child and a club hostess. The tabloid press would still have a field day at her expense, but today's jury, furnished with as much information as has subsequently come to light, might take a more generous view.

Self-defence is a complete defence to murder and means a defendant walks free from the court if it succeeds. It is permissible in law for someone to act in self-defence if placed in immediate peril and if some instant reaction is necessary to avert the danger. If the attack is over, or is not imminent, then the employment of force may be seen as revenge, or punishment, or the settling of an old score. The force must also be reasonable. The use of a knife, a heavy weight or a gun is often a crucial handicap for a woman, since a weapon may be regarded as involving excessive force and the act of securing it can allow for the argument that her behaviour was calculated or not in immediate response to an attack. Yet many women are incapable of defending themselves without having a weapon to hand.

When men determined what is acceptable conduct in response to attack and what might constitute self-defence, they were thinking of other men, of similar stature and strength, locked in even combat, where the introduction of a weapon would be bad form, stacking the odds on one side. The law takes insufficient account of the disadvantages women feel in the face of male strength. It is illustrative that the most common murder weapon used by wives is the knife, and the scene of her crime is most often the kitchen, while men kill their wives with their bare hands in the bedroom.

An element of subjectivity has been introduced to account for the race, sex, or special characteristic of the person in the dock. This is the narrow opening into which arguments about the history of domestic violence could be crammed, but women are still hamstrung by the spectre of the vengeful wife. It is in the ancient legal authority of Blackstone's *Commentaries* that we find the clear statement that revenge is no defence. The classic pronouncement in modern times, which is used daily to guide us in the courts, comes from Lord Morris of Borth-y-Gest, and in the ordinary case it is a perfect statement of the present law:

It is both good law and good sense that a man who is attacked may defend himself. It is both good law and common sense that he may do, and may only do, what is reasonably necessary. But everything will depend upon the particular facts and circumstances. Of these a jury can decide. It may in some cases be only sensible and clearly possible to take some simple avoiding action. Some attacks may be serious and dangerous. Others may not be. If there is some relatively minor attack, it would not be common sense to permit some act of retaliation which was wholly out of proportion to the necessities of the situation. If an attack is so serious that it puts someone in immediate peril, then immediate defensive action may be necessary. If the moment is one of crisis for someone in immediate danger, he may have to avert the danger by some instant reaction. If the attack is over and no sort of peril remains, then the employment of force may be by way of revenge or punishment or by way of paying off an old score or may be pure aggression. There may be no longer any link with a necessity of defence.

The problem with that statement is that battered women feel incapable of leaving, incapable of taking the commonsensical steps which may be possible between equally matched men. They are no match for their husbands, not just pound for pound in the weighing scales but in their feelings of powerlessness, in the weakness of their low self-esteem. Seeing one event of violence in terms of immediate peril or as a moment of crisis which passes is contextual distortion; when the abuse is constant it is inappropriate to pull out one single fragment of that history. This is a perfect example of a law that by its letter seems fair but in application is anything but. Treating as equal those who are unequal only creates further inequality. Battered women should not be expected to play by the Marquess of Queensberry rules, and it should be recognised that the peril has not passed for a woman and her children when a wife-beater is merely resting before the next round.

The immediacy principle makes no sense when the provocation takes the form of long-term abuse. When a person lives with persistent violence and alcoholism she often becomes overwhelmed. Her whole life is out of control. She would not be thinking rationally for some time, and her feelings often would not manifest themselves as 'snapping', in the form of the crazed outburst, but may seem more controlled: a snapping in slow motion, the final surrender of frayed elastic.

Any study of women who kill their husbands (a crime which in former times was indicted as treason) exposes a history of cumulative violence. Most women who kill a spouse or partner have suffered long-term abuse; yet a significant number would fail the test for provocation. Fortunately for most of the women – or unfortunately from another perspective – the toll of violence usually means they are able to invoke a defence of diminished responsibility, suffering as they almost invariably are from depressive illness or post-traumatic stress disorder as a result of the abuse. By and large this reliance on their psychiatric state takes the sting out of the weakness of the other defences, because the women are then sentenced with appropriate compassion, though there will always be women who slip through that net. There is also the principled concern that women should not be pushed so readily towards a pathological explanation for their behaviour, an argument which seldom troubles women looking at prison bars, who understandably value their liberty and the welfare of their children above all else.

On 9 May 1989 Deepak Ahluwalia had yet again beaten his wife and terrorised her with a hot iron. There was a well-documented history of domestic violence. He had hit her, tried to strangle her, brandished knives at her, pushed her downstairs, sexually abused and raped her, and constantly threatened to kill her. The attacks often took place in the presence of their children, who cowered in fear of him. Kiranjit

Ahluwalia had obtained court injunctions against her husband twice but had failed to get them enforced after threats from his family. Like so many battered wives, she could sense his mood swings and could read the signals which meant the onset of an attack, but she usually felt powerless. That night she could take no more and, when he fell asleep on the bed, she poured petrol over his feet and set it alight.

Deepak's death led to a charge of murder against his wife, a woman who had put up with long-term violence because of cultural constraints.

This is the essence of my culture, society and religion, where a woman is a toy, a plaything. She can be stuck together at will, broken at will. Everybody did what they wanted with me, no one ever bothered to find out what kind of life I was leading after I married – one of physical and mental torture.

The culture into which I was born and where I grew up sees the woman as the honour of the house ... In order to uphold this false 'honour' and glory she is taught to endure many kinds of oppression and pain in silence. Religion also teaches her that her husband is her god and fulfilling his every desire is her religious duty. For ten years I tried wholeheartedly to fulfil the duties endorsed by religion. For ten years I lived a life of beatings and degradation and no one noticed; now the law has decreed that I should serve a sentence for life. Today I have come out of my husband's jail and entered the jail of the law.

For Kiranjit Ahluwalia, diminished responsibility was not argued as there were varied opinions on the nature of her depression after suffering the effects of years of abuse. The problem for Kiranjit Ahluwalia's lawyers was that she had waited for him to fall asleep, and it was this aspect of the evidence that was emphasised by Mr Justice

Leonard. M. J. Willoughby, an American academic lawyer, expressed the opinion that on this view of battered women who kill their sleeping partners 'society gains nothing, except perhaps the additional risk that the battered woman will herself be killed, because she must wait until her abusive husband instigates another battering episode before she can justifiably act'.

The requirement that a battered wife must wait until assault is under way before her apprehensions can be validated in law is an acceptance of murder by instalment. If a person being held hostage killed a terrorist captor, the fact that he was sleeping would be of no consequence. The prison of the violent marriage is hard to contemplate for those on the outside.

In July 1992 Kiranjit Ahluwalia's case came before the Court of Appeal. Attempts were made by my colleague in chambers, Geoffrey Robertson QC, to contextualise his client's behaviour against the background of prolonged violence. He tried to press the argument that immediacy has been an evidential development and that no such requirement exists in law. On 31 July the court quashed Kiranjit's conviction. The three judges, headed by the Lord Chief Justice, Lord Taylor, ordered a retrial, on the grounds that new medical evidence, which might have proved a defence of diminished responsibility, had not been brought forward, and should be tested in court. Lord Taylor went to great lengths in his judgment to say that any alteration in the existing legal definition of 'provocation' as 'temporary and sudden loss of control', must be a matter for Parliament, not for the courts, since it involved changing 'a particular principle of law [which] has been confirmed so many times and applied so generally over such a long period'.

The case of Sara Thornton came to symbolise all that was wrong with the system and set in train some important shifts in the judicial approach to provocation. Sara Thornton stood trial in February 1990 charged with murdering her husband, Malcolm, having attacked him with a knife as he lay drunk on a couch. The Crown accepted that her alcoholic husband was deeply violent towards her, but maintained that she had attacked him in a calculated way, having deliberately gone into the kitchen and sharpened the knife. Because she had had periods of mental breakdown in the past and because of the delay between her husband's last threat and her strike, Sara's trial lawyers saw this as a case of diminished responsibility, but her plea to that effect was not accepted by the Crown, and she was convicted.

The psychiatric evidence of the defence was that Sara Thornton was in a state technically described as a 'fugue' at the time she killed her husband. This term would seem to describe an interval where the person is not in control. In answer to questions by the prosecutor the psychiatrist agreed that this was not a treatable condition. What Sara Thornton was undoubtedly suffering from was the cumulative effect of domestic violence and the psychological demands of dealing with a chronically alcoholic partner. She had only been married to Malcolm Thornton for 10 months, but those months had taken their toll. She was, in the language of provocation, no longer mistress of her own mind at the time of the killing, hence the 'fugue' state, but she was not fulfilling the definition of diminished responsibility: an abnormality of mind. She was functioning in conformance with the classical provo-cation scenario, except that there was no word or deed triggering her action. It was an accumulation of abuse, evoked as her husband lay on the couch, which drove her to violence.

Unlike English law, which viewed the elements of suddenness restrictively, Australian law would have had no problem with the delay which preceded Sara's action. Judges there have long recognised the concept of cumulative provocation, acknowledging that a series of incidents, which may in themselves be trivial, could constitute serious provocation if viewed collectively. It is accepted that deliberate preparations for killing may be made while in the heat of passion and that such deliberations are distinguishable from cases of pre-planned killings.

The common law in Australia has been developed in a way that is attuned to women's lives, and the judges' decisions have been consolidated in legislation which specifically stipulates that the provocative conduct of the deceased is relevant, 'whether it occurred immediately before the act or omission causing death or at any previous time'. The statute states unequivocally that provocation is not negated as a matter of law where 'the act or omission causing death was not an act or omission done suddenly'.

However, counsel for the Crown in Sara Thornton's case maintained to the jury that an acquittal would provide Sara Thornton, and I suppose any like-minded women, with 'a licence to kill'.

At her appeal in July 1991, Sara's new counsel, Lord Gifford, argued that 'the slow-burning emotion of a woman driven to the end of her tether ... may be a loss of self-control in just the same way as a sudden rage'. However, this argument was not accepted in Sara's case; her appeal failed because the court remained influenced by the fact that she had equipped herself with a sharpened knife and had in the week before his death threatened to kill Malcolm Thornton. At a later appeal she was released, but on the grounds that her mental state at the time amounted to diminished responsibility.

Other women have fallen foul of this same problem; their behaviour was seen as premeditated because, evidentially, delay before action is interpreted that way. However, in the context of the abuse, and because of the genuine belief in the omnipotence of the abuser, the killing seems to the woman like a rational and coherent response.

In the same week that Sara Thornton's first appeal failed, a trial judge accepted Joseph McGrail's plea to manslaughter of his wife on the grounds of provocation and passed a suspended sentence. McGrail had lived with Marion Kennedy for more than 20 years. They had two sons, both handicapped and both in care. Ten years previously Marion had begun to drink and eventually became addicted to sleeping pills. When she had been drinking she used to insult her husband and swear at him. She was a scold, a nag.

One day in February 1991, when McGrail returned from work to find her drunk again, he could stand no more. He kicked her hard enough to cause her to die of internal bleeding. The judge commented that living with Marion 'would have tried the patience of a saint'.

In March 1992 Rajinder Bisla, having strangled his 'nagging' wife in front of his three children, was also given a suspended sentence. No doubt, like Joseph McGrail, he snapped, and we should welcome the humanity which was shown to him. Justice for women does not have to be secured by denying it to men. However, the willingness to recognise the male experience is a reflection of the male nature of our courts. Nagging is seen as the female equivalent to violence. Yet men married to intolerable women usually have many more alternatives available to them and find it easier to leave.

However, from the early nineties the courts in fact shifted the parameters of provocation in response to the urgings of women seeking justice. Cases like that of Emma Humphreys educated the judiciary, politicians and the public about the law's shortcomings. In 1985 Emma Humphreys, aged 17, was jailed for the murder of her violent boyfriend and pimp, Trevor Armitage, who had introduced her to prostitution. After suffering months of physical, sexual and emotional abuse, she stabbed him when she thought he was about to attack her again – but did not tell the trial about the abuse. In 1995, after 10 years in prison, the Court of Appeal reduced her conviction to manslaughter and she walked free. As a result of these cases, a jury was directed to put themselves in the shoes of the woman on trial and to consider the context of events. There came a recognition that the courts must acknowledge cumulative provocation, where after a history of abuse the final act which tips a woman over the edge may not seem very grave but may be the last straw. The question of the time frame was also widened so that judges made it clear to a jury that 'immediacy' should not be interpreted literally. While clearly a woman would not be entitled to go days later to kill her abusive partner, a delay before acting did not preclude the defence. What was not allowed, though, were acts born of revenge rather than anger or despair.

By the early 2000s, attitudes towards women accused of manslaughter where abuse played a part were changing.

In 2001, my client Michaela Wrenn stood trial for the murder of a young man called Justin Chant. The allegation was that she, along with her older partner, Stephen Sullivan, and a young man called Lee Smith, had held Chant captive and starved him to death. The facts were horrifying, describing a cruelty beyond measure. What Chant experienced would have constituted torture in any international tribunal – food deprivation, no drinking water, deafening sound, a freezing cold shower, confinement in a space where the tiniest movement was impossible, no sanitation so that he had to sit in his own excrement with no inkling of what might happen next. He was kept in the dark and then brought cowering into the light to be subjected to verbal abuse, intimidation and aggression. The level of fear engendered was so great that Justin Chant did not ever cry out for help, not a sound. These activities, which compared to the behaviour of Latin American death squads and torturers, were taking place in a council flat in Essex.

The orchestrator of this prolonged punishment was Sullivan, a small-time crook and drug dealer, who reigned like a tyrant over his tight coterie of confederates. All the people he drew around him were vulnerable; boys like Justin Chant who had been in care, like Lee Smith who was physically disabled and lonely, or his girlfriend Michaela Wrenn who had been abused by her stepfather and run away from home when she was only 16 to be with Sullivan, a man twice her age. Stephen Sullivan's persecution of Justin, who was already treated like a slave, was for some trifling misdemeanour. The prosecution case was that Sullivan was indeed the central killer, a malevolent, dangerous man, but their argument was that Wrenn and Smith had willingly participated in the torture and death by doing nothing to secure help or to alleviate the torture of their victim.

However, as the Crown prepared their case an extraordinary picture of Sullivan came to light. More and more women gave statements telling of their suffering at his hands, though they had to be compelled to do so. His own mother had been battered by him when he was still a boy. His sisters lived in terror of him. One after another 10 women gave accounts of the most horrifying abuse against them and their children. The judge ruled that the Crown could not use the material as part of their case as it was so prejudicial to the accused, but for Michaela Wrenn and Lee Smith the evidence was vital as it explained their terror of and manipulation by Sullivan. After lengthy legal arguments during the trial, the judge conceded that the evidence was admissible to support the defence of Michaela Wrenn that she was a battered woman who was so paralysed by fear for her own life that she could do nothing to help Justin Chant. The fear Sullivan generated, even after many years without contact, meant that witness summonses had to be issued; the women with whom he had relationships were so afraid to come to court, so afraid to face him, even when he was in the dock between two prison officers and behind a security screen, that the court had to order their attendance.

Once there, the women recounted violence and cruelty of such magnitude that it was hard to listen to. Some of it was indescribable. He had shoved his hand into one woman's mouth and forced it open with such ferocity that it tore, leaving a scar which extended up the side of her face. He had beaten, kicked and humiliated these women when they were expecting his children. He had broken into their homes after they dared to change locks. When they tried to escape he found them. The women had no connection with each other but patterns emerged, creating a vivid picture of a controlling, domi-nating bully who surrounded himself with pliant, vulnerable people many years his junior, who became enslaved to him out of terror. The evidence showed a man who never reached maturation, driving around in flashy vehicles, spending hours cleaning them or getting others to do so, touring the streets with loud 'look at me' music blaring from his woofer; his obsessional concern about clothing, insisting that seams were pressed on his T-shirts, that his socks were ironed, that the soles of his trainers were cleaned; his bragging connections with criminals; his demands for constant attention that meant he was even jealous of a woman's child; his extraordinary control of women by impregnation. This was a man who had fathered 18 children, as if tattooing himself on these women so that they could never be beyond his power.

A number of the women described attempting suicide because of their despair. Some of the hardest pieces of evidence for the jury related to children: the smashing of a child's face for crackling a crisp packet; a small boy, little more than a baby, hiding wet pyjama bottoms for fear of the punishment that would be exacted – being locked in a dark cupboard; a hungry baby being left to scream while its mother wept because Sullivan decided when babies were fed; the pouring of a child's antibiotics down the sink. One mother described the day her daughter did not return home. She watched the clock and knew with each passing minute that she had run away, that her daughter was free. Although she had lost her child, she was happy for her because 'at least she had got away.'

Michaela Wrenn remained under Sullivan's spell until shortly before her trial, because even from prison he was able to exert control over her. It was with the support of decent, kind people that she began to recover her self-worth and to see that she could be free of him. Her greatest act of courage was going into the witness box and testifying against him. It was one of the most moving cases I have ever conducted.

The question for the jury was whether Michaela Wrenn, as a free agent, was a party to the murder of Justin Chant. But the jury had no difficulty acquitting her and also Lee Smith. They knew that she was no more able to stop Sullivan's cruelty towards Justin Chant than she was able to stop his cruelty towards her. Stephen Sullivan was sentenced to 23 years' imprisonment. Most of the women he had abused came to see him sentenced, to be sure that he was really going to jail. I was embraced by them all at the end of the case.

This was a case at the extreme end of the scale but only because one woman after the other told her tale. Had any one of those women appeared in court as a solitary complainant of abuse, they would have faced the same old claims of exaggeration and invention and they would have been asked sceptically 'if it was so bad why didn't you leave?'

Prosecutors and police find it hard to understand that a woman may be battered by more than one partner, and they draw from such a history the conclusion that the woman must make the men batter her. It is her fault. What is so often misunderstood is that men who abuse usually have a radar system, drawing them to women who will have underlying vulnerabilities – women who have had rotten lives, who think they deserve no better, who have been sexually abused or traumatised in childhood. It is not always so. Women from a secure and stable background can also be battered or psychologically abused, but it is often the case that abusive men seek out women who feel fortunate to be loved at all. Their unerring antennae takes them straight to women who are less likely to walk away at the first slap.

Since the turn of the century there has been a quantum leap in the court's understanding of the forces which drive women to kill. Cases are now being handled with increasing comprehension of domestic violence, which is invariably the backdrop to domestic homicide, whether it is a husband or wife who is in the dock. Judges and juries can be greatly assisted by hearing from experts like the psychologist Sandra Horley, who as chief executive of Refuge has worked for years with battered women, counselling over 3,000. Psychiatrists like Dr Gillian Mezey and Dr Nigel Eastman have now extensive experience of dealing with cases of women who kill after a history of domestic violence and they regularly testify in court about the dynamic which is set up in abusive relationships and the consequent post-traumatic stress disorder or battered women's syndrome which victims of abuse suffer.

Women have also been helped by the fact that that prominent actor in the dramatis personae of the courtroom, 'the reasonable man', took his final bow when the new statutory defence of loss of self-control was created in 2009 in the Coroners and Justice Act. His long journey on the Clapham omnibus came to an end. 'Of course, we all know there is no such thing as the reasonable woman,' was always the law lecturer's cheeky joke. The fictional 'reasonable man' was frequently invoked in criminal trials whenever juries were asked to apply a common-sense standard of acceptable behaviour. The new defence of loss of self-control which can reduce murder to manslaughter required a qualifying 'trigger' to cause the loss of self-control that resulted in the killing. The jury would then be asked if a person of the same sex and age as the accused with a normal degree of tolerance and self-restraint would have acted similarly in the circumstances. This statutory defence gave us a modern reshaping of the old provocation defence and I like to think that my argument for law reform set out in *Eve Was Framed* laid some of the groundwork for this legal change. The Act also expressly provides that the defence cannot be triggered by the victim's infidelity.

Some campaigners feel that it is unjust that a woman is convicted of manslaughter after killing a manifestly brutal partner and have argued for a new defence of 'pre-emptive strike' self-defence. This would provide a woman with a complete defence if she kills her partner when he is asleep or drunk because she has become so convinced that he is going to kill her when he wakens. The very language replicates George Bush's justification for breaking international law and waging war on Iraq and I am deeply opposed to it. His position was that waiting for Saddam Hussein to take definitive offensive steps towards the West was unnecessary so he was entitled to bomb Baghdad to blazes. But that argument was not persuasive to most of the world. Similarly, most people would not be enthusiastic about a perfectly rational woman planning and then blowing out the brains of her sleeping husband, even if she was terrified of him. They may be content to see her culpability reduced to manslaughter in the right circum-stances but not to see the killing vindicated. Legal reform must always be undertaken while looking in your wing mirrors; otherwise ghastly coaches are driven through your best intentions.

Despite these advances, women are still convicted of murder where many have felt it should have been manslaughter. Especially where women are young and vivacious it is hard for juries to accept their high levels of fear. I was in a taxi not long ago where the taxi driver recognised me and said he had been on my jury in a case where my battered client had been acquitted of murdering her husband. He told me that the women on the jury had been the ones who delayed in reaching a not-guilty verdict; they thought it possible that my client had provoked her husband's violence by her flirtatious conduct. Sometimes women can be tougher on their own gender than men. However, the solicitor Harriet Wistrich believes in some of the plausible cases of miscarriage of justice the failure is related to the poor preparation of the woman's case and the failure to secure good psychiatric assessment by trial solicitors and counsel who know nothing about the effects of long-term abuse or domestic violence.

A root-and-branch review of the homicide laws is still needed. Judges complain that current rules force them to treat all people convicted of murder in the same way. The mandatory life sentence should be abolished. It fails to reflect the wide variations in crimes now classified as murder – at one extreme, the sadistic killing of a child, and at the other, the assistance given to a patient who is dying and begs for the pain to be ended. Life should be made the maximum sentence, rather than mandatory, and it should be left to the judge to sentence according to the circumstances. However, the government is committed to the mandatory life sentence because the law-and-order lobby holds too much sway and the mandatory life sentence was the price for abolishing capital punishment.

Given the intransigence on the mandatory life sentence for murder, there should also be a new partial defence created of 'killing in extremis', which would cover a carer who kills purely to end the suffering of someone who is terminally ill, or someone who kills in circumstances where there is extraordinary mitigation, such as after rape or the murder of one's child. Such mitigatory circumstances should reduce murder to manslaughter. This suggestion is likely to be highly controversial but I make it only as an alternative to the ending of the mandatory life sentence, which I consider preferable. This new mitigatory defence could cover situations where a woman deliberately killed her partner after terrible abuse but was not able to invoke diminished responsibility or loss-of-control defences.

Murder is the most serious crime of all. That is why we have to progress with caution when it comes to reform. But we also have to keep remembering that women rarely kill, yet they are frequently murdered.

8

WICKED WOMEN

I n almost every culture and every period of history, a she-devil
emerges as an example of all that is rotten in the female sex. This
Medusa draws together the many forms of female perversion: a
woman whose sexuality is debauched and foul, pornographic and
possibly bisexual; a woman who knows none of the fine and noble
instincts when it comes to men and children; a woman who lies and
deceives, manipulates and corrupts. A woman who is clever and
powerful. This is a woman who is far deadlier than any male, in fact
not a woman at all.

The perversion of the human spirit that underlies crimes of
desperate cruelty invokes an atavistic desire to punish till the end of
time those who inflict such pain, not just on the victims, but on the
scarred families who are left to mourn. It is tempting to characterise

all women criminals as victims, because so many of those who go through the system have themselves been at the receiving end of criminal behaviour. There has been a tendency in fighting the women's corner for feminists to go into denial about women's capacity for cruelty and wickedness. However, there are women who commit crimes as terrible as any committed by men. They just happen to be the outliers. Men enter the pantheon of monsters more often than women; one thinks of John Christie, Peter Sutcliffe, Denis Nilsson. But those convicted of killing who do not belong to the dominant culture are more likely to be mythologised. The imprisonment of Myra Hindley has come to stand for more than simple punishment for an abhorrent crime; her long incarceration symbolised our fear of returning to a more primitive past. In an increasingly secular world, a woman like Myra Hindley is the vessel into which society pours its dark secrets; like a war criminal, such a 'she-devil' is a reminder of what is horribly possible.

Myra Hindley was and remains the embodiment of all that is unnatural in women. Yet if you ask people under 50 what she actually did, they are uncertain, apart from a hazy appreciation that children were killed and that the case had sadistic sexual overtones.

It is impossible to fathom what corruption or disturbance of the human spirit can account for the horrible crimes Ian Brady and Myra Hindley committed, and no lawyer is going to be able to provide the answers.

The investigation began in October 1965 when David Smith, the brother-in-law of Myra Hindley, informed Manchester Police that he had been witness to the savage murder by Ian Brady of a 17-year-old youth. On the information he provided, the police went immediately to the address of Ian Brady and Myra Hindley and found the boy's dead body cleaved by an axe. Brady maintained at his trial that the boy was homosexual and that he had picked him up with Smith to 'queer roll' him for money, and that the death resulted accidentally when the boy struggled.

In a notebook discovered in the house was a list of names, including that of John Kilbride, a 12-year-old boy who had gone missing two years before. The police sensed that they might be dealing with a complex investigation and scoured the couple's property for information of John Kilbride's whereabouts. They found a quantity of photographs taken on the nearby moors, and with the assistance of a neighbour's child the location of a number of other photographs was identified. A search of Saddleworth Moor unearthed the body of another missing child, Lesley Ann Downey, who had disappeared the previous year.

The case began to come together when David Smith also recollected that he had seen Ian Brady remove two suitcases from the house which could not be found. They were discovered in the left-luggage office at the city's central station and contained crucial evidence linking the pair to the body of the little girl. Days later, the body of John Kilbride was also found on the moors.

The contents of the cases included books on sexual perversion, coshes, photographs of Lesley Ann naked, and a tape-recording of her screams, pleading not to be subjected to whatever was happening. The voices of Ian Brady and Myra Hindley are clearly audible, remonstrating with the little girl, telling her to shut up and to cooperate. The child is threatened and told to put something in her mouth. The playing of that tape in the court did more than any other piece of evidence to secure the convictions.

At their trial in 1965 at Chester, Myra Hindley was presented by both Brady himself and the prosecution as his faithful lieutenant. In the popular press she was described as his sex slave, and there was little doubt at the time that, while her role was criminal and appalling, she was not the prime mover in the murders. The trial judge, Mr Justice Fenton Atkinson, suggested she might be capable of reform. He said: 'Though I believe that Brady is wicked beyond belief without hope of redemption, I cannot feel the same is necessarily true of Hindley once she is removed from his influence.' Yet as the years passed she moved centre stage. Brady's psychosis became well established, and he ended up serving his sentence in a penal institution for the mentally insane until his death in 2016. The mad dog was safely caged; whatever power he once wielded, he became, we are told, a pathetic, demented specimen.

Not so Myra Hindley, whose survival and persistence in seeking parole right up to her death in November 2002 was seen as a testament against her. Her academic success and her support from prominent campaigners like Lord Longford and Lord Astor served only to compound public perceptions of her as a highly intelligent, scheming woman and put paid to any suggestion that we were dealing with a psychiatric case here.

I acted for her in 1974 when she pleaded guilty to plotting with a prison warder to escape from prison. The warder was a former nun called Pat Cairns, who had fallen in love with Myra. Their affair, which lasted three years, created a media-feeding frenzy of prurience about lesbianism, and the papers paid former inmates for stories about alleged sexual trysts in the chapel at Holloway Prison. Here, they inferred, was further proof of deviance. It has more recently come to light that senior police became fixated at the time of the escape plot with the possibility that this was an even wider and darker conspiracy than was made public, combining whole swathes of the most feared women in the system, including members of the Angry Brigade and the IRA. A detective chief superintendent at Scotland Yard called Frank McGuinness compiled a report making very tenuous connections between Pat Cairns and a couple of women who had spurious links to the Angry Brigade, who were in turn deemed supporters of the IRA. From this wild concoction of surmise, he suggested in a report recently opened by the National Archive that the prison escape was going to throw open the gates of Holloway also for the Price sisters, who had been convicted of the Old Bailey bombing in 1973. It was the stuff of misogynistic nightmares.

In 1994 Myra Hindley published a letter, begging: 'After 30 years in prison, I think I have paid my debt to society and atoned for my crimes. I ask people to judge me as I am now, and not as I was then.' She claimed in 1998 that she had been abused by Brady, who had threatened to kill her mother and grandmother and sister if she did not participate in the killings. She applied again and again for parole but successive Home Secretaries refused to relent, knowing that the public would be enraged. Even when she was dying of cancer she remained in prison.

Dreadful crimes challenge belief in fundamental goodness, and if there is no understandable motive, such as jealousy or greed or a response to some form of provocation, we cannot comprehend them. We are disturbed at our failure to categorise the conduct, beyond accepting that it falls well beyond the bounds of moral acceptability. We are happier cataloguing the deed as a result of madness, because we do not then have to deal with the troubling concept of wicked-ness. Madness, for all its elusiveness, is a label which gives us comfort in the face of inexplicable behaviour. Yet there is ambivalence about how it is used. The public want murderers convicted as 'murderers' rather than madmen if they have killed in cruel and vicious ways; they want lunacy to be diagnosed after the magnitude of the crimes is recognised, not before. The catharsis of public condemnation has to be ritually experienced.

In the case of Peter Sutcliffe, the Yorkshire Ripper, the judge felt that the issue of the accused's sanity should be tried by a jury. It would have been wrong for a decision about the state of Sutcliffe's mind to have been resolved by a cabal of lawyers and medical men, even if their opinions were completely sound. Public involvement in such decisions is crucial, because it maintains a balance between the vox populi and the law. If it had been decided that Peter Sutcliffe was not guilty by reason of insanity and he had been sent to Broadmoor, a secure hospital, under section 60 of the Mental Health Act, the public would have felt aggrieved. That a serial killer who had stalked women, attacked them, sexually assaulted, mutilated and killed them, and also put all women in fear of their lives, should not carry the label murderer would have seemed like an affront. In fact, the jury decided that he was not criminally insane, but since his initial incarceration he has been transferred to Broadmoor in recognition of his deep psychopathy.

Many lawyers in the Temple felt that the trial was a show put on for public consumption; they thought it was an abuse of the process, as Sutcliffe's psychiatric state should have been recognised. Psychiatrists of considerable reputation were publicly undermined, and it was subsequently shown by his move to a mental institution that what they were saying was true. It is all too easy to be sceptical of a defendant's descriptions of hallucinations or divine injunctions to commit crime, but psychiatrists with a wealth of experience do know when they are dealing with a psychopath. Although the jury had no hesitation in deciding that in their view Sutcliffe was not criminally insane, that does not necessarily mean they doubted his madness. What they wanted was the law to acknowledge his wickedness and they were unable to contemplate returning verdicts of not guilty to murder but guilty of manslaughter. The label of murder was important. I am sure, however, that the jurors who listened to the roll call of Sutcliffe's violence ultimately found it reassuring that his crimes could be attributed to some deep-seated mental abnormality.

There is a conflict between seeking an explanation for the inexplicable in madness and an unwillingness to allow madness to become an excuse. When we ask ourselves, how could someone do that to another human being, to an innocent child? we want someone to make the behaviour intelligible to us. We hope that psychiatry might have all the answers and that evil might be rendered obsolete, but the medical profession is not as magical or all-powerful as we like to believe. Explanations for deliberate acts of criminality are sometimes not available; although these occasions are comparatively rare, there are motiveless crimes with no suggestion of diagnosed disease of the mind. And, of course, if they are denied by those charged with their commission, no insight comes from the offender.

Evil as a concept is resisted by some people, but the majority do accept the idea of evil and want punishment for its perpetrators. Sexual depravity as a component in killing heightens our revulsion, and our inability to understand becomes the more pressing if children are involved. However, countless men have been convicted of revolting crimes, beyond the imagination of most people – raping and mutilating, torturing and killing, severing and dismembering – in a nightmare of atrocities that make one long for the simple bullet in the head or the knife wound. These men fill the chambers of horrors, but few of them are remembered by name.

We feel differently about a woman doing something consciously cruel because of our expectations of women as the nurturing sex. The adage is that women who commit crime are mad, bad or sad. The bad may be few in number but once given the label there is no forgiving. It defies explanation that someone, especially a woman, stood by and allowed torture to take place, but it is important to remember that women did it in the concentration camps and evidence is emerging that women are doing it in Syria and Iraq with IS. Mary Bell, the 10-year-old girl who said she strangled two small children 'for fun', also perplexed and terrified the British public because her behaviour contradicted the sugar-and-spice make-up that little girls are expected to have. Yet in every child's fairy story the delicate heroine is contrasted with a wicked woman who is there to put fear into the hearts of little boys (and girls), a reminder of corrupted womanhood. Wicked witches, old crones, evil stepmothers and ugly sisters leap from the pages in greater numbers even than the giants and ogres. Terror is a man, but wickedness is a woman. These women, who either have a cruel beauty like the stepmother of Snow White or are as ugly as sin, insinuate themselves into positions of power over children and grown men, luring them to danger, plumping them up for a final devouring, cutting them to pieces.

Most police mugshots are less than flattering, but the photograph of Myra Hindley which is forever used in the press is in a class of its own, and bears little resemblance to the woman I acted for in 1974. The female who looks out from that photograph with steely eyes has badly dyed, dishevelled hair and a heavy face. Her mouth is tight and mean. This is a woman to hate.

In 1986 the moors murders case was reopened when Ian Brady was said in the press to have confessed to reporters that he had also killed two other young people, Keith Bennett and Pauline Reade. In the prison interviews with the police which followed this disclosure, Ian Brady refused to help, but Myra Hindley admitted that they had been murdered. She described the unbearable pain of confessing to crimes of such enormity, but wanted the whole thing to be laid to rest for herself and for the families. Her years of imprisonment had provided ample opportunity for self-analysis and introspection, and she was able to describe the fierceness of her passion for Ian Brady, who had such a powerful hold upon her at the time, but her attempts at explanation only fuelled the cynicism of police and public. The lucid explanation that Myra Hindley herself put forward to explain (but not excuse) her involvement in the killings – that she was then a naive young girl totally in the thrall of a complex, experienced man – missed its mark because of the very coherence with which it was expressed. From the knowledge of her as the woman she had become, the public found it hard to extract a sense of the woman that she was then.

An obsessional quality, which she continued to possess, was clearly revealed in the personal diary that Myra Hindley kept when she first met Ian Brady at their place of work. The entries are a catalogue of childish desperation for him to show some interest in her, and since they were not written for public consumption and were penned before the spiral of degradation was under way, they support her contention that she was deeply immature. But it is hard to see beyond the strength of character and force of will which she came to exude in middle age. Her all-too-late confessions of guilt in relation to the original charges and the further admissions of two additional murders were hard to interpret as genuine repentance, and appeared rather as part of calculated machinations to get herself released. Press revelations of her lesbian relationships in prison, in an era of deeply ingrained hostility to anyone who was gay never mind a convicted felon, had further stoked the fires of abhorrence.

There are very few female serial killers, by which I mean people who murder strangers successively. The closest we have seen in the UK is Joanna Dennehy, who pleaded guilty to the Peterborough ditch murders in November 2013. She had stabbed three men to death and dumped their bodies in ditches outside the city. She was assisted in the disposal by two male friends. She also pleaded guilty to attempted murder of two other male victims, having on her own account to a psychiatrist for the Crown got the taste for killing and found it 'more-ish'. She would not give those prosecuting her the satisfaction of a trial and her sister claimed Joanna Dennehy's plea of guilty to all charges was to control the situation, as she liked people to know she was boss.

One of the men she killed was her lover, a man called Lee; the others were his housemates. So these were not the killings of strangers. The dead body of Lee had been clothed in a sequin dress by the accused. The attempted murders, which followed soon after this killing spree, were also of men known to her. She had a star tattooed on her face and self-harmed while in prison before her appearance in court. She had told psychiatrists that she would not kill any woman, especially the mother of children. While the Crown produced psychiatric reports, diagnosing her as a psychopath, the defence did not seem to get very far in finding out what dark matter lay behind her conduct. Despite her plea of guilty no motive was offered for her crimes. Even murderous psychopaths usually have some distorted rationale for their killings but none was forthcoming from Joanna Dennehy. As she was sentenced for the murders at the Old Bailey, she also pleaded guilty to further charges of preventing the lawful burial of her victims and said in challenge to the judge: 'I've pleaded guilty and that's that. I'm not coming down here again just to say the same stuff. It's a long way to come to say the same thing I've just said.'

Joanna Dennehy was a spree killer and undoubtedly a psychopath but not a serial murderer as they are normally understood. I am aware of no case where the killer is a lone female operator, who stalks successive prey with whom she has no connection whatsoever. Despite efforts by Hollywood to create movies along those lines, there seems to be no female Boston Strangler or Yorkshire Ripper. The one woman who has come closest to this systematic taking of life was the American prostitute Aileen Wuornos whose pathetic life was immortalised in the film *Monster*. Wuornos was severely abused as a child and as an adult sex worker killed a succession of male clients, though the evidence was that she committed the murders in the company of her girlfriend. There are other bizarre instances of multiple killing like Mary Beth Tinning, an American, who gave birth to nine babies in fourteen years and killed them all, year after year, or when women carers, such as nurses or keepers of old people's homes, kill their charges. When the nurse Beverly Allitt stood trial in 1991 for the killing of babies and young children the public were horrified. She was diagnosed as suffering from Munchausen's syndrome by proxy in which women use the ostensibly caring role of mother, nurse or nanny to inflict harm on children. While she was clearly shown to be highly disturbed and dangerous, the degree to which her offences were treated with disbelief and then moral panic reflected the extent to which she, as a nurse caring for children, had shattered the image of womanhood held most sacred by the general public.

Men who commit multiple homicides against women are usually involved in a misogynistic power-play deriving from a deep-rooted anger against the opposite sex, often directing their perverse rage at women they perceive as bad. The blame for the criminality of the serial killer is frequently put on his maternal relationship or lack of one. Powerless women do not seem to seek indiscriminate vengeance against men in the same way.

On the few occasions when women have played a role in serial killings, as in the moors and Manson murders, they have functioned as handmaidens to a master. This is not the same dynamic as the battered wife who submits or colludes because of her own passivity in the face of violence. These are women in the power of strong-willed men who kill to express their scorn for humanity, men who see themselves as superior and are empowered by exacting the ultimate price from their victims. Some women feel perversely flattered at being chosen by such men, as though they had been singled out from the ordinary run of womankind.

There are people whose sexual make-up seems to require a relinquishing of personal will; it implies never having to face moral responsibility for sexual indiscretion or having to accept guilt if your deviance becomes criminal. It may be that at that time in her life Myra Hindley needed Brady's sexual control just as much as he needed a witness to his atrocities, and that they then became welded together by their mutual knowledge.

No one should be surprised at Myra Hindley's reconstructing of the past. We all do it, and the enormity of her shame must require some delusion. But every attempt she made to explain her acts only fed the view of her as a devious, manipulative woman. Her own gender is especially repulsed by her crimes.

Rosemary West has now replaced Myra Hindley as the female monster within our jails. She is still an enigma because she failed to testify at her trial and has withdrawn into silence. Frederick and Rosemary West were arrested in February 1994 after their garden was dug up during a search for their daughter, Heather, who had gone missing seven years previously. The police unearthed more than one body. In interview, Fred West admitted having killed his daughter and two other young women but insisted that Rose knew nothing at all.

However, in the excavations of the house which followed, six other bodies were found. Fred was not a novice at murder when he met Rose; he had killed before they ever met. He admitted murdering his first wife and a previous lover and hinted that other bodies were buried in shallow graves but it was in his relationship with Rose that a campaign of sexual depravity reached its apotheosis. Together they would lure hitchhikers into their car – young women reassured by the presence of a woman. Then they would abduct their victims, violate them sexually and then kill them. The vile torture to which the women were subjected was so terrible that the press felt inhibited about printing all the details. Rosemary West may have been drawn into killing because of her infatuation with Fred but she could not claim immaturity as Myra Hindley did. Rose took part in serial killing over many years. There was direct evidence that she herself was a sexual abuser and not just an aider and abetter. On New Year's Day 1995 Fred West committed suicide in prison leaving Rose to stand trial alone in October 1995. She was convicted on 10 counts of murder and sentenced to life imprisonment.

The idea of contemporary witches may seem laughable, but women who murder summon up a special revulsion, especially if they do not present in a sympathetic way. Ruth Ellis did not cry in court. Myra Hindley did not cry. Joanna Dennehy actually laughed. Real women cry. Yet even when they do, it can be met with scepticism. When Ian Huntley stood trial in 2003 for the murder of Holly Wells and Jessica Chapman, two 10-year-old girls, his girlfriend Maxine Carr was also in the dock, charged with providing him with a false alibi. Carr's account to the police was that she was upstairs in the bath when the little girls came to the house asking for her. She claimed that she heard Ian speak to them outside but that they then left without anything untoward happening. She was in fact 100 miles away in Grimsby. In the week before being arrested she helped Ian Huntley clean the whole house from top to bottom, which meant that possible forensic evidence was unavailable.

At her trial Maxine Carr admitted lying but described her relationship with Ian as one in which he was controlling, jealous and at times violent. She said that she had provided an alibi for Huntley at his insistence because he had been falsely accused of rape in the past and said he might face the finger of unjust blame again because of that history. She said she could not let herself believe that he had killed the girls. However, Detective Chief Inspector Hebb, number two in the inquiry team, was unimpressed by Carr's tearful performance in the witness box, still convinced that she must have had her suspicions about what Huntley had done. 'Rather cynically is how I view it,' he told the *Observer* in December 2003. His view so publicly expressed fed into the general vilification of Maxine Carr in the press. Public vitriol was such that she had to be given a fresh identity and placed in a safe house on her release from prison.

This outrage reaches fever pitch when women commit crimes against their own children. On 19 February 2008, Karen Matthews reported her nine-year-old daughter missing from her home in Yorkshire. A huge search operation was mounted by the police and local community, during which Matthews made televised pleas for her daughter's safe return. Widespread public sympathy turned immediately to vitriol when it was discovered that Matthews herself had drugged her daughter and was hiding her at the house of an accomplice called Michael Donovan. Both Matthews and Donovan were sentenced to eight years' imprisonment for their horrific hoax. Yet while Donovan was portrayed in the media as a loner and an oddball, the real vilification was reserved for Matthews. It was 'Britain's most hated mum' who had committed that additional crime seemingly reserved only for women, and which we've seen over and over again in this book, that of failing to display the natural maternal instinct supposedly innate in the female sex.

One of the cases which dominated the news in the last decade and which created a new she-devil in criminal iconography was that of Amanda Knox, who was initially convicted of murdering Meredith Kercher in Perugia, Italy, in November 2007. Ultimately she had her conviction definitively quashed in 2016 by the Italian Supreme Court of Cassation but not before every detail of her sex life had been minutely examined and laid before the public via the Internet and the tabloids.

Meredith Kercher, a British student of politics and Italian at Leeds University, was undertaking a year of study abroad as part of her degree. She was brutally murdered. Her throat was cut with such ferocity her head was almost severed. She was found semi-naked in her bed in a house she shared with Amanda Knox.

Knox, an American, and her Italian boyfriend, Raffaele Sollecito, were interrogated and eventually charged with the murder. A man called Rudy Guede was also charged with murder and tried in parallel proceedings.

However, it was Knox who captured the salacious fascination of the media when her diary was leaked from the prison to a journalist and her sex life was revealed in lurid detail. She said she had recorded her relationships because she was wrongly informed by the Italian prison authorities that she was HIV-positive and she was cataloguing those with whom she had had sex. The Italian prosecutor claimed that Amanda Knox's motive for killing her housemate was Knox's 'lack of morality'. She was filled with a desire 'for pleasure at any cost' and marks on Meredith showed the knife had been wielded 'teasingly' with the point piercing the neck before being plunged into the young woman whom he alleged was Amanda Knox's victim.

Rudy Guede was convicted of murdering Meredith and of sexually assaulting her. Guede was a known burglar and his bloodstained fingerprints were found on Meredith's possessions.

When Amanda Knox was filmed after her eventual reprieve, she spoke about how she came to be perceived. 'I was some heinous whore – bestial, sex-obsessed and unnatural.' She pointed out that she had had sex with seven men – not a world record. There is no doubt that her sexual desire as a young woman was used to implicate her in the murder. She was asked on prime-time television whether she was into deviant sex. Throughout the case, judgements about Amanda Knox were being based on how we perceive female sexuality and what it says about a woman if she has multiple lovers. It is these extraneous factors which make justice processes for women so much more fraught with risk and injustice.

In her authoritative book *Women Who Kill*, Ann Jones suggests that moral panics about women and crime coincide with the periods when women make strides towards equality, and that such panics may be a crude and perhaps even unconscious attempt at controlling these advances. She cites the cases of two 20th-century American examples of the female criminal, Ruth Snyder and Alice Crimmins, in support of this view, placing both historically in times of dynamic change for women. Ruth Snyder was tried with her lover Judd Gray in 1927 for the killing of her husband, who had been bludgeoned to death with a sash weight. Alice Crimmins was tried in the late sixties for the murder of her two children.

Ruth Snyder was described as having no heart, being a bad woman, a bad wife, a bad mother, who did not even look like a woman. Comment was made on her dyed blonde hair, her 'masculine' jaw and her mouth, which was 'as cold, hard and unsympathetic as a crack in a dried lemon'. Ruth Snyder and Judd Gray went to the electric chair.

Again, Alice Crimmins did not look like a decent woman, let alone a proper mother; she was described as a 'sexy swinger' who wore tight trousers and had affairs and, like Ruth Ellis, had been a nightclub hostess. The police officer in the case took one look at her and decided he had his murderess. He escorted her to the scene where her little girl's body had been found and showed her the corpse. She failed the test because she didn't cry, although she did faint. It took him two years to put together a case against her, and it later came to light that this had involved bribing and suborning witnesses. After two trials and an appeal she ended up being sentenced for manslaughter.

It is difficult to assess accurately whether Ann Jones's theory about moral backlashes against female advances holds true in Britain. Serious crime by women here is still sufficiently rare to invoke horror whenever it happens, and it is hard to link the outrage to specific periods in history, but a number of notorious cases are remarkably similar in their facts and in the response they evoked to the ones cited by Ann Jones.

Edith Thompson was hanged at Holloway Prison in January 1923 at precisely the time when women were being admitted to the professions, having successfully secured the vote. She had been convicted of murdering her husband.

The Crown alleged that the Thompsons were walking home on a dark road in Ilford, Essex, in October 1922, when a figure emerged from the shadows and stabbed Mr Thompson to death. The assailant was later proved to be Frederick Bywaters, a young ship's purser and Edith's lover, once a lodger at her house. From the moment of her arrest, Edith Thompson denied all complicity in the killing and insisted that she had no idea that Bywaters was anywhere in the vicinity or had any intention of harming her husband. Bywaters himself confirmed this. However, the core of the evidence against her at her trial at the Old Bailey was her correspondence to the man she loved while he was at sea. The love letters seemed to indicate that she was learning about poisons and wanted him to send her something to do away with her husband. The defence was able to show that much of the contents were fanciful, that she was merely using the letters as a means of indulging her fantasies of being free to share a life with Freddy. The autopsy report from a celebrated pathologist, Sir Bernard Spilsbury, proved that her claim to be adding broken glass to her husband's food was a nonsense, wholly unsupported by the find-ings at the post-mortem. The picture that comes clearly across today is of a woman apped in a loveless marriage to a less than admirable man who physically abused her, but she received little understanding from the trial judge, Mr Justice Shearman, and his bias against her repeatedly filtered into his summing-up. The same old judicial formula was used whereby judges absolve themselves from any responsibility for prejudicing a jury when they indicate their own interpretation of the evidence. Mr Justice Shearman invoked this when he chose to assert his view, and followed it with the rider that the final decision was, of course, in the hands of the jury: 'That is for you and not for me.' He was clearly convinced that Edith Thompson was culpable of inciting Frederick Bywaters to murder. Even if she was not privy to the fine detail of the ulti-mate plan or its execution, it was she, as an older woman, who had to be held responsible. His moral outrage on behalf of husbands was obvious, and he was particularly offended by the descriptions of the defendants' great love.

At the end of one of Edith's letters to Freddy, she referred to her husband as having 'the right by law to all that you have the right to by nature and love'. Mr Justice Shearman vented his spleen:

Gentlemen, if that nonsense means anything it means that the love of a husband for his wife is something improper because marriage is acknowledged by the law, and that the love of a woman for her lover, illicit and clandestine, is something great and noble. I am certain that you like any other right-minded persons will be filled with disgust at such a notion.

His Lordship also suggested that some strange chivalry, rather than an expression of the truth, might account for Freddy's exculpating Edith.

In the press, Edith Thompson was portrayed in a covert way as the New Woman; she earned her own living as a supervisor in a clothing manufacturer's, taking home more than her husband, who was a city clerk. She was portrayed as a flapper, who liked to go to a show in the West End and have a port and lemon with her girl-friends. She showed little interest in having children. Was this the kind of woman society wanted?

Poor Edith went to the scaffold amid some public concern about her conviction. Horrible stories were told in the press alleging that she disintegrated emotionally at the point of hanging, that she fought, kicked, screamed and protested her innocence to the last, and that five warders had to hold her down as she was carried to the gallows. It was even suggested that 'her insides fell out'. As late as 1956, during the death penalty debate, the then Home Secretary denied these accounts, but accepted that she had to be given seda-tives before the hanging. Recent investigations into the case suggest she may have been pregnant at the time of the hanging, but her Home Office file has been withdrawn without reason and is no longer available to the public.

As we have seen, the trial of Ruth Ellis took place in 1955, when women were being shooed back into domesticity after the war. But where Ann Jones's theory perhaps has most potency is in the legal response to women who are involved in political crusades or are fighting for equality. The women who have most seriously confronted the male authority of the court are those whose offences emanate from their political beliefs. In the 1970s and 80s we saw many waves of political women coming before the courts, involved in anti-nuclear campaigns like the women's peace camp at Greenham Common, or feminist demonstrations such as Reclaiming the Night and Women's Right to Choose on abortion. These public campaigns echoed the suffragette campaigns of the beginning of the century. The response of the court had changed remarkably little, and women voiced very similar criticisms of the patronising and paternalistic nature of the system as the suffragettes did.

The operation of the criminal justice system in public order cases always produces feelings of anger. The mass processing involved in dealing with so many cases arising out of the exercise of political freedom inevitably creates a sense of injustice. In most circumstances the response of the court is no different whether you are male or female, but some other component does come into operation when the demonstration is actively organised by women for women.

In the early days at Newbury Magistrates' Court, where the Greenham campaign cases were tried, the celebratory atmosphere of women coming together demanding peace penetrated the courtroom. The magistrates were perplexed and unsettled by the motley collection of women who appeared before them: women of all classes, ages and marital status, gay women, nuns, mothers. I always remember being instructed to appear for a group of peace women. After making the legal argument in relation to the right of way and not succeeding, we had agreed that I would withdraw and no longer act so that the women could make their own political statements. I stayed to watch, and it was quite extraordinary to see the way in which the traditional regimented courtroom procedure was changed. One after another, the women gave forceful explanations of why they were involved. Their large numbers together in the dock meant that they were not intimidated and were able to express themselves freely in what is normally an inhibiting male theatre. They gave each other encouragement and support.

Apart from the male magistrates and a few police officers, the only other man in the court was the court interpreter, who was there to translate the incantation of the Japanese Buddhist nuns. He had learned his Japanese in a prisoner-of-war camp and he entered into the spirit of the event as few interpreters do. Instead of sounding like the speaking clock, he charged his translation with some emotion and enthusiasm, and spoke with deep feeling about the horror of war. The women were all found guilty, but my last memory of the courtroom was of a great festival of kissing and hugging, with the interpreter getting his fair share of the affection.

However, this female insurrection had to be contained, and a decision was made to separate the women so that only one or two were tried at any one time. The variety of the women involved was soon homogenised by the popular press into the 1970s stereotype of the political woman in dungarees, spiked hair, non-matching earrings and no trace of lipstick. The legend was created that this or that woman was a man-hater, an iconoclast with no respect for the institutions, a woman who abandoned her responsibilities of home, hearth and children to haunt the perimeters of legitimate male activity in defending the realm. The antagonism towards the Greenham women was soon tangible in the courtrooms; in the most minimal of obstruction cases, questions would be asked about whether the women had children and who had been caring for them at the time of their arrest.

No miner on a picket line would ever be asked to account for himself in this way.

Greenham moved from being portrayed in the press as legitimate peace campaigning to a side show, and eventually a freak show. This process of marginalisation was completed in the courts. However, contemporary politics threw up a different kind of political she-devil.

The trial of the Price sisters in 1973 for bombing the Old Bailey court was the first of a number of cases against women involved in Irish republicanism. The surprise and sense of horror that women were playing a prominent role ran right through the trial and the publicity which surrounded it. The headlines on 11 September 1973 blazoned the significance of their leading roles: DOLOURS BOSSED THE IRA BOMB SQUAD (*The Times*); THE TERROR GANG WAS LED BY A GIRL CLAIMS QC (*Daily Mirror*) – and she was 'a pretty 23-year-old redhead' to boot, according to the *Sun*.

The terrorist woman is a different category of female offender, in that she challenges the pathos of so much female crime. Her attack upon the state is dual, assaulting the institutions both directly, in bombing attacks, and indirectly, by confronting the traditional role of woman as a cornerstone of established society.

There seems to be a sexiness about the combination of young women and power; the words 'cold', 'calculating' and 'ruthless' are often juxta-posed with 'attractive', 'vivacious' and 'pretty'. The men involved in these cases – police, lawyers, judges and reporters – were titillated by images of the Armalite rifle in feminine hands, but they were also fearful of its implications. Running through most of the cases of IRA activity involving women is a sense of horror that women should use the very attributes which make them so appealing to men to undermine their guard.

The rush to judgement on people who may be linked to terrorism always risks getting it wrong. In 1974 Judith Ward was convicted of the M62 motorway coach bombing, an explosion which killed Corporal Clifford Houghton, his wife and two young children, as well as eight other British soldiers. She was given 12 sentences of life imprisonment plus 30 years for that and two other bombings. Her father disowned her after her trial. The press had a field day about her wickedness. Until her release by the Court of Appeal at the end of April 1992, she was the longest serving woman prisoner in Britain or Ireland for offences connected with the Irish conflict. Like the Guildford Four, the Maguire family and the Birmingham Six, she had never been acknowledged by the IRA as one of its adherents. For years people hardly knew her name, and while serving her sentence she received little media attention or campaigning interest over the 18 years of incarceration. Judith Ward did not campaign or write letters over the years but quietly maintained her innocence. Prison officers and probation officers involved with her had deep misgivings about her conviction, but felt that she became resigned to a course of biding her time in hope of eventual release on parole. She had to settle for a fate she felt she had brought on her own head.

The evidence against Judith Ward was paralleled by that in the Birmingham Six case. She made confessions which were deeply flawed and in significant respects unreliable and fantastical. At trial her defence lawyers described her as a 'Walter Mitty' character who made claims which were manifestly untrue. Forensic evidence was supposed to show that she had been in contact with explosives. However, the expert was Dr Frank Skuse, also of the Birmingham case, who was forced to resign in 1985 because of his 'limited efficiency'. He used the infamous Griess test for detecting the presence of the explosive nitroglycerine on swabs taken from Judith Ward's hands. This simple presumptive test was called into serious doubt in the Birmingham case because positive reactions can also be obtained from innocent material such as soap, Formica and the coating on cigarette packets. It is usually followed by a more sensitive procedure called thin-layer chromatography. When the more sophisticated process was applied to Judith Ward's swabs, the results were negative.

While the mental state of women is usually leapt at to explain their aberrations, at her trial the emotional vulnerability of Judith Ward was never allowed to explain her behaviour. This was terrorism, where different rules seem to apply. She was questioned extensively by police over many days without a solicitor or outside contact. Sixty-three interviews took place, an unbelievable number, and outside the experience of any lawyer I know. Thirty-four of those interviews were not disclosed to those who defended her at her trial, and the jury heard nothing about them. The failure of the Crown to disclose this evidence was quite extraordinary.

Dr James MacKeith testified at Judith Ward's appeal that she was at the time of her confessions suffering from a personality disorder which had developed into mental illness by the time she was charged. The disorder manifested itself in attention-seeking, memory problems, mood swings and depression – a condition of 'hysteria' making her removed from reality. His assessment was based on interviews with her, her family, and people who knew her, but also on police and prison records and all the documentation which had subsequently come to light.

The medical officer at Risley Prison, where she was held on remand, prepared a pre-trial report (which juries do not see). It said: 'Ward cannot be described as a very truthful person in that she has changed her story to me several times ... She is a most difficult person to evaluate. At times she is feminine and well-mannered. At other times she is rough, foul-mouthed and coarse.' In the months just before trial Judith Ward was so mentally ill she attempted suicide twice; the defence lawyers were never informed.

When giving evidence at the appeal, Dr MacKeith said that it would not have been reasonable to expect the jurors in her trial to be conscious of Ms Ward's mental state. The full body of interviews showed clearly how disturbed she was, but the jury and defence were never availed of that information, having heard less than half the possible evidence. The lawyers were putting together a jigsaw with most of the pieces missing.

On 4 June 1992 Judith Ward's convictions were quashed by the Court of Appeal as unsafe and unsatisfactory; the judges, in an excoriating judgment, made clear their disgust at the non-disclosure of important evidence by the Crown, a doctor in the prison service and the scientists in the case. It is hard to resist the conclusion that the willingness to cut corners was all the greater because she was seen as an outlier, a thoroughly bad and dangerous woman.

Women like Ulrike Meinhof and Gudrun Ensslin, who led the German Baader–Meinhof group of urban guerrillas, Bernardine Dohrn and Kathy Boudin of the American Weather Underground, Anna Mendleson and Hilary Creek of the Angry Brigade, or Patty Hearst, have all provoked more interest and speculation than their male comrades. All were educated, middle-class women who became involved at the extreme end of the radical politics which grew out of the anti-Vietnam War movement. However, it was their sexual liberation, rather than their class analysis, that seemed to interest the male voyeur.

This response may have been influenced by some of the cultural images which were prevalent at that time, in the late 1960s and early 1970s, images of leather-clad Diana Rigg in *The Avengers* or 'Pussy

Galore' in the James Bond films, physically able to floor men without losing any of their sexual charms. These women also functioned along-side men, introducing exciting possibilities about what they got up to sexually, in contrast to women-only politics like Greenham Common, which were at best boring and at worst involved sexual activity that few wanted to hear about.

The theatrical convention, from Jean Genet to *Monty Python*, in which the judge indulges his fetish for sadomasochism with some beautiful, scantily clad dominatrix spanking him in the wings of the court, has its roots in the complicated relationship between sex and guilt, punishment and power. These elements charge the atmosphere at the trials of political, independent women, and as a result subtle and insidious inferences undermine the proceedings. There is no differ-ence in the way women are sentenced – the courts cannot be criticised for inequality on that score – but the sense of alarm that they should be involved in such warlike activity infects the rhetoric of the courtroom.

Although the IRA women invoked complicated responses, their commitment to their cause was understood, even at the time. The calculated nature of their offences means they acquired the 'bad' rather than 'mad' label, but their motive was appreciable. The support they received from their own community helped them maintain dignity and self-esteem, and they were acknowledged as a special category of prisoner within the penal population itself. They may have been perceived as a monstrous regiment, but they do not fill the nightmares of the public in the way that Myra Hindley, Rose West and female child abusers do.

The women striking terror into hearts now are those involved with IS and other extreme Islamist groups. The most prominent is the 'White Widow', Samantha Lewthwaite, the daughter of a former soldier who was born and brought up in County Down, Northern Ireland, but came to London to do her degree and converted to Islam. She was the wife of Germaine Lindsay, who blew himself up on a Piccadilly Line train between King's Cross and Russell Square stations, one of the four 7/7 suicide bombers who caused multiple explosions in London on 7 July 2005, killing 52 people and injuring more than 700 others.

Samantha Lewthwaite and her children were at the receiving end of a revenge arson attack on their home when her identity as a terrorist's wife became known. She disappeared soon after and is believed to be in Somalia, where she married the warlord Habib Wahid. She is now designated the most wanted woman in the world and subject to a global manhunt because of her own terrorist activity. There is an Interpol Red Notice warrant for her arrest in existence. She is said to have been the mastermind of many terrorist attacks including the bombing of a bar in Mombasa in 2012, where tourists and locals were watching a Euro cup football match. It is claimed she ordered the assassination of two Muslim clerics and two Protestant preachers. She was also linked to the bombing of the Westfield Mall in Nairobi in 2013 and the massacre at Garissa University College in Kenya, where 148 were killed. In September 2016 three women jihadists stormed a police station in Mombasa and after one attacked a police officer with a knife, a petrol bomb was launched. All three women were shot dead. One had with her an unexploded suicide vest. Laptops and emails belonging to the three women were found at their homes, which indicated they had been in communication with Samanatha Lewthwaite, also known as Umm Sherafiyah or the Mother of Holy War. Security services claim that she is involved in the grooming and training of large numbers of women using the Internet, encouraging many to leave their families and travel to places like Syria or Somalia to participate in the struggle and creation of Islamic states. Al Shabaab, the group she is associated with, is based in Somalia and was linked to al-Qaeda and the Boko Haram, but recent outrages in the region have been claimed by IS. There is now speculation that she may be dead.

Another woman flagged on the most wanted terrorist list until 2017 was Sally Jones, otherwise known as Umm Hussein al-Britani. She was a single mother of two living in Kent when she began communicating online with a young Muslim hacker, Junaid Hussein. He drew her into Islam and when he decided to go to Syria he urged her to join him there. During the 2013 Christmas school holidays, she left the country with her nine-year-old son Joe, leaving behind her older son who was 18 and chose to remain in the UK. Sally Jones married Hussein the day she arrived in Syria, converting to Islam. Joe's name was changed to Hamza. They then travelled to Raqqa where Junaid Hussein embarked on military training and Sally Jones was inducted into Islam and the Islamic State's extreme interpretation of sharia law.

Soon after, Hussein took for his second wife a young Syrian woman half Sally's age. Most of the fighters had more than one wife but they usually took and enslaved Yazidi, Christian or Shiite women. On social media Sally Jones boasted of her wonderful life under the Caliphate. Intelligence reports claimed she had recruited dozens of young women before her accounts were shut down and according to defectors who have been providing intelligence to the West she quickly rose to a prominent position because of her success in encouraging followers to carry out attacks against the West. Whether there is substance in these claims is unknown and untested.

Junaid Hussein was suspected of being behind some of IS's notorious hacking attacks as well as being the recruiter of sympathisers in the West to carry out lone-wolf attacks. It is believed that it was he who installed IS radar technology. As a result he was high profile and at the top of American hit lists. In August 2015 he was killed in a US drone attack.

Sally Jones did not remarry but it is claimed she moved into a high-level training role as a jihadi widow. She is believed to have trained a special unit of European female recruits in the use of firearms and bomb-making and showed them how to plan and execute suicide attacks on the West. French intelligence linked her to the arrests of a cell of three women led by Ines Madani, who were found in possession of gas canisters and other material in central Paris in 2016.

Sally Jones and her son were killed in a US drone strike close to the Iraqi border on 12 October 2017.

Reports in May 2017 estimated that 50 British women headed for Syria and Iraq in the preceding year, some travelling with husbands and even children but others travelling alone or with friends, drawn by the heady mix of romance, adventure and piety. Others believe that the numbers are greatly underestimated. The call to women to come and help build a new Islamic State captured the imaginations of many jihadi brides. A CCTV camera captured three girls from a Bethnal Green school in London setting off for Syria via Istanbul and the image is seared in the memories of the British public. They remain missing or are presumed dead according to press reports in August 2017.

Undoubtedly, some of the women are as politically committed as the men but very many were brainwashed into believing they were going to create an ideal Islamic state; this may well include these three girls. They must have been psychologically scarred by what they found awaiting them and may have had second thoughts but had no way out. Within IS, women are commonly bought, sold or traded. They are used as tools to retain disillusioned troops, made to police the women in local populations, forced to produce children for the cause, and made to accept their place as one of several wives. Evidence being taken from Yazidi women in refugee camps and in asylum refuges in Germany describes the horrors of watching their fathers and brothers massacred and then they themselves being multiply raped by their captors. Sadly, they recount also being ill-treated by IS women.

As Islamic State has been slowly beaten back, many of the IS women are now being held in prison camps in the area of Syria controlled by the Syrian Kurds. Government ministers in the UK would prefer that the fighters, including the women, never return, or that they are prosecuted for war crimes and terrorist activities in the countries where they were captured. But the latter is hard to pull off given that European countries like the UK are opposed to the death penalty and are not confident that countries like Syria and Iraq can hold fair trials. A Kurdish state does not exist so there is no justice system by which the women can be tried. If they do return to their families in the UK, though they can be prosecuted for giving support to terrorist groups, it would be difficult to prosecute them for the serious crimes many of them have committed while in Syria or Iraq. There is unlikely to be much sympathy for jihadist women when they return but the struggle is to make the system rise above such visceral responses. Travelling to join a terrorist organisation is in and of itself a crime, and some girls were stopped by the authorities at airports before leaving the country. Careful decisions were made as to whether prosecution was necessary and usually it was not. But when women return and there is evidence of complicity in terror, recruitment, cruelty to enslaved women, or other criminal actions, the women will face trial and if convicted they will rightly receive long prison sentences.

However, being part of the Irish trials over a couple of decades and seeing the human cost when legal standards are lowered and wrongful convictions follow has taught me the imperative of keeping the bar high. The profound misogyny of IS means that some of these women will themselves have been victims of terrible abuse and will have been subjected to duress and coercion. The legal system will have the difficult role of charting a course through uncorroborated accounts, fragile evidence and strong public hostility to determine where real guilt lies. This is the complex terrain of justice and it requires our utmost vigilance.

9

GIRLS, GIRLS, GIRLS

The Rotherham child sexual exploitation scandal rocked Britain. This was exploitation that had gone unchallenged from the late 1980s until a prosecution in 2010 of five British Pakistani men opened the floodgates. The accused were convicted of sexual offences against girls aged between 12 and 16 but the men in the dock were not the ringleaders, who miraculously avoided prosecution. Risky behaviour was first documented when social workers in care homes noticed that some of the children in their care were being picked up by taxi drivers. From 2001 onwards there were memos and reports passed between police and social services alleging abuse and naming alleged perpetrators, a number of whom were from the same family, but nothing was done. The 2010 prosecution would have seemed like a single isolated case to many on the outside but in 2011, Andrew

Norfolk of *The Times* wrote an electrifying piece reporting that abuse in the town was widespread and that the police had known about it for 10 years. A trial then took place in 2012 in which it transpired that a child sex abuse ring was also operating in neighbouring Rochdale. Alarm bells were ringing in many towns and cities and it prompted the Home Affairs Committee in Parliament to hold hearings which led to the creation of an independent inquiry led by Professor Alexis Jay, a distinguished sociologist.

The Jay Report was published in 2014 and concluded that at least 1,400 children, most of them white girls aged 11–15, had been sexually abused in Rotherham between 1997 and 2013 by predominantly British Pakistani men. Taxi drivers had indeed been picking the girls up from care homes and schools and using them for sex; sometimes the children were passed around men running takeaway outlets. The abuse was horrendous – gang rape, forcing the children to watch the rape of others, dousing them with petrol and threatening to set them alight, threatening to rape their mothers and sisters and to traffic them to other towns or cities. From time to time the girls would get pregnant so there were abortions, miscarriages and babies taken from their child-mothers causing terrible trauma. Many of the girls were barely adolescent.

The failure to address the abuse was a toxic combination of race, class and gender. Police and council decision-makers were utterly contemptuous of these working-class girls. They were mere children who had no sense of their own self-worth, who had disturbed and problem backgrounds, but they were being treated as 'white trash' by people whose sexism was only matched by their desire to watch their own backs. The police were afraid that the ethnicity of the perpetrators would lead to their being accused of racism and they would have to handle the fallout in poisoned community relations. The Labour-led council to its eternal shame did not want to make waves among the town's ethnic community leaders because it relied too heavily on their votes.

Rotherham Council's chief executive, its director of social services and the Police and Crime Commissioner for South Yorkshire all resigned. Dame Louise Casey was asked to inspect Rotherham Council and when she reported in 2015 she concluded that the council had a bullying sexist culture of covering up information and silencing 'whistleblowers'. In February 2015 the government replaced the council's elected officers with a team of five commissioners. Further prosecutions took place in 2016 and 2017 and 19 men and two women were also convicted of sexual offences dating back to the late eighties. A ring-leader was jailed for 35 years.

One of the women was a radio operator at a minicab firm. She and the other female accused were convicted of false imprisonment and conspiracy to procure prostitutes, having befriended the girls, listened to their problems, given them alcohol and then insisted they repaid their debt by providing the men with sex.

The complicity of the police was plain in the trial when evidence was given that a young victim was in a car with an abuser when a police vehicle approached and asked what was going on. The abuser replied, 'She's just sucking my cock, mate', and the police left. No doubt it caused hilarity down at the station as well as at the minicab office.

One victim who had been groomed from the age of 12 and was raped for the first time when she was 13 told Radio 4's *Today* programme her harrowing story. She said she was raped once a week, every week, until she was 15. That police 'lost' clothing she had given them as evidence and that she had feared for her family's safety.

The attitude of the men involved was displayed when one was interviewed before he was charged. He blamed the victims, saying that the problem was that 'these days these young girls are dressed up, that is miniskirts, stuff like that; they're going into the clubs and ending up going with blokes and they're waking up next morning and scream rape. Or groomed.' He blamed social services for having let the girls out in the first place.

The systemic failures of police and councils were repeated all over the country. Rotherham opened the door to a flood of investigations which might otherwise never have taken place.

Oxfordshire County Council failed to stop a grooming gang that plied girls, some as young as 11, with alcohol and drugs. The men beat and raped the girls and sold them for sex. A court heard that the men had acted 'under the noses' of the authorities who showed 'almost wilful blindness'. Seven men were convicted and sentenced to a total of 95 years in June 2013 for offences including rape, facilitating child prostitution and trafficking.

In Derby nine men were convicted over three trials of systematically grooming and sexually abusing teenage girls in 2010. Many of the victims were given alcohol or drugs before being forced to have sex in cars, rented houses and hotels across the Midlands. CCTV footage had the men driving round Derby stopping girls on the street.

The case in Rochdale involved a sex ring of nine men who were given sentences ranging from four to 19 years after being found guilty of conspiracy to engage in sexual activity with a child. The men, from Rochdale and Oldham, were found to have exploited girls as young as 13.

Seven men were jailed in Telford after a series of court cases relating to a child prostitution ring. The charges included rape, trafficking and prostitution, sometimes involving girls as young as 12. According to West Mercia Police the group had targeted more than 100 girls between 2007 and 2009.

In 2014 and 2015, 10 men were brought to trial at Peterborough Crown Court for committing sexual offences against underage girls, some as young as 12. They were found guilty of rape, child prostitution and trafficking for sexual exploitation. The men were of Pakistani, Iraqi Kurdish, Czech and Slovak Roma heritage.

In September of 2017 a grooming gang was investigated and jailed for sexually abusing vulnerable girls in Newcastle after plying them with drink and drugs, including mephedrone. There were estimated to be 780 victims.

The scale and nature of this abuse, and the systemic failure to investigate and support the victims, reflects a complex set of competing prejudices in our society. Black men and men from other minorities often face prejudice in their dealings with the authorities from the police to many other state institutions as well as potential employers. The racism within our society is regularly exposed. Since the Macpherson Inquiry in 1999 into the death of Stephen Lawrence, the police have been regularly challenged about the embedded attitudes which inform their decisions as to stop and search, their approach to investigation and to arrest. The issue of race is now so much higher on the policing radar and this undoubtedly weighed with the police in the choices they made in the Rotherham case and others. But would the police have stepped back from investigating organised robberies by men from ethnic minority backgrounds if allegations were brought to them? Would they have been so sensitive to racism if the allegations were of organised drug trafficking? Their negative sexist attitudes about the girls, the kind of girls who went with minority men, outweighed issues of racism.

The critique by many on the right that the failure in policing was about political correctness has to be challenged. The capture of language is one of the ways in which those with power maintain their supremacy.

So too is the refusal to adapt language. Political correctness came into being to make people think before they made racist or sexist utterances. The term PC is now being used as a slur to permit bigoted and hateful views. How dare you take away from me my right to say what I want about blacks and lesbians, Muslims and slags?

It is important to acknowledge that the use of girls for sex is commonplace. Thousands of girls in the UK are subjected to sexual exploitation by male-run gangs. Youth and community workers increasingly see girls and young women passed around different male gang members for sex, with rape used as a weapon in conflicts between rival gangs and in initiation ceremonies. The gangs are sometimes white; sometimes black; sometimes youth gangs and sometimes organised crime syndicates. In their desire for approval and acceptance, the girls themselves become complicit and have been known to set up friends for rape. Edward Boyd of the Centre for Social Justice conducted research with XLP, a charity working to create positive futures for young people, and their report said that society is often oblivious to the 'desperate plight of girls embroiled in gangs. They live in a parallel world where rape, carrying drugs and guns is seen as normal.' And it starts when girls are very young, mostly because there were problems in their home life. The report estimated that 12,500 girls and young women could be involved in gangs. One girl described being drawn in because she had no one to depend on. Her mother was a drug addict and she was on her own. She explained that she initially associated with gang members to be protected. Another described wanting to be accepted and gang members feeding on that need. She too spoke of home problems, running away and being out by herself, 'hooking up with a load of older people' who abused her.

The Foundation 4 Life is a charity which works with girls in gangs; many of those involved are ex-gang members themselves. One of the workers, Isha Nembhard, says that social pressure and the increasing sexualisation of young women has changed the nature and severity of a problem that was always there. The girls are used by male gang members to carry guns and knives and to hide drugs or weapons, or take drugs to customers because they attract less police interest. They are also used to bring drugs and phones into prisons. They can be paid well but are also expected to supply sex readily. The girls often become drug-dependent or suffer other mental health problems. Again, it cannot be emphasised enough that a person is a child under our law until they are 18, although a girl can consent to sex at 16.

The double standards experienced by women in the courts are also prevalent in the youth justice system. The remit of the youth courts goes beyond that of adult courts because it is concerned with the well-being of children and young people. This means that sanctions can be brought into operation for behaviour that is not technically criminal but likely to affect a young person's development. Children can be taken there for truanting, for being neglected or in 'moral danger' or beyond parental control. Many girls are thus brought into the system for non-criminal offences or trivial misdemeanours when they are not conforming to notions of proper behaviour. Girls are often referred to the youth courts for different reasons than are boys, and are dealt with differently. A son's overnight absence will earn him a knowing wink, and drunkenness will be seen as a natural part of his growing up – boys will be boys – but 'ladette' behaviour by a girl calls down other responses. There is a clear preoccupation with the sexuality of teenage girls and an overemphatic concern with their moral welfare. If she fails to come home on time, hangs around the wrong part of town or adopts dubious friends, a girl is far more likely to be declared in moral danger, for which, at the instigation of her parents, school, social worker or the police, she may be taken into the care of the local authority. The same behaviour in boys does not evoke the same response from the courts. These young women start off in the penal system having committed no crime at all, but once it is on their record that they have been locked up, a cycle of imprisonment begins, and offending often follows.

Girls who have been sexually abused within the family are frequently rejected, even by their mothers, when they make the abuse public. They often absent themselves from school, run away, go on the streets and end up in care. They feel such self-loathing and lack of worth that abuse by other men follows or they prostitute themselves to survive. The police are now required to involve social services and avoid criminalising the girl if she is underage. But it is not uncommon to hear the police complain that for some of the 16- and 17-year-olds it is a lifestyle choice and instead of being prosecuted for offences they are getting away with it. But young women who are on the game rarely have a happy story to tell about their home life. Girls who need to be taken into custody – because they have committed violent offences – should be placed in the secure units run by local authorities but there are few places, and custody orders are often made where there is no violence at all, just repetition of offending. Girls who are arrested and have nowhere to go still sometimes end up in adult prisons, despite proof that it is damaging to lock up the young with people who are older.

The story of our young and the criminal justice system is not comforting. Young people between the ages of 16 and 24 years old are more likely than any other age group to be the victims of crime according to the 'Bromley Briefings' published by the Prison Reform Trust in 2013, and many of those who are the victims of crime are the very ones being locked up in prisons. In August of that same year, there were 1,229 children in custody: 736 were white and 468 were BAME; 50 were girls.

Seventy-six per cent of children in custody or care have an absent father, 33% an absent mother and 39% have been on the child protection register or have experienced neglect or abuse. One in eight children in custody or care have experienced the death of a parent or sibling. Although less than 1% of all children in England are in care, looked-after children make up 33% of boys in custody and 61% of girls.

One in 10 girls in custody have been paid for sex according to research by the Prison Reform Trust. Almost half of them were 14 or younger when last in education and 60% arrive in custody with a drug problem. The numbers who have been sexually abused or brought up in households where there was domestic violence are very high. Fifty-three per cent of adult women in prison have experienced emotional, physical or sexual abuse in their childhood. Thirty-five per cent of girls between the ages of 13 and 18 in custody have been identified with depression and 19% have post-traumatic stress disorder.

According to research by Ewan Kennedy for HM Inspectorate of Prisons in 2013, young girls not only felt isolated from friends or family when incarcerated but they had no one in prison to turn to for support. A large percentage of girls felt unsafe and were victimised while in custody both by other prisoners and by staff. Thirty per cent of children in custody were held over 50 miles away from their homes, including 10% held over 100 miles away. Forty-two per cent of girls experienced trouble with sending and receiving mail and only 19% of girls said it was easy for their family to visit. As a result of these revelations, later in 2013 it was decided to stop imprisoning girls in actual jails. All girls under 18 are now detained in secure training centres or secure children's homes but the same sense of insecurity and fear persists. The secure children's homes are run by local authorities scattered around the country so research into the girls' experiences is harder to undertake. What is clear is that girls in care suffer high levels of stress, anxiety and depression, and often go on to petty crime and prostitution. Half of the secure children's homes have now been decommissioned which means that children are being held further and further away from home or from people who might care about them. They are also under-resourced and understaffed. We are just transporting the victims of one type of abuse or neglect into another environment of abuse and neglect.

But it is not just girls with backgrounds of abuse or very troubled families who suffer mental health problems. According to a major study published in September 2017 and conducted by University College London, one in four teenage girls believe they are suffering from depression. The research tracked 10,000 teenagers and found widespread emotional problems with misery, loneliness and self-hate rife. Parents were more likely to pick up signs with sons because they were more likely to display behavioural problems like fighting and rebellion compared with girls. Why are girls suffering in this way?

Children are not born aware of skin colour or gender but all too soon our world invades that innocence. Black children have a moment that brings awareness of racism into their lives; sociologists call it the 'encounter'. It is an occasion where they are subjected to abuse or differential treatment or see racism happen to a parent, and it is like a tremor that shifts the earth's tectonic plates. Afua Hirsch, the mixed-race journalist and author, describes minor feelings of otherness as a child in her book *Brit(ish)*, but the full force only hit her when as a girl in her early teens she entered a small boutique in Wimbledon where she lived and was followed around the shop; she realised her blackness made her an automatic suspect for shoplifting. She says that to this day she always makes a conscious display of her hands when in shops and does it routinely despite her success and privilege. The world immediately changes in a significant way when people become aware of racism; their own ways of seeing and feeling are changed.

Something similar happens to girls of all races, though. Ideas of what it means to be a girl or boy surround children and imbue deep attitudes that are hard to uproot. Boys learn a sense of entitlement about their wants and needs from an early age. However, growing up for a girl is about learning to be afraid of what can happen. You come to know you inhabit a body that is vulnerable. You learn that if you allow something to happen you will be punished. Women discover by watching and listening that when something like sexual assault happens it is their fault.

Girls also feel huge pressure from ever earlier ages to conform to commercially driven ideas of attractiveness and size. The most recent work of the psychoanalyst Susie Orbach, concerning the human body, has revealed that girls as young as six talk about dieting. The compulsion to be model-thin has led to an epidemic of eating disorders among girls, and the toll on female self-confidence caused by the barrage of media images extolling the only acceptable body type is immeasurable. But pressures to be the right kind of desirable woman take other forms. Girls are coerced into providing sexual favours at ever earlier ages. Getting down on their knees to boys is for many girls their initiation into sexual intimacy. Teachers describe the constant sharing of pornographic imagery on mobile phones and the shoving of it under the noses of the less worldly in the classroom to shock them and then mock them. Pictures of bestiality, the penetration of multiple orifices, gang sex – the full panoply of extreme imagery is so readily available.

Sexting produces particular anxieties. Sexting can be a kind of foreplay but it more often descends into coarse descriptions of what people want to do to each other, pornographic rather than erotic. What people do not recognise is that once sent they are no longer in control of what happens to the messages or the attached photos. It is illegal, however, to post sexual images online of people under the age of 18 – an important threat teachers and other adults can use when insisting that pictures on the phones of pupils are deleted.

Cyberbullying is not against the law but harassment or threatening behaviour is. If someone keeps making someone feel scared online and they are doing so intentionally, what they are doing could be illegal. The important thing for someone being bullied online to do is to keep a record of when something occurred and what happened and to seek help from a trusted adult.

Online bullying is now a serious problem for the young with hateful comments and messages being posted that are then shared and endorsed by others with a 'like'. Rumours are spread on Twitter which reach hundreds. Trolling has become a new form of playground bullying with the constant posting of derogatory comments or doctored images and other gross abuse. Trolls incite others to join in what is described as virtual mobbing. A girl with Down's syndrome and her mother experienced trolls photoshopping their images onto pornography and then posting them on Facebook. It was reported in 2016 that one in four teenagers had suffered abuse online over their sexual orientation, race, religion, gender or disability. The Internet should not be an anonymous place where people can post abuse without any consequence, but while the Crown Prosecution Service has created new guidelines saying it will prosecute, few recorded cases have followed because of the evidential difficulty in identifying perpetrators. This aspect of modern life is posing serious problems for law enforcement. Freedom of speech means that simply putting up postings that are nasty or offend is insufficient for prosecution.

A new law was introduced in April 2015 to deal with revenge porn – the situation where someone maliciously shares sexually explicit pictures of former partners. In the first year there were 1,160 reported incidents including a victim as young as 11. There were 200 actual prosecutions. Scotland passed similar legislation in 2017. Threats to publish material is also part of the coercive control that is now a crime. The new technology which turns our phones into tracking devices is now being used by abusive men.

The misery and self-loathing induced when someone is humiliated or when the pack turns on a vulnerable person has led to increased suicides and an epidemic of self-harming. Self-harm is more prevalent among girls than people imagine, with gay, lesbian and bisexual people all figuring high in research. Prisoners, asylum seekers and veterans of the armed forces all have a high incidence of self-harming, and 96% of transgender youth self-harm. When people self-harm – cutting themselves, taking overdoses – they are almost always struggling with intolerable distress or unbearable situations and sometimes it is because they have experienced bullying, pressure to conform, physical or sexual abuse. Inflicting physical pain is a way of releasing the mental pain and tension. It can also be about punishing yourself. Care homes and prisons are full of women and girls who injure or mutilate themselves. But so too are our schools, universities and colleges. Self-harm is not by any means confined to women but boys are more inclined to externalise their emotional distress.

None of it points to a world that is a woman's oyster.

And for girls from some cultural backgrounds, that world is even more distant. The horrifying tradition of female genital mutilation is euphemistically called female circumcision to put it on a par with male circumcision because that is a practice widely accepted and without the same assault on a person's sexuality. FGM involves slicing into the genitalia of girls and frequently the removal of the clitoris. It can lead to haemorrhaging, chronic pain, bladder and menstrual problems as well as psychological harm. It is usually performed by community women on little girls when they are between the ages of seven and twelve, often without anaesthetic and using a razor blade. I have visited health education programmes in Ethiopia and have met with women who perform these ritual incisions; I have also spoken with many women who have gone through the ordeal as well as male leaders who still think it is a cultural practice which is good for women and for their society because it stops promiscuity, helps preserve virginity until marriage and makes women more passive. They actually say that is one of its purposes. Little girls become more subdued and less bois-terous and troublesome.

I remember in 1997 going to a hospital in north London at the invitation of a consultant obstetrician who was concerned about the prevalence of the problem and the failure of current policy to prevent it. Women would arrive at the clinic expecting their first child and he would find they had had their labia removed and the vagina stitched so that the opening was a tiny aperture through which she would never be able to push a baby. Women would have to be told that at the time of birth they would need an episiotomy to cut an opening wide enough for the baby to emerge and that afterwards their vagina would be repaired, but not closed up as it had been before as to do so would be contrary to British law. The women would listen intently as it was explained that it was not healthy to have a closed vagina. They often gave histories of painful periods and excruciating intercourse, as well as urinary tract and other infections. They would cry as they spoke of unsatisfactory sex lives and the pain of penetration. Sadly, after a healthy birth and delivery and a vagina returned as near as possible to normal, the women would invariably come back to the hospital for their second birth with their vagina reinfibulated. The doctors at the clinic knew that these operations were being performed in the community by elderly women or that the women had had it done back in the country from which they had originally come. They were persuaded that their husbands would not want them with open vaginas. British-born girls with family origins in numerous West African countries, as well as Egypt and the MENA region, now speak out about the practice and describe being taken out of school for a holiday and having the practice performed back in their parents' villages. Although there has been legislation in the UK for 27 years there have been few prosecutions. The law was extended in 2003 because there had been until then no prosecutions whatsoever. The new law made it an offence to enable such a practice to be performed on another, so that family members who arrange for it to be done can be prosecuted too.

An asylum case conducted by my own chambers was the 2006 case of Fornah, involving a woman who had fled Sierra Leone during the civil war there. She was just 15 when her father rushed the family back to his own village from the city seeking sanctuary from the conflict. She had overheard elders expressing horror that she was uncircumcised and talking about subjecting her to FGM. She ran away but was captured by rebel forces, raped repeatedly by their leader and became pregnant. She managed to escape and came to the UK to an uncle's family. Her attempt to obtain refugee status on the basis that to be returned put her at risk of FGM was opposed by the British government, and even the Court of Appeal turned down her application on the basis that FGM was not discriminatory as it did not set aside from the rest of society those who were subjected to it. Most women in Sierra Leone underwent the procedure and indeed most women accepted it as a cultural practice. It was not a defining characteristic of the particular group, namely women. A group could not be defined by the kind of persecution to which they might be subjected, said the majority on the court. One judge dissented – Lady Justice Mary Arden.

The Supreme Court overturned that decision and I have no doubt that Baroness Brenda Hale played an important role in the discourse which preceded the ruling. Lord Bingham, who led the court, made remarks of far-reaching significance. He said that the women of Sierra Leone did share a common characteristic, which without fundamental change in the social mores is immutable, namely a position of social inferiority compared with men. And it was true of all women, whether those who accepted their socially inferior position or those who did not. He pointed out that FGM is an extreme and very cruel expression of male dominance. The court agreed.

The decision has been followed by many other cases involving the nature of the culture in countries from which women are fleeing and seeking asylum: Liberia, Kenya, Sudan, Uganda, Ivory Coast. It has now been used as an authority in non-FGM actions – where the culture embeds the social inferiority of women.

The case is an example of why we need women in our higher courts in significant numbers. It is about changing the nature of judicial discourse. Lady Justice Arden's minority judgment in Fornah laid the ground for the debate in our highest court where Baroness Hale, in partnership with enlightened men, was able to create a vitally important precedent which is having ramifications around the world. This is how the law changes and how larger shifts in legal thinking come to pass. A diverse judiciary means different perspectives are brought into the courtrooms and the law is enriched by that broader experience.

However, there is still a very long way to go. For example, three cases referred to the Crown Prosecution Service in the last seven years were not pursued because there were evidential problems. One case against a young doctor failed because there was no evidence that he was performing FGM deliberately; he was not of a culture that followed such practices and through inexperience and lack of supervision stitched the woman along her original scar seam. In that same trial the husband of the woman was also in the dock for complicity but was also acquitted.

In November 2017 a man was charged in Bristol with two offences contrary to section 1 of the Female Genital Mutilation Act 2003 alleging that he excised, infibulated or otherwise mutilated the whole or part of the labia minora of a girl. He was also charged with alternative offences of wounding the child and three separate counts of child cruelty. The alleged offences took place between five and seven years ago. Again the case failed because it transpired that the prosecution arose after he was deliberately engaged in conversation about FGM by a passenger in his minicab who was an anti-FGM activist. It was claimed he had admitted having his daughter cut. However, examination of the girl did not in the end support the allegations.

The problem with FGM prosecutions is that those who perform such operations are almost invariably not qualified medical professionals but people in the community here or back in Africa who have become practised in doing it. Unsurprisingly, girls do not want to testify against their parents or other family members, and although people whisper the names of those who perform such operations on kitchen tables, they aren't prepared to give evidence. It is estimated that 100–140 million women worldwide are living with the consequences of FGM, which is tantamount to torture. Many new African constitutions such as that of Somalia prohibit the practice. It is said that as many as 24,000 girls under 15 in the UK are at risk of FGM. This will be an estimate based on ethnicity and the fear that unless adequately challenged girls of identified communities will be forced to undergo the procedure. I have spent time in Ethiopia working on health and human rights projects addressing the issue. It is still strongly linked to ideas of chastity and marriage and also to child marriage arrangements, where families betroth or marry off very young girls, who may even be prepubescent. In most countries child marriage is now contrary to law and it is recognised that early marriage and pregnancy lead to serious health hazards and mortality for babies and child-mothers. However, the persistence of customary practice is the problem. A chaste woman is of high value both in practical and moral terms. The best advocates against FGM are the courageous young women of Somalian, Kenyan and Ethiopian background who are leading campaigns to end the practice. What is also needed is the clear direction from imams and priests that myths about the practice being religiously required are totally untrue as many believe it is sanctioned by their holy books.

Proper sex education in schools is one of the ways to engage the young in discussions about relationships and mutual respect, about sexual activity and consent, and it should start early. At the moment personal, social, health and economic education (PSHE) is not a statutory part of the curriculum in the UK, although schools are expected to provide it. In 2017 the Department for Education announced that relationships and sex education (RSE) would be compulsory in all secondary schools but as yet the content cannot be agreed. The usual religious concerns will be urged upon ministers and the right to remove young people from classes will be preserved. Those who get withdrawn are often the most vulnerable and the least likely to get good information from their parents. Schools need to have professional sexual health experts come into the classroom and provide regular advice on what a healthy sexual relationship looks like; consent workshops are needed and misogynistic ideas around women's bodies and about relationships should be challenged. Work also has to be done on the stereotyping of what men and women are supposed to be and do, which feeds homophobia and transphobia. It is unfair to expect regular teachers to talk about sexual pleasure and mutuality in sex. That is invariably cringeworthy and ripe for taking apart by embarrassed pupils. There are now great vlogs on sex education available on YouTube which the young are using to get the information they do not get elsewhere, but if you are only getting your sex education from videos you might not be getting a rounded view of what good sex is like and what values you might want to bring to your choices. Some aspects of sex education are already compulsory and are taught in science like an anatomy lesson. The last time guidance on sex education was updated was in 2000. It really is time that the UK recognised the full import of good sex education in creating awareness and confidence as well as ultimately changing a culture in which sexual predation thrives.

And nowhere, perhaps, is that sexual predation more in evidence than in the rise of modern-day slavery. It is one of the shocking consequences of globalisation and has become a fact of life in the UK in ways that we would never have imagined only a decade or two ago. Child exploitation, child labour and the sale of children for sex were things that happened elsewhere, or so people thought. The true scale of trafficking is still difficult to assess but more than 5,000 potential victims of trafficking and modern slavery were reported to UK authorities in 2017, the highest on record so far. More than a third of all potential victims of trafficking are children under the age of 18. Many of those children are actually British child-citizens, sometimes runaways, used as drug mules by criminal gangs to take drugs from one place to another for potential buyers. Girls are most often utilised, as the assumption is that they draw down less police attention. They are also exploited for sexual purposes by gang members and the criminals who are involved in these forms of exploitation also operate online, particularly on adult services websites, where they promote their illicit 'wares'. Almost half of the cases reported – 41% – involved the possible exploitation of a child aged under 18. These figures come from the National Referral Mechanism, the system for identifying victims of trafficking.

London is a prime destination for human traffickers. Reports in November 2016 from a child trafficking NGO Ecpat UK and the charity Missing People found that significant numbers of children go missing from local authority care and gravitate to central London, where they are picked up by traffickers and moved around the country. Other children arrive, ostensibly unaccompanied, at ports of entry, stations and airports, but in fact they have been brought in by traffickers. The traffickers know the children will be taken into the care of local authorities but they have such a hold on them that before long the children are spirited away from foster parents or care homes into the dark underworld of domestic servitude, nailbars, cannabis cultivation and sexual servicing. The NGOs found that 167 of the 590 children suspected or identified as child trafficking victims in the year from September 2014 to 2015 vanished from care. An additional 593 of the 4,744 unaccompanied children placed under the protection of local authorities also went missing at least once in the same period. Of the 760 children who have disappeared, 207 have never been found. It is believed that this data is only the tip of the iceberg as many local authorities have not responded to researchers.

British children and EU nationals are dealt with by the National Crime Agency's modern slavery human trafficking unit, while non-EU cases are dealt with by the Home Office. Many professionals suspect that there is bias against recognising people as victims of trafficking if they are from countries where their right to residency in the UK is not pre-established. There is a belief that in a department which had a policy of creating a hostile environment on immigration matters and a culture of scepticism, there is a failure to see trafficking where it exists. A new expert body has been created in the Home Office but in fact the most effective way to build a firewall between victim identification and immigration concerns would be to move the process out of the Home Office altogether.

Investigating these cases is very hard as the whole system relies on high levels of fear and threat. The young are too frightened to testify and are terrified for the safety of their family. The worst traffickers move readily across borders and Europol, Eurojust, and the EAW are all crucial in bringing them to justice. Yet here we are, putting in jeopardy these collaborative and effective ways of dealing with cross-border crime by exiting the European Union. The only way to deal with trafficking is to do it in partnership with other nations, especially our closest neighbours.

CONCLUSION

The stark conclusion from this review of women and criminal justice is that despite the dramatic changes which have taken place in women's lives over the last four decades, women are still facing iniquitous judgements and injustice within the legal system. All the legal reforms have produced only marginal advances. Myths and stereotypes still pervade the courts. Women still have to struggle for credibility, their perceived deceptiveness is not yet a thing of the past, they are confronted with unspoken beliefs of 'double deviance', where they are not just breaching criminal law but also ideas of appropriate womanhood and femininity. They are not the gender most judges have in mind when they think of the 'reasonable person'; that person more often than not remains intractably male. In rape cases, women continue to face unacceptable cross-examination and with the arrival of social media are even more at risk of having their past sexual conduct paraded in front of the jury.

In the last 25 years women's organisations have turned up the volume on their discontent with the law. The arrival of greater numbers of women in Parliament has undoubtedly shifted the debate. These women MPs, from all parties, have fought hard to place women's issues on the agenda and, despite ridicule and accusations of political correctness, they have instigated legal reform. The former Cabinet minister Harriet Harman led the way. Maria Miller and Anna Soubry have taken up the banner.

But some of the reform has had poor outcomes. Blanket bans do not work and banning the use of sexual history as evidence lacked nuance and consideration of the rare but real circumstances when sexual history is relevant. While we learned that old-fashioned gendered language sustained subordination, what women in Parliament did not realise was that 'neutral' language carries pitfalls too. In public documentation and reports the language is now frequently made gender neutral, using 'he/she' in reports about domestic violence or rape, for example. Domestic violence is certainly perpetrated against men, as is sexual abuse and stalking and rape. But how often? Most domestic violence and abuse and sexual violation is perpetrated against girls and women. Girl children experience more childhood abuse. Girl children are killed more than boy children. Serial killers prey on women; they do not prey on men unless they are men who are deemed by patriarchal values to be lesser men – namely homosexuals. Men are sexually harassed but not often. So what has happened is that gender-neutral language has masked those facts. In hiding the workings of gendered inequalities behind a curtain of ungendered language, we sustain patriarchal ideas and practices.

We have spent a lot of time in recent years pulling down the barriers to women's achievement and trying to ensure that places of power have women there in significant numbers. It is without question vital to have women in senior positions in decision-making bodies and reforming the judiciary must remain a matter of urgency. We know that diversity produces different and more equitable outcomes. However, that also means moving beyond the safe, already acculturated appointee. There is a default position in most organisations never to appoint those who might rock the boat, when rocking is precisely what is needed.

But in trying to drive change at the top, too little attention has been paid to the lives of ordinary women and the pay differentials they face, the uncertainty created by zero-hour contracts and the gig economy. We have always known that financial independence enables women to make choices; it means they do not have to accept abusive relationships either in their private lives or in their places of work. They can move on. But the current miserable economic system which has driven down wages, disempowered workers in the name of flexibility, made housing unaffordable and largely destroyed the welfare system has been disastrous for women. There can never be equality under the current economic system where market fundamentalism rules our lives. There is nothing liberal, liberating or generous-spirited about neo-liberal economics. It has led to the disgraceful enrichment of a few at the expense of the many and created a culture in which money has become the supreme value. Masculinity and male potency are now confused with big bucks. This is why genuine gender equality will only ever be achieved if we pay attention to wider inequality.

Gender and other forms of discrimination are particularly prevalent in those aspects of our social organisation which have deeply forged hierarchies: police forces, armed forces, highly structured corporations, any place where progress upwards can be dependent on patronage or appraisal by superiors whose tendency is to replicate what has gone before. Such organisations, and this includes big law firms, should be on their mettle when it comes to their processes for advancement. In combatting modern-day slavery, companies and firms and all public bodies are required in their annual reports to document the active measures taken to ensure exploitation and slavery are not taking place in their supply chains. Those same companies and bodies should be expected to report on the progress of women and people from minorities in their workforce, not just on the pay gap but on their promotions to senior level.

There have been incredible changes to women's lives – social, political and economic – but these have not been accompanied by great change in underlying attitudes. Conventional gender norms persist because they are sustained by deeply embedded power structures. They keep women under-represented in the highest echelons of law and business, politics and the media by undervaluing women and marginalising them. The same power structures also expose women to disproportionate levels of poverty and sexual exploitation and make them vulnerable to violence. I have little doubt that women's progress in education and work and their greater claim on power is a factor in the increase of harassment and sexual violation on our streets, campuses and on social media, in clubs and the workplace. It is a means of informal social control. Women are expected to adjust their behaviours to deal with potential transgression. Not men. They are called upon even by other women not to drink too much, not to go out late, to avoid certain places, to dress appropriately, and this is part of what women are taught from girlhood.

Patriarchy persists because power does not readily cede its clout. People who have known entitlement are rarely keen to surrender it. Unless we recognise that the world itself is engineered in ways that do not fully nurture women and determine to change some fundamentals, law will fail to deliver just outcomes. We can monsterise individual men like Savile, Weinstein and Worboys, but the hard work is the more difficult task of changing attitudes and cultures and of building an equitable system for men and women both.

Women are angry and we have to harness their rage against male misconduct and malfeasance into a grander ambition for change. To turn men into the enemy is futile. I do not believe we will ever see true equality if our society is constructed around ideas which create huge chasms between men and women, or between those who have and those who have not. Understanding this female anger is hard for men. Most men also face inequality but of different kinds. Many black women have resisted feminism for a long time because for them the experience of racism, which they share with their menfolk, is usually a source of greater pain. They have watched their men being emasculated and disrespected by white men and women, by police and other sources of power, and they understand why such racism makes them reach for hyper-masculinity, as an expression of their maleness, even if they as women often pay the price. We hear criticism of black absentee fathers but not why they are absent. We rarely discuss how masculinities are constructed and how cultural and class experiences lock us into certain ways of behaving that give us some sense of a powerful self.

Working-class women frequently have similar emotions about gender roles and can also be leery about feminism because they see their husbands, partners and sons losing face, without meaningful work after deindustrialisation. Yes, they are in jobs but crappy jobs, doing work that carries no respect, with none of the camaraderie that bound men of previous generations together. These women cannot see contented futures for their sons; instead they see drug abuse and disrupted relationships. My own father was a dispatch hand in newspapers, an unskilled job that is now mechanised, but his self-respect came from his role as a trade unionist, collecting dues, organising workers to ensure their welfare was considered and their wages fair. He liked looking after the members of his chapel, as his branch was called. The destruction of trade unions disempowered people, particularly working-class men, and if ever there was an opportunity to bind men and women together in the creation of better working conditions it is now, when work is being casualised and protections for workers destroyed. Men who feel the wheels coming off the vehicles of their power often cling hardest to old-fashioned manifestations of maleness, wanting to retain rigid demarcation of roles.

A man in an audience I was addressing asked what would happen to men in this new equal world I was advocating, as though, like a redundant shipyard or steelworks, they would be dismantled and sold for scrap. He was having difficulty imagining how there might be any fulfilment for men in a society where there is gender equality. While it is right that all of the jobs and roles currently held by men should be open to women, and some of the preserves of men and the social goods they claimed for themselves will have to be shared, it would not be bleak for them either. The sex might be better for them too.

If we un-gender work and pay decent wages so that many more men might be encouraged into the caring roles, which an ageing society desperately needs, we might solve some of our biggest societal challenges. We should be training many more men as counsellors and social workers, youth workers and community leaders, nursery staff and classroom-support staff, ancillary workers in hospitals. It is women who have been raised to look after others, to feed them, to tend to their needs, but it should not be so any longer. We need large numbers of men in these roles. We need to recalibrate wage claims and working hours so that more people work less and have time for play and for family. But all of that means a rebooting of the welfare state and an ambitious use of the public purse, which in turn requires fairer taxation and no one at the top taking vast salaries and bonuses. We have serious skills shortages, with too few electricians, roofers, plumbers, engineers, construction workers and plasterers, which women and men could be meeting. It fills me with gloom that we are spending £50 billion on Brexit when it could be spent on creating a world-class health service, or housing for everyone, or training places so that people can acquire new skills.

The right to our bodies and to a sexual life – whether gay, straight, bi, trans or fluid in our identity – is another vital part of equality. And we should be tolerant of difference. It is about experiencing our bodies in the world as active participants not as passive receivers. Our sexuality is integral to our sense of self, just as it is for men. Sexual equality means completely respecting the sexual autonomy and integrity of the other in any sexual interaction. It isn't complicated and should be seen as fundamental to human relations. Men are facing a shake-up in what they took for granted. If they have to think first before making a move on a woman or another man, that is all to the good. That is how behavioural change starts and predatory or exploitative conduct ends.

Women's anger at the system's failure is wholly justified; and let us be clear, the #MeToo campaign is a form of civil disobedience. Women have broken the normal rule of turning to the law when it comes to abuse. They are choosing to cut out the law and due process because they have been affording them little comfort. When they complained about rape, sexual assault or sexual harassment they have been traduced as liars or fantasists or bullied into secret settlements. Now they are blowing the whistle, naming and shaming on social media. They are prepared to risk libel suits and civil lawsuits, saying 'Come and get me if this is not true.'

However, that cannot be the way forward. I have spent a large part of my life asking questions about which parts of law are man-made concoctions to maintain male ascendancy and which infantilise women and maintain their second-class status. I have looked for ways to reform those dynamics and achieve fairness. However, I believe there are some rules in our system which are not gender specific and which have to be maintained. High standards of proof, and the obligation that the state carries that burden of proof, are non-negotiable if we are to preserve liberty – the liberty of women *and* men. These protections are in all our interests. Punishment without trial is dangerous. People should not lose their liberty or suffer other detriments or carry the stigma of an accusation without due process to establish the accuracy of the claim. That is a human right.

Feminism is about justice if it is about anything, and that means for men as well as women. Justice for women is not secured by reducing justice for men. I do not want to see women calling for a lowering of the standard of proof to gain convictions in rape cases, nor do I want to see men losing their jobs for minor transgressions like commenting on clothes or being overfamiliar. There has to be due process. We have to put in place proper systems of complaint with proportionate remedies. I do not think the answer to crimes against women is about throwing away the key and simply imprisoning more men for longer, except where there is a pattern of behaviour indicating a continuing risk to women. We have to find better ways through this morass. Reaching for authoritarian 'law and order' responses always rebounds on women too.

The law has been confronted with its failures and should now be looking for ways to address its massive shortcoming. However, the system is in crisis. In 2016 the Public Accounts Committee told MPs that the criminal justice system was at breaking point. After 20 years of successive brutal and counterproductive cuts, the system is now broken. Since the introduction of austerity policies in 2010, the Ministry of Justice has lost 40% of its budget, more than any other Whitehall department, which is an indicator of the value the government attaches to justice. Legal aid has been slashed and women have suffered the consequences disproportionately because of the effects on family law, welfare, immigration, prisoners' law and crime. Access to justice is now being framed as a welfare issue and not as a fundamental right – which is what it should be.

Unsurprisingly there is a consequential recruitment and retention crisis at the criminal bar. The level of debt new entrants have to deal with, the collapse in fee levels and the toll taken by conducting cases which are inadequately resourced has resulted in a haemorrhaging of young lawyers from the profession, particularly women. There is little incentive for debt-saddled lawyers to opt for a career in legal aid work. More than a third of criminal barristers are reconsidering their employ-ment options as criminal practice offers such a poor income and a miserable work-life balance. The situation is particularly acute for those lawyers with caring responsibilities because of the demands placed upon barristers and solicitors outside of court hours and the fact that childcare often costs more than you are paid for a hearing in the criminal courts. It is often forgotten that barristers are self-employed so there is no holiday pay, no parental leave pay, no sick pay, no pension and you pay a huge whack of your earnings into chambers for clerking. Solicitors are facing a similar withdrawal from criminal practice for all the same reasons. The cuts also mean that cases are ill prepared for prosecution as well as defence. Corners are cut. Money is not available for experts or translators. Evidence is not analysed for want of time and resource. There is non-disclosure of evidence by police and pros-ecution that can be vital to a case. People are appearing in court unrepresented. As a result, the guilty walk free and the innocent are wrongly convicted. Judges are in despair and lawyers are suffering really low morale. The only way to save the system from irredeemable decline is to have a serious independent review of what is happening and restore the legal aid system.

The idea of securing greater justice for women in this climate is remote. There has to be a cultural shift within society if we really want equality, but it will only be achieved if we constantly call out the practices that sustain inequality. This is a job for men and women together. Real reform will only come about when men join women in calling for it. The law has a powerful part to play. Change involves consistent intellectual effort. People resist it; it is only human to cling to long-held beliefs, but we have to keep making the argument that this is about our shared humanity. This is about human rights. This is about justice.

ACKNOWLEDGEMENTS

I am a woman blessed. Although I am a lawyer, my life has not been confined to law. While my central passion is the business of justice, I have also had the good fortune of spending time in the worlds of education, politics, science, the media and the arts. How lucky is that? Those experiences have not just enriched my life but infused it with the belief that everything is interlinked. It also means I have the most wonderful friends across all walks of life. They are young and old, well off and poor, black and white, religious and non-religious, and they all enrich my life beyond measure. They provide me with insights and perspectives which help me see my own professional world in a different light. They keep me facing outwards, which is so vital if we are to avoid complacency; they keep me questioning how everything works, especially the legal system. Professions and institutions hate criticism; yet if we do not listen, especially to the young, we are doomed to fail those who need the law most. Having such a broad and wildly creative body of loving friends is something I wish on everyone. It means that solutions to problems can be found in the cross-currents.

In giving thanks there is always the profound risk that some of those who have helped me over the years and months will escape the net. I have been given so much intellectual sustenance by women friends and colleagues. My sisters in law at Doughty Street Chambers are extraordinary. They are the most brilliant, compassionate and enlightened group of lawyers you could hope to find. And the men are pretty good too! I especially want to mention Caoilfhionn Gallagher QC, a legal Amazon whose work on human rights especially for women has been groundbreaking. She led the legal team on abortion rights for the women of Northern Ireland all the way to the Supreme Court and with such commitment that we should be raising statues to her. She also instigated the annual lawyers' event which Doughty Street Chambers runs on Women and the Law. This has kept me on top of the raw experience of women in the courts, as lawyers and as clients. It is all too easy when you become senior in the profession to see the best of what the system has to offer in the highest courts and to be immune to the reality of what is really going on elsewhere. I also want to thank the amazingly gifted women working on the international front, especially my colleague Amal Clooney, who shares my engagement on the issue of trafficked women and children, and who has been deeply immersed in the cases of the Yazidi women enslaved by ISIL in northern Iraq. Also my fabulous colleagues Kirsty Brimelow QC, Jen Robinson and Angela Patrick, all of whom have provided invaluable advice and intelligence on the current state of play in the profession and the courts.

I could not have made a start on this book without the updated material provided by the most wonderful American intern I had the good fortune to engage two years ago, Arielle Littles, a marvellous scholar from Columbia University, New York. She systematically scoured the chapters of *Eve Was Framed* and charted the changes in law up to that time. However, as it turned out I did not have the hours in the day at that point to write a new version of *Eve Was Framed*. I started the earnest work last year and this time the formidably clever Ciar McAndrew helped me identify the changes in statistics and law since last time around and was an invaluable source of ideas and input. She is now launched into practice as a barrister and is undoubtedly bound for higher things.

I am also indebted to Andrea Coomber, the extraordinary Director of Justice, the legal NGO, who curates some of the best work you will find on legal reform; and her colleague Jodie Blackstock whose knowledge on the criminal justice system is encyclopedic. And another laurel to Martha Spurrier the stunningly articulate Director of Liberty who was also a Doughty Street woman. And Afua Hirsch, yet another who went on to be a leading commentator on the law and is now a celebrated author and journalist. I have learned from them all. Heading the list of influences are many women in the world of academic law: Professor Christine Chinkin of LSE, Kate O'Regan, the director of the Bonavero Institute of Human Rights at Oxford University, and Aileen Kavanagh also at Oxford, Erika Rackley of Birmingham University and my wonderful friend and awesome inspiration Professor Nicola Lacey QC, scholar of All Souls and LSE. The list is much longer but would become unwieldy and includes many great criminologists. I thank them all for providing me with the theoretical basis for my professional life. I also want to thank two close friends, Dr Estela Welldon and Professor Susie Orbach, who have taught me so much about the workings of the human psyche. And any such list of influences must include the wonderful woman who is president of our Supreme Court, Brenda Hale, who to my delight has no hesitation in describing herself as a feminist.

I will always be indebted to my agent, Faith Evans, who was on one of my juries thirty years ago and wrote to me afterwards, persuading me to write. She has remained a source of encouragement in my life and I thank her yet again for all she has done. And then to my editor, Becky Hardie, for whom most tributes are inadequate. Her insight, intelligence, skill and support were fundamental to the making of this book. Teasing out the arguments with her was invigorating and took me to new places.

No woman survives without the support of a troupe of friends who share evenings of laughter and well-filled glasses. Friends who cheer us on, send us encouraging texts and cards, and offer advice and wisdom. They know who they are. Thank you from my heart. I also confess that I could not function without a great PA. Hilary Hard is my right arm and I love her like a sister. I also had the great support while principal at Mansfield College, Oxford, of Jane Buswell, another terrific PA and supportive woman, who kept me on the straight and narrow in that part of my life.

And finally, my eternal gratitude goes to my family, which has grown in recent years. To Keir, Reem, Tai, Clio, Calum, Noa and Roland, thank you for being so wonderful and such a source of joy. And to my husband Iain Hutchison, you have filled my life with love. Thank you.

INDEX